Night

I'll walk with God

Count your Blessings.

What a Friend we have in Jesus

ON HIGHEST GROUND

ON HIGHEST GROUND

Surveying your resources in Christ

A DAILY DEVOTIONAL

DERICK BINGHAM

AMBASSADOR

Belfast Northern Ireland Greenville South Carolina

ON HIGHEST GROUND
© 1999 Derick Bingham

ISBN 1   84030 068 X

Ambassador Publications
a division of
Ambassador Productions Ltd.
Providence House
16 Hillview Avenue,
Belfast, BT5 6JR
Northern Ireland
www.ambassador-productions.com

Emerald House
1 Chick Springs Road, Suite 203
Greenville,
South Carolina 29609, USA
www.emeraldhouse.com

*For Kathryn and David
on their wedding day
December 23rd, 1999
with deepest love and affection*

INTRODUCTION

We all have a favourite place which, when reached, gives us a magnificent view of the surrounding countryside. Maybe we can get there by car or maybe only by foot. The journey, though, is always worth it. We drink in the scenery and turn to our daily tasks refreshed. Even mountaineers who get to the summit of great mountains consider the journey more than worthwhile

One of the most magnificent views in Scripture is given in Paul's letter to the Ephesians. In it he surveys the Christian's resources in Christ which bring us, amongst many other things, salvation by grace, redemption through His blood, forgiveness of sins, adoption into God's family, sealing by the Holy Spirit and incomparable power for living, the very same power as raised Christ from the dead.

Here is power to overcome ethnic divisions within society, power to transform relationships between husband and wife and between parents and children. Here is the definitive definition of what a Christian is and what the Christian church is all about. Here is unity which is indivisible. Here is an armour which can withstand all the fiery darts and intents of the evil one.

This book covers Ephesians verse by verse in a Daily Reading form for eight months of the year. I have then added two months readings from the life of David, first when he was hunted on the mountains by Saul and then when he eventually brought the ark to Zion's hill. A further month is devoted to studies in the biblical teaching about the eagle, who nests in high ground and finally December's readings are devoted to Christ's final lessons to His own before He ascended from the Mount of Olives, far above all.

Writing this book in the last year of this millennium, through busy days of teaching and preaching God's Word, has enriched my mind and spirit more than I can find words to express. The experience has redefined for me what true Christianity is about and as I have surveyed all the resources I have in Christ I turn to the future absolutely convinced that Jesus Christ is the answer to the deepest needs of my heart and life and the hearts and lives of people in every corner of the earth.

Derick Bingham
Autumn 1999

JANUARY

At the mouth of the Cayster River between the mountain range of Coressus and the sea lay the most important city in the Roman province of Asia, on the West coast of what is now Asiatic Turkey. Ephesus served as a great export centre and also as a natural landing-point from Rome. At the foot of Mt. Ayasoluk, 2 km from the main part of the city, stood the largest building in the Greek world, dedicated to the goddess, Diana, who was worshipped by people all over the world.

The Gospel, preached by Paul in this pagan city, infiltrated the culture of Ephesus with all its prostitution, sorcery, exorcism and magic arts. Here a new counter-culture arose, a counter-culture of Christians who no longer looked to Diana but to the living Saviour. Their resources and blessings in Christ are yours, Christian, as you begin this New Year and face all that it will hold.

January *first*

> **"Paul"**
> (Ephesians 1:1)

In Western society people use their name to sign off a letter. Paul, though, begins with his. What follows is some of the most sublime teaching ever penned in history but he still puts his name up-front.

There's a lot in a name. For Christians in the early church the mention of Paul's name filled them with feelings of terror, of fear, and of loathing. He was a religious bigot and in this world there is nothing more frightening. Paul did not hesitate to have Christians put in prison and done to death. Now, unashamedly, he puts his name to Christian teaching. Was such a thing credible? Yes. Why? Because of what the grace of God had done in his life.

Is your name sullied by all sorts of dark things in your past behaviour? Now that you have become a Christian do you wonder how you are ever going to hold credibility? You will. How? The same grace that lifted Paul's head up has lifted up your head, too. No matter how dark the past, your future is bright in Christ. If being sinless was a qualification for Christian service no-one, anywhere in the world, would be involved in Christian service. If the impact of Paul's name could be changed so powerfully by the Lord in his day, so can yours.

January *second*

> **"An apostle of Jesus Christ"**
> (Ephesians 1:1)

People spend a fortune today trying to discover who they really are. Even wars are constantly fought across the world over the question of identity. The psychoanalysts are kept busy with people searching for self-identity.

Paul had no problem with his own identity. Had he? He tells us he is an apostle of Jesus Christ. We shall discuss later in this book the whole question of the gift of an apostle but what the verb "apostello" means is to "send".

I think of a Chinese girl I know. She has taken the name Jess to help her friends in the West over the difficulty of pronouncing her name! She told me that an American lady came and joined the English faculty at her university in China. She was a great lecturer and teacher and Jess watched her very carefully. She showed constant kindness to her students and, even when showing them videos, if something questionable came up she used the fast-forward button. After a particular incident where this lecturer had shown great self-control and courtesy in a difficult situation Jess could endure it no longer: "What's different about you?", she asked. "If there is any characteristic in me that is different", answered the lecturer, "it's Jesus in me". "Who's Jesus?", asked Jess. Her life was turned around when she found the answer to that question. Interestingly, the lecturer had never once mentioned the name of Christ up until that point. She had been sent, in the will of God, to that university and lived a Christ-like life. So, sent one, preach the Gospel wherever you go, and only use words when necessary.

January *third*

"By the will of God"
(Ephesians 1:1)

There is a loving hand behind the universe. That same loving hand is behind your life. The one who has "measured the waters in the hollow of His hand" and "measured heaven with a span" has the hairs of your head numbered. All the things that happen to you are not good but they all work together for good. You'll see.

Paul says he is an apostle by the will of God. He didn't call himself. A church didn't call him. God did. Isn't God capable of calling you? Doesn't He know your address? Didn't His eyes see you being formed in the womb and, as King David put it, "The days fashioned for me when as yet there was none of them"? Are not His thoughts toward you, if you could know them, more in number than the sand? Paul's C.V. isn't very long, is it? His credentials are very short. "An apostle by the will of God", he says. God has willed you to be where and what you are. So why aren't you content?

My friend, Mrs. Carol Cordiner of Aberdeen is very gifted at appliqué work. Recently I noticed she had stitched some words into a cushion in her home. They read, "Contentment is not the fulfilment of what you want but is the realisation of how much you already have". Put that cushion under your head tonight.

January *fourth*

"To the saints"
(Ephesians 1:1)

The word makes us all shudder a little. Christians have an aversion to being called saints because they have such an unrealistic concept of what a saint is. We think of a saint as being an extraordinary human being. "I am a Christian", we say, "but I am far from being a saint". To claim to be a saint would be the height of arrogance to many Christians.

Tell me: are the people this letter addresses all exceptional people? Are they all great leaders of humanitarian causes, or outstanding Biblical scholars, or great teachers? No. Here you have a New Testament term used to describe what constitutes a Christian. They are saints. Saints are not a minority: they constitute the whole international Christian community. Every Christian is a saint.

The word refers to people who are "set apart". They are different in mind-set and outlook because they belong to the Lord Jesus. Rather than cowering from the term, Christians should appreciate what it means. To be "set apart" for the service and glory of the Lord Jesus has got to give to life a purpose that nothing else can.

January *fifth*

"To the saints who are in Ephesus"
(Ephesians 1:1)

To be a "set apart" one in Ephesus is a contrast hard to imagine. Ephesus, the great trading city with its marbled street off the Arkadiane which ran from the theatre to the harbour was most famous for being sacred to the goddess Diana. Worship of Diana found expression in the famous temple. It had vast dimensions and contained extended colonnades, many statues and paintings and its sacred effigies made it one of the wonders of the world.

Sorcery was connected with the worship of Diana and a host of priestess-prostitutes served in her temple. The city was the greatest centre in all Asia for the practice of communication with the dead, exorcism and magic arts.

Silversmiths made their livelihood manufacturing silver shrines, images and minature replicas of the temple. They were revered by people in their houses or carried by travellers. Ephesus was, on Paul's first visit, a completely pagan city.

Who would ever have imagined the Christian Gospel flourishing there? The fact is that it did and if it could flourish in Ephesus it can flourish where you are no matter how godless your surroundings. The fact that there were "saints in Ephesus" is a starlight of encouragement for Christian witness as we live in a new millennium, in God's will.

January *sixth*

"And to the faithful in Christ Jesus"
(Ephesians 1:1)

This text informs us that in the environment of Ephesus where, by the thousand, people had exercised their faith in the goddess Diana, others had exercised their faith in Jesus of Nazareth. Jesus said to doubting Thomas, "Do not be faithless but believing". The word "faithful" in today's verse is equivalent to believing.

In our generation millions will say that "seeing is believing" but with the Christian "believing is seeing". To have faith in something somebody must make a promise, there must be a very good reason for believing that person and then there follows an assurance that it will be as they said. The promises of God are what faith feeds on. There is absolute reason for believing what God has promised in Christ. So you have believed, too? Your faith in Christ will lift you out of mediocrity and help you overcome insuperable difficulties. It doesn't matter who or where you are, faith is possible to you. Think of them: Moses the Egyptian prince, Gideon the farmer, Ruth the gleaner, Deborah the judge, David the shepherd, Samuel the prophet, the little boy with his lunch, the young maid in Namaan's household, a sinner like Mary Magdalene, a guileless Nathaniel and, of course, the believers in the evil-soaked Ephesus. So, Christian, wherever you are: all things are possible, only believe.

January *seventh*

> *"In Christ Jesus"*
> (Ephesians 1:1)

What is your identity? To a lot of people their identity is all tied up in social status. The car they drive is their "calling card". The house they live in and the location in which it is placed is extremely important to them. The people they know, the college tie they wear, or the uniform or badge, all add up to how they see themselves in the world.

The Christian, though, has an identity which is more deeply satisfying than any social or political identity. It is an identity which will surpass and survive all other identities. It is is to be "in Christ". Once a person becomes a Christian they are united to Christ, the Scripture teaches, as branch to a vine, as a husband to a wife, as the Father, Son and Holy Spirit in the Trinity It is not a mere formal attachment, it is a living union of shared life and love with Jesus Christ. The Buddhist doesn't claim to know the Buddha nor the Confucianist, Confucius, nor the Muslim, Mohammed, nor the Marxist, Karl Marx but even a little child in Christ will tell you without a blink that they "know Jesus".

In the New Testament church there were people who believed in baptism but they did not call themselves Baptists. They believed in presbyters but they weren't called Presbyterians. They believed in the gifts of the Holy Spirit but they were not called Pentecostalists. They believed in salvation but they were not called the Salvation Army. They had bishops but they were not called Anglicans. They referred to "the brethren" but without a capital 'B'. They trembled at God's Word but they weren't called Quakers. They had method but they were not called Methodists. They believed the church to be truly international but they did not call it Catholic nor Roman. The bottom line and the top line was that they were "in Christ". It was enough. It still is.

January *eighth*

> *"Grace to you"*
> (Ephesians 1:2)

Grace. It is a word which sets the whole of Christian truth on fire. Without it the very Gospel is lifeless. It is the very beginning of our faith. It comes from the same Greek word from which we get our English word "charm". It is unmerited favour from God and reaches down to us long before we ever think about reaching up to Him.

It has been said that the greatest heresy on earth is to lay the emphasis on what we do for God instead of what God does for us. Millions of people follow that emphasis. They try to earn salvation when the whole message of the Bible is that it is a gift. Honestly? Of course. "For by grace you have been saved through faith and that not of yourselves it is the gift of God", Paul wrote later in this Ephesian letter. There it is: you and I are undeserving and yet unconditionally loved because of God's grace. There is nothing that chokes the life out of legalism like grace. For years I wondered why the unconverted often seem to go to work whistling while some of the converted are often miserable, inflexible, colourless and unbending. Now I know. They ignore the freedom Christ won for them. Come Christian, truly let grace into your life and find out just how charming it is.

January *ninth*

> *"And peace from God our Father and the Lord Jesus Christ"*
> (Ephesians 1:2)

Are you fretting and worried? Are you filled with anxiety and fear? Are you being eaten up with tension and stress by the unknown ahead of you and the circumstances around you? You haven't gone looking for trouble, it has come looking for you.

How often have you and I heard that peace is not the complete absence of war? As long as we live in this world there will be trouble but in the midst of it all we can have a peace from God grounded in His promises and presence and that comes as a result of believing prayer. We need to switch today from our worry list to our prayer list. We need to hand all those anxieties and worries to the Lord one by one. Go on, do it. My motto for this year in which I am writing this book is "Be anxious for nothing". Those little birds around you have accidents, face predators, have to search for food in bad weather and catch diseases. Do they care for their responsibilities? Try and touch their young and see if they care. But what marks them? They are without anxious care. "Look at them", said Christ. You can be without all that anxious care, too. You can be at peace with God, at peace with others, and at peace with yourself.

January *tenth*

"From God our Father and the Lord Jesus Christ"
(Ephesians 1:2)

If God is going to bless us then He does it through the Lord Jesus. By Him everything consists. Everything that claims to be Christianity without having Christ at the beginning and at the centre and at the end is a denial of Christianity. It can be called by whatever name it likes, it is not the real thing. He is everything to the church. He is the church's head, He is her foundation, He is her life, He is her inspiration, He is her mediator, He is her message, He is her guide and He is her salvation. The very gates of Hell cannot prevail against her because they cannot prevail against Him. Death cannot close over the church because Christ lives in the power of an endless life. He is everything to the Christian and He is everything to the Christian church.

Let us learn it once and for all - He will have no rival. If we pollute His church by trying to link Him with other pseudo saviours He will spit our testimony out of His mouth. As Augustine put it: "He values not Christ at all who does not value Christ above all."

January *eleventh*

"Blessed be the God and Father of our Lord Jesus Christ"
(Ephesians 1:3)

Paul is about to list many of the blessings that are given by God to the Christian. What is about to be listed is one of the most profound spiritual outpourings ever penned but first, before he looks at the nature of the blessings, he worships God. That is always a very healthy thing to do.

I was in a store one day with my wife and was passing through a particular department in the store. It had some beautiful and very expensive goods on display all of which were under a very famous brand name. A lady went by and sighed to us as she passed saying how frustrating it all was! Gently I reminded her of the blue sky outside and the beauty of the creation around her and how the Creator never put His name on any of it!! She smiled, relaxed for a moment and said cheerfully, "That's our thought for the day".

The thing is, in the pace of modern living where advertising is huge and where brand names bring so much clout, is it not worth stopping for a moment and realising where the true source of our blessings lie? Who made the sheep that produced the wool that made your carpet? Who created the trees behind the wood of your furniture? Need I go on? The source of all is God but the greatest designer, artist, and architect hardly gets a mention in our everyday language. Let's get, like Paul, our priorities right.

January *twelfth*

"Who has blessed us"
(Ephesians 1:3)

Ephesians 1: 3 to Ephesians 1:14 is, in Greek, a single complex sentence. There is not a single full stop. Paul speaks of God's blessings in a continuous cascade. I have noted various phrases used by writers to describe this amazing statement of blessings. Here are some of them. "A magnificent gateway". "A golden chain of many links". "A kaleidoscope of dazzling lights and shifting colours". "A snowball tumbling down a hill picking up volume as it descends". "Like the preliminary flight of an eagle, rising and wheeling round as though for a while uncertain which direction in his boundless freedom he shall take". "Like an overture of an opera which contains successive melodies that are to follow".

In our local church there is a very enthusiastic and gifted Christian lady called Dot Irwin. She was busy hoovering the premises where our local church meets after a service recently and quipped, as I passed, "We are blest!". Right on, Dot.

January *thirteenth*

"With every spiritual blessing"
(Ephesians 1:3)

The Holy Spirit, who is God, is the one through whom all the spiritual blessings we possess are mediated. You need him in your life in order to appreciate the spiritual blessings Paul is about to list. Paul spoke of such things as redemption, forgiveness and holiness and the hope of glory. Speak to those who do not have the Holy Spirit indwelling their lives and they will surprise you with their indifference. "The natural man receives not the things of the Spirit of God", says the Scripture, "for they are foolishness to him; neither can he know them for they are spiritually discerned".

Do not be disheartened, though. While people around you may have more interest in the latest fashion, the latest novel, the state of politics, their favourite musician or sports person or team or whatever, more than they ever would have in the things of the Spirit, things can change. The Holy Spirit can use your witness to bring them to Christ. He can "quicken" them spiritually. So speak up for your Lord and watch the Holy Spirit work.

January *fourteenth*

"In heavenly places in Christ"
(Ephesians 1:3)

The phrase "heavenly places" is not confined to the future state of the believer. It refers to the realm of invisible reality which you can't see or touch at this moment. It is like Elisha's servant who thought all was up until the Lord opened his eyes to see the chariots of God manned by myriads of angels. It is from heavenly realms that our blessings come as we face the huge pressures of modern living.

Science, of course, only deals with what it can see or quantify. Philosophy tries to explain, to elucidate. The heavenly places are a mystery to science and philosophy; they are not a mystery to the Spirit of God. He can bring spiritual blessings from the heavenly realm to you even this morning as you face the problems of today, or tonight as you gnaw over the decisions of tomorrow. Have faith that the resources of the heavenly realm are available to you in the earthly one. As all colour is hidden in sunlight, waiting to be drawn off by the flowers so all the Christian's blessings are stored up in Christ.

Draw from those resources constantly and you will be victorious. Draw only from the earthly and you will ultimately be disappointed. You doubt me? Look at the book of Ecclesiastes and you will find that all under the sun is vanity. You will also find that all that lies behind the sun is the source of all truly fulfilling blessing.

January *fifteenth*

"Heavenly places in Christ"
(Ephesians 1:3)

The true story is told of the old minister, Dr. Davidson in Drumtochty in Scotland. It was Christmas day and after a busy time preaching and visiting he was having supper at the manse with one of his elders, a man called Drumsheugh. Suddenly he became very thoughtful and said: "You and I, Drumsheugh, will soon have to go on a long journey and give an account of our lives at Drumtochty. Perhaps we have done our best as men can, and I think we have tried; but there are things we might have done otherwise, and some we ought not to have done at all. It seems to me now that the less we say on that day of the past the better. We shall wish for mercy rather than justice and we would be none worse, Drumsheugh, of a friend to say a good word for us in the Great Court".

It turned out to be Dr. Davidson's last conversation. He showed his elder to the door and watched him walk away in the snow and the next morning the Doctor was found dead in his chair.

To be "in Christ" is to have a friend in that world of unseen reality. We need Him now, as we live in the Shadowlands, we will need Him then when we enter that amazing world where the final word will be given on how we have served Him. No wonder the term "in Christ" is one of Paul's favourite expressions. It is still gloriously applicable to Christians from Ephesus to Drumtoghty, is it not?

January *sixteenth*

> *"Just as He chose*
> *us in Him"*
> (Ephesians 1:4)

How many arguments have raged around the subject of predestination? Many people get into a real corner over it. I once came across a Christian who had stood every week in the thoroughfare of a great city with some evangelistic literature in his hand. He wouldn't give it out but stood there waiting until people took it from him. Such was the impact of his views on predestination!

The most helpful statement I have ever come across regarding the subject of predestination comes from the great Victorian pastor C. H. Spurgeon. He once said;

"It is a difficult task to show the meeting place of the purpose of God and the free agency of man. One thing is quite clear, we ought not to deny either of them, for they are both facts. It is a fact that God has purposed all things both great and little; neither will happen but according to His eternal purpose and decree. It is also a sure and certain fact that oftentimes events hang upon the choice of men and women. How these two things can both be true I cannot tell you; neither probably after long debates could the wisest person in heaven tell you .... they are true facts that run side by side like parallel lines .... can you not believe them both? And is not the space between them a very convenient place to kneel in, adoring and worshipping Him whom you cannot understand?"

January *seventeenth*

> *"Before the*
> *foundation of the*
> *world"*
> (Ephesians 1:4)

Imagine a geologist at work. He digs and finds footprints or fossils of animals long extinct. Then deep into his excavation imagine he finds a rock with his name engraved on it! That certainly would make the headlines in the news media across the world. It would be the biggest discovery of his life and he would tell the story everywhere.

According to the Scriptures God saw "my substance being yet unformed" and in His book they all were written, "The days fashioned for me, when as yet there were none of them". That implies that God knew all about the very characteristics of my personality long before I was born. Today's verse, though, implies that He chose me in Christ long before the world was formed! No human being had anything to do with that original choice. So, Christian, if this is true of you, why are you so worried about what other human beings think of you? Why do you set your agenda by theirs? Selah.

January *eighteenth*

"That we should be holy"
(Ephesians 1:4)

There is a goal behind God's choosing of us in Christ. It is that we should be holy. For millions of people in our world the very word conjures up an image of pale-faced, miserable individuals who are negative about most things and who are trying to be negative about the rest! The Lord Jesus takes a very different view. He taught that in knowing Him we could become like a bunch of grapes on a vine. If I know anything about grapes, they are most refreshing, very attractive and can re-invigorate anybody's day. Of course it is true that holiness has a negative side. A surgeon, for example, has a very negative attitude to germs or cancer cells. There would be something seriously wrong with him if he didn't. His aim is to make his patients healthy and strong.

The aim of holiness is to make us beautiful in our lives, to have beauty like that of our Creator. For this to happen holiness has a negative attitude to anything that would dishonour Him. Does it work? Just look at Christ's disciples when they first came under His leadership and then look at what they became. It works.

January *nineteenth*

> *"And without
> blame"*
> (Ephesians 1:4)

Is there any more haunting accusation than for someone to say: "You are to blame for it all". Worse if the accusation is true. To be cleared of all blame is a blissful condition. The wonderful thing is that every Christian has been declared blameless. In what sense? In the sense that God has cleared the Christian of guilt by imputing his righteousness to us. What does that mean? It means that God attributes to us that which is not naturally or characteristically ours. How? By the death of the Lord Jesus on our behalf. Positionally we are blameless because He took the blame at Calvary. Practically, though, we are to live so that people will not be able to point the finger of blame at us for wrongdoing. The position we hold in Christ is just wonderful, the practical effect is the challenge.

January *twentieth*

> *"Before Him in
> love"*
> (Ephesians 1:4)

Just as the priests of the Old Testament tabernacle served "before the Lord" for his satisfaction and enjoyment, so do we. I feed from God and God feeds from my worship and service. Really? Read Revelation 3: 20 and you will see that it teaches that God says, "I will dine with him and he with me". Got it? There is a double feeding.

Truly there can be no greater lifestyle than to live out my life before the Lord. In the university, in the hospital, in the school, in the home, in the shop. According to this statement of Paul's the whole purpose of God inventing the universe was that we should find redemption, live out our lives before Him for His satisfaction and, eventually, be before Him forever.

I don't read about that in the "Lifestyle" sections of national newspapers. Do you? I don't see that as the goal before millions of men and women and young people across the world. Few scientists tell me that is the goal of human existence. Yet, in a few small words Paul sums up the ultimate reason for existence. Let God's satisfaction be your goal in whatever you do, today.

January *twenty-first*

"Having predestined us to adoption as sons"
(Ephesians 1:5)

No other New Testament writer uses the term "adoption" other than Paul. Jews knew nothing of the term. Paul was a Roman citizen and he knew that adoption was a means used in the Greco-Roman world of bringing a desired person into one's family. That person in Roman society was male, so Paul uses the term, 'as sons', but the honour of Biblical adoption is given equally to men and women.

It is interesting that in the eyes of Roman law an adoptee was a new person, he completely lost all the rights of his old family. All debts and obligations connected with his previous family were abolished as if they had never existed. An adopted child had the right to the name and to the property of the person by whom he had been adopted.

Recently a friend of mine was dying. She had been adopted when only a baby of ten days old and as she approached death the theme was deeply on her mind. Suddenly, one morning in her daily devotions, she had discovered the Biblical doctrine of adoption. She realised for the first time her position as an adopted person in God's family. "So", she said to me one morning, "I have been adopted twice!" The fact that she had been "a child of His choice" brought her immense comfort as she faced death. Let that truth bring you comfort as you face life.

January *twenty-second*

"By Jesus Christ"
(Ephesians 1:5)

Who of us with children are not brought up short by noticing certain hereditary factors in our offspring? We wish we had control over such things but we have none! When we are adopted the Holy Spirit comes within us and that Spirit begins his mystery work of conforming us to the image of God's Son.

All this is made possible through the work of Jesus Christ. No work ever attempted was more perfectly completed. "It is finished", He cried on Calvary and bowed His head and died. Most people die and bow their heads but this death was different. They could not take His life from Him. He gave His life a ransom for many. When He paid the debt we could not pay then, and only then, did He bow His head and die. The price for our adoption was met, the work necessary for its implementation was accomplished. Adopted by Jesus Christ. Now, there's something!

January *twenty-third*

"To Himself"
(Ephesians 1:5)

I know that Christ has gone to prepare a place for us and that He will come again and receive us to Himself, that where He is we will be. That hope inspires me, it keeps me going. But what about today? What is my position, now? Jesus told His diciples in the Upper Room, "If anyone loves Me, he will keep My Word: and My Father will love him and we will come to him and make our home with him".

The Lord Jesus promised that one day He would bring us to the Father's home but in the meantime He will bring His Father to make His home in our hearts, now. And not only that, the Holy Spirit will take up His abode in our hearts. And what is more, the Lord Jesus has adopted us to Himself. He too will take up His abode in our hearts. Notice the phrase, "We will come to him and make our home with him". Christ does not propose to wait until we get to Heaven before He introduces us to His Father or the Holy Spirit. He proposes to bring them into our hearts and lives now. You may be lonely, today, but you are most certainly not alone.

January *twenty-fourth*

"According to the good pleasure of His will"
(Ephesians 1:5)

The creation of the world brought God great pleasure. On the seventh day He rested from His creation. God saw everything He had made and behold it was very good. It must have been work involving great energy and needed rest. The intricacy of it all, from the tiniest flower to billions of stars is awesome. If we enjoy it all can you imagine the pleasure it brought him?

The life of Christ also brought God great pleasure. "This is my beloved Son", He said at Christ's baptism, "in whom I am well pleased".

But you, Christian, bring God great pleasure. He brought you into His family according to the good pleasure of His will. He loved you long before you loved Him. He set His love upon you even before the world was and through all the circumstances of your life draws you to Himself. He willed your adoption but willed it out of love and not out of sheer determination. This is not dry theology: it was incalculable, indefinable, indescribable love that came after you. God is not passive. He is active. Facing problems today? Walk with the conscious knowledge that you are beloved of the Lord.

January *twenty-fifth*

> *"To the praise of the glory of His grace"*
> (Ephesians 1:6)

A man approached me after a church service once, and told me a fascinating story. He was in Shetland in Scotland and was in charge of some mentally handicapped people waiting in a line to meet Diana, the Princess of Wales. It was a very cold morning and eventually the Princess arrived and began to cheerfully greet those who awaited her. Suddenly one of the mentally handicapped patients began to stroke her hair. "Don't touch the Princess!", he pleaded. "Don't worry", said Diana, "it's all right. They can touch me". The gentleman in question was deeply moved by this aspect to Diana's personality. It had been, of course, a feature of her life. AIDS patients, lepers, the dying, victims of landmine explosions, people all across the world in dire situations were touched by her. She was a gracious lady. Love that stoops is grace.

We often praise the late Princess for her ability to stoop to touch those in need. It is our abiding memory of her. Yet, what of God who stooped to not only touch but to save? We praise the glory of His grace.

January *twenty-sixth*

> *"To the praise of the glory of His grace"*
> (Ephesians 1:6)

We all know what it is to be shut out or shunned by individuals. But, to be cut off from God is to be without hope. The Lord Jesus, though, interposed between God's wrath and us and put away sin by the sacrifice of Himself and has now entered into the Holiest of all to become our merciful and faithful High Priest. We are accepted by God "in the Beloved".

I would have to say, though, that sermons I heard in my youth led me to believe that God loved me for Jesus' sake. This truth was particularly taught from the life of David. When David became king he asked "Is there not still someone of the house of Saul to whom I may show the kindness of God?" He was told, "There is still a son of Jonathan who is lame in his feet". They brought Mephibosheth the son of Jonathan, the son of Saul to David and he immediately fell on his face and prostrated himself. Then David said to him, "Do not fear, for I will surely show you kindness for Jonathan, your father's sake and you shall eat bread at my table continually". The teaching was that David showed kindness to Mephibosheth for Jonathan's sake and that this was an example of what God did regarding us; God showed us kindness for Jesus' sake.

We were taught that the intervention of Jesus at Calvary was such that God was moved towards us because of Christ. This is simply not true. Why? Because we cannot separate between the Father and the Son for God is one. Jesus revealed to us what God was like. In fact He revealed to us what God was always like. God did not love us because Jesus died but Jesus died because God loved us. Before the world began God loved us. The death of Jesus was necessary in order that the claims of a broken law might be satisfied but such an action does not cloud the fact that God's love was reaching down to us long before we ever thought of reaching up to Him . His love is an eternal love.

January *twenty-seventh*

> *"By which He made us accepted in the Beloved"*
> (Ephesians 1:6)

The Beloved is a beautiful title for Christ. In the great prophesy of Isaiah we read, "Behold my servant whom I have chosen, my Beloved in whom my soul is well pleased ..... a bruised reed He will not break, and smoking flax He will not quench till He sends forth justice to victory. And in His Name Gentiles will trust".

In the bloom of a reed there is no beauty. There is no strength in its slender stem. Not many in our world would take a long journey in search of a reed and even less in search of one that is bruised and crushed, but this Beloved one does not break bruised reeds. Do you think that nobody cares? Would the selfish crowd ignore and break you? Not half, you answer.

And what about smoking flax? Sparks do not streak across its fibre. It smoulders. You wouldn't use it to kindle a fire, for sure. Are you like that smoking flax? Fitful? Irregular? Does no contagious spiritual flame flow from your life?

It is the "smoking flax" of this world and the "bruised reeds" that our Lord is deeply concerned about. Isn't it incredible that we are accepted in the one whom God loves, in whom His soul delights? Who is He? He is the one who specialises in not quenching smoking flax or breaking bruised reeds.

January *twenty-eighth*

> *"In Him we have redemption"*
> (Ephesians 1:7)

If your car breaks down by the side of the road and I come along and give you a new one, that is not redeeming your car, is it? I would need to fix your car and give it back to you in order to redeem it.

So, in Christ, we have redemption. Not only do we have the redemption of our souls but our very bodies will be, one day, like His body of glory. And that is not all. The earth will also be redeemed. It will be called "a new earth", so there must be something of the old one in it. This earth will melt with fervent heat, we are told, but even if you burn something you do not destroy its atoms. The new earth will be the old earth redeemed. God is greener than "the Greens" (environmentalists). Our new bodies will be our old ones redeemed. That is why we will know one another in heaven. There will be something of us that is recognisable, forever. Redemption is a much bigger thing than any of us realise.

January *twenty-ninth*

> *"Through His blood"*
> (Ephesians 1:7)

"Take this piece of paper", he said, "and put it on your door in Ireland and you will have peace". The paper had blood on it. "Our priests cut themselves while in a trance", he explained, "and that is their blood on the paper". "I don't need their blood", I said, as I stood outside that temple on that hill in Hong Kong. "Why not?", he asked. "Because about two thousand years ago the Lord Jesus, God's Son, shed His blood for me outside Jersualem at a place called Calvary and He made peace through the blood of His cross".

He looked at me. "I have got to work in this temple after my daily work is done to try to get my ancestors out of Hell", he said, "I hope my children will come here and work for me to get my soul out of Hell. You're lucky, all you have to do is believe".

Lucky? Not so. The message goes out to him as much as to me that on repenting toward God and putting faith in the Lord Jesus redemption is available. "Make much of the blood of Christ", my dying mother said to me, "For when you come to where I am now it counts".

January *thirtieth*

> *"The forgiveness of sins"*
> (Ephesians 1:7)

It has been said that everybody thinks forgiveness is a good idea until they have someone to forgive. There could be no release from the indictment of a sin had not sin been righteously dealt with by the Lord Jesus at

Calvary. Who could possibly describe the absolute bliss of having one's sins forgiven? The blood of Jesus Christ His Son cleanses us from all sin and we are incredibly forever forgiven.

There once was a great Christian preacher called George Whitfield. His effect upon the generation he lived in was immense. Long before the days of public address systems Whitfield would preach to literally tens of thousands of people in the open air. Multitudes were converted to Christ through his ministry. I love the answer he gave to the man who approached him and asked him what he would do if someone rose in one of his audiences and told the people that he was going to tell the people bad things about his past. Whitfield replied that he would tell him to tell them the worst about him and then he would follow by saying that he knew more than what had been exposed because only he knew his own heart! It is to such a depth that forgiveness of sins by God reaches.

When God forgives He does not forgive stintingly. His forgiveness is proportioned to the wealth of the riches of His grace. And of course he does more than forgive; He says "Your sins and your iniquities I will remember no more for ever". This does not mean that God is not aware of sin. He does not look across Heaven and see the wounds in the hands of the Lord Jesus and say that He cannot for the life of Him remember what caused those nailprints. The "Remembrancer" was the one in the Royal Court who brought news of events that had happened in the kingdom to the king. There will be no "Remembrancer" in Heaven to bring up our past again. It is forgiven.

January *thirty-first*

"According to the riches of His grace"
(Ephesians 1:7)

An old Navhajo Indian had become very rich because oil had been found on his property. He took all his money and put it in a bank and his banker became very familiar with the habits of the old gentleman. Every once in a while the Indian would go to the bank and say to the banker, "Grass all gone, sheep all sick, water holes all dry". The banker wouldn't say a word because he knew what needed to be done. He would bring the old man inside and seat him in the vaults. Then he would bring out several bags of silver dollars and say, "These are yours". The old man would spend about an hour in there looking at his money, stacking up the dollars and counting them. Then he would come out and say, "Grass all green, sheep all well, water holes all full". What was he doing? He was reviewing his resources!

The resources out of which you have been redeemed and forgiven, accepted and blessed with every spiritual blessing flow from the riches of God's grace. The old Indian could count his resources but you'll never count yours. They are incalculable.

FEBRUARY

S ome folk never seem to look up! Bogged down with the cares and troubles of this life they don't lift their eyes to the hills. Of course, even when they do, they think that all they see is all there is. Christians, though are very different. They lift their eyes to the hills from "Whence cometh" their help. Their help comes from the Lord who made heaven and earth.

There are more eyes than your physical eyes, though. You have inner eyes, called by Paul "the eyes for your heart" where the mainspring of feeling, faith, words and actions lie. When the Holy Spirit gets to work enlightening the eyes of your heart an incredible change takes place. Things all around you are perceived in a different way. In answer to prayer those eyes of your understanding, Paul emphasises, can be opened up. You can then understand what is the hope of your calling and the power that is available to you. May you experience that spiritual eye opener during February days. See if it does not even change your very attitude to the everyday happenings of your life.

February *first*

> *"Which He made
> to abound toward
> us"*
> (Ephesians 1:8)

Grace is lavished upon us. Grace to save you! Grace to keep you going! Grace to bear persecution! Grace to take misunderstanding! Grace to overcome temptation! Grace to wait when no answer from God is forthcoming! Grace to live and grace to die!

"Of His fullness", wrote John, "we have all received, and grace for grace". What does that mean? It means that when one supply of grace is exhausted, another is available. It is wave for wave. It is showing us that it is foolish to rest on past or present experiences. Are you at a turning point in your life? Is the future uncertain and even the present blurred? Have you known grace to be adequate for all you have known in the past? Then why can you not turn now to the future with confidence? Why should God dry up resources of His grace which have abounded to you up until now? It is impossible. God never stints. You are going to be enriched forever. It's too good to be true you say? No, it is too true not to be made good to you. His grace is sufficient for you in what the next few weeks and years and eternity holds. Let me write it again; wave for wave. Honestly!

February *second*

> *"In all wisdom and
> prudence"*
> (Ephesians 1:8)

The consequence of the lavishing of God's grace upon us is that we receive the gifts of spiritual wisdom and discernment. I broadcast weekly, at this time in my life, on satellite across Europe. My task each week is to draw from current events and apply the Scriptures to them. I am constantly staggered by the fact that week after week the Scriptures prove so powerfully adequate for throwing light upon events that are happening all around me.

Oscar Wilde said, "You give the criminal calender of Europe to your children under the name of history". That was Oscar's summary of what history was about. "The universe is indifferent", said Andre Mamos, "who created it? Why are we here upon this puny mudheap, spinning in infinite space? I have not the slightest idea, and I am quite convinced that no-one else has the least idea". In truth I am quite convinced of the opposite.

Here in Northern Ireland we are blessed in that the famous African Children's Choir has a base in Newcastle, County Down. The special wisdom and discernment of these children, many of whom have been through incredibly traumatic experiences in Africa, would stagger you. I have seen a friend of mine humbled, challenged and transformed by the display of God's grace in these children's lives.

The youngest or most mature believer can grasp something of God's purposes in the ages as well as in their day and generation and can know their place in it all. No wonder Philip Yancey asked, "What's so amazing about grace?"

February *third*

> *"Having made known to us the mystery of His will"*
> (Ephesians 1:9)

In our day, as in Paul's, there are plenty of societies and cults that demand that their members make solemn promises not to reveal their secrets to the uninitiated. Those societies and cults love to be surrounded by a sense of mystery.

In the New Testament a mystery is something which has been concealed up until now but which has now been revealed. Here the great mystery of God's will through the ages is revealed at last. Notice the mystery has been revealed "to us". It was revealed to Paul first (Ephesians 3: 3) and then through him to the church. The story of God's grace is a story to be told. The message of the Gospel, given to the church to declare is not to hold as concealed mystery only for the initiated. It is to be carried to the ends of the earth, to every clime and culture and tongue. It is a truly international message as relevant to Washington, Peking, Moscow, Pretoria, London or Delhi as to Ephesus. Share the great story with someone, today.

February *fourth*

> *"According to His good pleasure which He purposed in Himself"*
> (Ephesians 1:9)

Who of us in Christ don't enjoy pleasure? The pleasure of a walk in the snow. The pleasure of a cappuccino with a good piece of writing. The pleasure of a child's laughter. The pleasure of sleep. The pleasure of creativity and achievement. The list is endless.

God, though, has pleasures. One of His greatest is the revealing of His purposes in Christ: this is the great mystery of His will. Everything He does is all tied up in the Lord Jesus. Hendriksen translates the verse: "The purpose which He cherished for Himself in Him". That is just beautiful. If you love the Lord Jesus you will find He is the key to revealing the mystery of God's purposes to your heart. What more perfect description of the purpose which He cherished for Himself in Him could you find than the words of Christ to His own, "I in them, and You in Me; that they may be perfect in one, and that the world may know that you sent Me, and have loved them as you have loved Me. Father, I desire that they also whom you gave me may be with Me where I am, that they may behold My glory which You have given Me; for you loved Me before the foundation of the world" (John 17: 23-24). If such a position brings us pleasure have you any idea of the pleasure it brings God?

February *fifth*

> *"That in the dispensation of the fullness of the times"*
> (Ephesians 1:10)

This phrase means "at the appropriate time". God is working to a plan. In all His actions through the ages He has a purpose. A teacher in the nursery school shows the children how to play with blocks and lays out tables for them to do their painting. A teacher in the sixth form also lays out experiments for his or her pupils studying physics. So a university lecturer teaches his or her students computer science. Now see the young adult setting up his or her computer programmes in the software company.

All of those stages were linked though at each stage the teacher was doing a different thing. Each stage was preparing the child for the next stage.

So God, at appropriate times, through history did different things. In Adam's time, in Abraham's time, in the time of the Judges, in David's time, in the time of the prophets, in the time of the apostles; God was revealing His nature and His plan. Now in our day and in our time He is doing new things. What He does at each stage is entirely appropriate.

And this principle in history also applies to your personal history. Has the Lord taken you through to a new stage of your personal history? Be glad of it. Be patient and you will find what God does at each stage of your life is exactly appropriate in His plan.

February *sixth*

"That .... He might gather together in one all things in Christ"
(Ephesians 1:10)

God summed up creation in Adam. So He will sum up history in Christ. This great climax of history is described by Paul in a rare verb. It means to sum up, as a great orator would sum up his argument. All around us is fragmentation and alien and discordant elements often break up harmony in our lives. Look around you and you will see that things do not seem to add up. But they will add up, one day, in Christ.

Are you feeling discouraged today? Do you feel there is no purpose in your life? Do you think, "What have I to contribute?" Please realise Christian, that you will be part of that final statement, that final summation that God will make. Your conversion and Christian life will be part of it. It not only benefits you; it is a huge corporate experience. The whole cosmos will be re-integrated into its original harmony in Christ. The cosmos will also be unified toward a common goal.

Think of the hopelessness of life without Christ. It is to live a life which does not bring glory to God. It is to perish eternally. To be in Christ, though, is part of something bigger than you and I ever dream of. Relish it!

February *seventh*

> *"Which are in heaven and which are on earth - in Him"*
> (Ephesians 1:10)

We have all seen it happen. People who are from very different backgrounds and situations become one in Christ. They say it is as though they have known each other all of their lives. If that can happen between people, it is, according to today's verse, going to happen with all things both in earth and in heaven.

Life is full of extremes, of joy and sorrow, of suffering and pleasure. Money is unevenly distributed and the gap between the rich and the poor is huge. Inexplicable and discordant things constantly crash into our lives. It is all very confusing.

Consider, though, Paul writing this amazing letter. He is under house arrest, chained to different soldiers as their guard times rotate but his mind and heart soars out of his difficult circumstances into eternity. He is not doubting the purpose of God in his and the world's circumstances. He is not saying that the world is governed by the blind will of an uncaring Deity. All things in the universe and on earth will one day be finally subjected to Christ's headship. Every knee shall bow and every tongue confess that Jesus Christ is Lord.

In a world where the United Nations mediates or the "International Community" polices and where there are constant wars and rumours of wars, let your mind soar to that coming day. It will save you being swamped with the often relentless grinding of the immediate.

February *eighth*

> *"In whom we have obtained an inheritance"*
> (Ephesians 1:11-12)

Paul is writing here about the Jewish age. They were the people who first trusted or hoped in the Messiah. For centuries they had been waiting for Him. They stood out like a beacon light in comparison to other religions and heathen philosophies. Think of the great centres across the ages. Centres like Ur or Babylon, Stonehenge or the Mayan, Incan or Chinese centres of religion. The history of the world is a religious forest of concepts and texts, of practices and languages, of teachers and preachers, of guides, gurus and gods from Easter Island to Newgrange or the Hill of Tara in Ireland, from the dualistic school of Saivism in South India to Shinto, the underlying value orientation of the Japanese people. Through it all the Jewish people were chosen as special; "For the Lord's portion is His people, Jacob His allotted heritage". This didn't mean, of course, that other civilisations or philosophies didn't contribute anything to anything but it meant Israel was chosen for a very special purpose. They were not perfect, they were not better than anybody else, they often behaved abominably but they witnessed to the glory of God and His coming Messiah in a very special way.

I know people argue that in our desperately suffering world it is hard to believe that God had been working out a purpose through the ages. Yet, would you like to believe the alternative? Would you like to believe that there isn't anybody saying anything through history? Do you say with Camus that the whole thing is meaningless? God forbid.

February *ninth*

"In Him you also trusted"
(Ephesians 1:13)

Into our world came the Messsiah so long witnessed to by the Jewish people. No-one ever had spoken like Him, no-one ever had behaved like Him. He showed clearly that history had not been going around in circles. He explained that it was all linked in Him. There was a heart behind it all. On the way to Emmaus after His resurrection He showed to the two baffled disciples in all the Scriptures the things concerning Himself. He had other sheep which were not of the Jewish fold. He must bring them too.

So it was that He brought you into His fold. Now you are part of His body, the church and as Israel trusted or hoped in her Messiah, so you now trust and hope in Him. And it is not "hope so", it is a living hope. How many of our hopes have you and I had to bury? Too many. Here is a hope that will never die. Let it lift your spirit. Let it fuel your recovery from bad decisions. Let it inspire you to wait for God to work things out. Let it remind you that the Lord is still in control. He cares about your school or college studies. He cares about your marriage. He cares about your every-day work. Hope in God. You will not be disappointed. The Christian hope is to desire with expectation of obtainment. It is the fresh air of survival!

February *tenth*

> *"After you heard the word of truth, the Gospel of your salvation"*
> (Ephesians 1:13)

We are living in an age when we are told that New Testament Christians were very limited in their knowledge. We are informed that it was a pre-scientific age they lived in and that's why they swallowed the story of the resurrection of Christ. We are informed they didn't know much about other religions and now we must be more inclusive.

What people forget is that when the New Testament Christians preached the resurrection, most of their audience didn't believe in the possibility of any resurrection of any kind; this included high ranking priests in the temple! Sadducees didn't even believe in an after-life of the human spirit never to speak of a human body.

It wasn't that Christians didn't know much about other religions and so they believed in the risen Christ as the only Saviour and Redeemer: it was because they knew too much about those religions!

There is something about a Gospel that stands out anywhere. It towers above all other messages in the uniqueness of its claims. Its truth survives all false gospels. It is because of the One about whom it speaks. When Sundar Singh was questioned by a Professor of Comparative Religions as to what he found in Christianity which he had not found in his old religion he answered, "I have Christ". "Yes, I know", said the Professor, "but what particular principle or doctrine have you found that you did not have before?" "The particular thing I have found is Christ", he replied ('The Christ of the Indian Road' by Stanley Jones, Hodder and Stoughton, p.64).

February *eleventh*

> *"In whom having believed you were sealed with the Holy Spirit of promise"*
> (Ephesians 1:13)

Alexander the Great once sent his emissary to Egypt. He travelled without weapons or military escort, carrying only the seal of Alexander. He met with the mighty king who stood with his army behind him and communicated Alexander the Great's message: "Cease hostilities against Alexander's interests", he said. The King of Egypt, wishing to save face, said he would consider the request and let the emissary know.

At that Alexander's man stepped forward, drew a circle in the dirt around the King of Egypt and said: "Do not leave this circle without informing me of your response".

What nerve! The emissary was unarmed and alone yet the King dare not touch him because he carried the seal of Alexander. To touch him was to touch Alexander. To disobey the emissary was to disobey Alexander. To affront him was to affront Alexander. The King assessed his options and said: "Tell Alexander he has his request", and stepped out of the circle.

The seal of Alexander the Great was powerful but the Holy Spirit is our seal. God has put his mark on our lives. You are, Christian, God's own possession and are proteced by His power and authority.

February *twelfth*

> *"Who is the guarantee of our inheritance until the redemption of the purchased possession to the praise of His glory"*
> (Ephesians 1:14)

These bodies of ours are going to have to be changed if we are ever going to get into Heaven. We are not yet fully redeemed. As a guarantee that God is actually going to complete the redemption process He has given every Christian the Holy spirit to live within them. That is his down payment. "We also have the firstfruits of the Spirit", writes Paul, "even we ourselves groan within ourselves, eagerly waiting for the adoption, the redemption of our body" (Romans 8: 23).

The Holy Spirit is the guarantee of our inheritance. He is the pledge given to believers by God to assure us that the glory of the life to come is a well founded hope. The gift of the Holy Spirit is the guarantee of coming immortality. This is a reality, not an illusion. Christians can enter now into the enjoyment of what is theirs forever. They have the foretaste of it. The Holy Spirit is the first instalment, the down payment of our coming inheritance. He is a deposit: the full remainder of the blessings of our inheritance will come. In modern Greek the word "guarantee" is used for an engagement ring. It is a promise of something greater. If all the blessings we have in Christ now are so wonderful what will the full consummation be like? And all to the praise of His glory.

February *thirteenth*

> *"Your faith in the*
> *Lord Jesus"*
> (Ephesians 1:15)

It was a costly thing for so many to have faith in the Lord Jesus. The very man writing these words was an ambassador for Christ but an ambassador in chains. The monster Nero was in power. Across the years Nero and other emperors' indiscriminate slaughter of multitudes of Christians was put into effect. Stories of tortures borne for the faith by young people almost surpasses belief. The church was purified of nominal Christians afraid to suffer.

At Ephesus too, as the book of Acts shows, to be a Christian was a dangerous thing. Yet slowly and powerfully the Gospel had its influence in changing attitudes to all kinds of things; the position of women, personal purity in marriage, slavery, abuse of children, licentious sports, human legislation and distribution of property. As Brace wrote, "The power of Christianity on the Roman world was especially the influence of a Person, of a pure and elevated character who claimed to be a supernatural Being in his relations to men and God. His nature alone, from its purity and elevation, seemed to sweep away unnatural passions from among men both in the Roman Empire and after".

So you too have faith in the Lord Jesus? There is no telling what it will affect around you. Keep going, my much pressured reader, keep going. You are on the winning side.

February *fourteenth*

> *"Therefore I also,*
> *after I heard of*
> *your faith in the*
> *Lord Jesus and*
> *your love for all*
> *the saints"*
> (Ephesians 1:15)

There are people who say they have faith in the Lord Jesus but love for all believers is not apparent in their lives. Of course some people are easier to live with than others but if what people call faith does not result in their becoming more loving people then theirs is not genuine faith. You simply cannot have faith in the Lord Jesus and not grow in love.

It is possible to give intellectual assent to Christian truth and not know real faith. It ties in with James' teaching that faith without works is dead. Notice how faith and love are qualities often mentioned together in Scripture (11 Corinthians 8: 7; Galatians 5: 6; 1 Thessalonians 3: 6; 11 Thessalonians 1: 3; 1 Timothy 1: 5, 14; Ephesians 3: 17, 6,23).

Strange, isn't it, how Christians find it so hard to love one another? Bought with the same blood, indwelt by the same Spirit, saved by the same grace, guided by the same Scriptures, heading for the same Heaven, adopted by God into the same family but they don't get on very well together. It is probably the greatest single hindrance to revival blessing. Let the coupling of faith and love in today's text search us all.

February *fifteenth*

"Do not cease to give thanks for you making mention of you in my prayers"
(Ephesians 1:16-17)

Paul is about to tell the Christians at Ephesus that he has been asking God for something more special for them. That there are greater, wider and deeper and even more profound things available as we progress in the knowledge of God is a fact. It is also a fact that while there are spiritual blessings ahead there are also spiritual blessings we already have for which we ought to be thankful.

I remember, one evening, pouring out my heart to God in prayer at a prayer meeting in Scotland that God would really bless us at some evangelistic services we were having. A Scotsman called Alec Easton approached me afterward and in a very direct way he simply said, "Derick, try thanksgiving!" I deserved it. As we seek for more and more of God's blessings let us be marked by gratitude. Paul says he did not cease to give thanks for the Christians at Ephesus.

It is also worth noting that Paul was not slow in writing encouraging letters to Christians. How about you? Why not send out an E-mail to someone today whose faith has inspired you? Why not praise God for that person and write a note to say how much you appreciate them? You would be amazed how much it would mean to them.

February *sixteenth*

> *"The God of
> our Lord Jesus
> Christ"*
> (Ephesians 1:17)

Paul is about to tell us that he has been asking God for something in prayer. Why do we need to pray? We need to pray because we are grateful. This is called thanksgiving. We need to pray because of who God is. This is Christian worship. We need to pray because we need forgiveness. This is called confession. We need to pray because we need help. This is Christian petition. We need to pray because others need help. This is called intercession. We need to pray because Jesus is Lord. This is called consecration.

All of these are good reasons to pray. There is another, though. We need to pray because the Lord Jesus prayed. He is our supreme example. He began His ministry with prayer, He prayed early in the morning and at the end of the day. He prayed before making important decisions. He prayed before accomplishing great miracles. He ended His ministry in prayer. He still intercedes for us today.

Who, though, did the Lord Jesus pray to? He prayed to His Father. The Lord Jesus depended on His Father to answer His petitions. So Paul prays to the source, whom he calls the God of Our Lord Jesus. This of course refers to Christ's subjection in His humanity to the Father; this took nothing away from His eternal deity. As you think of those answers Jesus got to His prayers let it inspire you to come to His Father and yours with your requests today.

February *seventeenth*

> *"The Father of
> Glory"*
> (Ephesians 1:17)

This is the second title Paul uses of God in this prayer of his. He is first "The God of our Lord Jesus Christ" but He is also the Father of glory. He is the great revealer. He reveals His glory. His glory? Glory is the outward shining of the inward being of God. Here is a God who in a million ways reveals who He is.

If I were to walk into your home I could tell what kind of a person you were by the kind of things that you have in it; the colours you choose, the pictures you hang, the CDs you listen to, the books you read, the furniture you choose. What you like is revealed.

Just take a walk around God's world and you will see His glory revealed. The stars declare His glory. The snowdrop declares it, too. God's creativity in creation reveals His mind. The glory of its intricate detail from the billions of stars in the galaxies to a baby's smile is awesome. And yet the greatest revelation of the glory of God comes through our lovely Saviour. "For", writes Paul in 1 Corinthians 4: 6 "It is the God who commanded light to shine out of darkness who has shone in our hearts to give the light of the knowledge of the glory of God in the face of Jesus Christ". The glory of God as seen in His creation is incredible but impersonal. If your heart is breaking because of a breakdown in a relationship or through bereavement or some huge problem that has come into your life, a walk under the stars will not comfort you. The knowledge of the Lord Jesus, though, will. Lean hard on Him today. He will hold you up.

February *eighteenth*

> *"That the God of our Lord Jesus Christ, the Father of glory, may give to you the spirit of wisdom and revelation in the knowledge of Him"*
> (Ephesians 1:17)

You cannot do anything to make God love you more. You cannot do anything to make God love you less. He already loves you totally and perfectly in Christ. You are chosen, redeemed, forgiven, enriched, sealed and secure. To understand all this, though, you will need more than human understanding. You need the ministry of the Holy Spirit. He can illuminate your mind, revealing, unfolding and unveiling spiritual truth to your heart and mind.

You cannot ask God to give the Holy Spirit to those who have already received Him and who have been sealed by Him. You can and should pray for His ministry of illumination and enlightenment. The philosophy of the world says know yourself. The ministry of God, the Holy Spirit, is to help you to know God. Ask God to give you through the Spirit an insight and understanding of the knowledge of Himself. What higher knowledge could you possibly have? May the end of this day bring you a deeper knowledge of God. Be assured that such knowledge will never be taken away from you.

February *nineteenth*

You have inner eyes. These are the eyes of your heart, the eyes of your inmost self where the mainspring of feeling and faith, words and actions lies. When the Holy Spirit gets to work enlightening the eyes of your heart and understanding change takes place.

A few minutes ago I was in a car centre and was speaking to a Christian I know who works there. He was talking to me of how his father used to gamble for money and he couldn't understand why his wife wouldn't take the proceeds. He got so angry he used to fling the money on the floor. He was into serious and heavy drinking and heading for death. Then a friend pointed him to Christ and the Holy Spirit began to enlighten the eyes of his heart. The change was incredible. His attitude to gambling and alcohol changed. His attitude to his wife changed. Everything looked and became different.

That's how it is when the Holy Spirit enlightens the eyes of your heart. Fear is shown up as being groundless. Jealousy is seen as pointless. The ultimate emptiness of lust is exposed. Our disappointments are seen to be God's appointments. Loneliness is replaced with the assurance that we are not alone. Grief sees that God is the God of all comfort. Pain is seen as transient, real, but ultimately passing. Truth becomes crystal clear in a world of falsehood, pessimism becomes optimism. Patience is seen as being more fruitful than impatience. In fact darkness becomes light. Rejoice that your body is the temple of the Holy Spirit. He enlightens like no-one else can.

February *twentieth*

He owned sixteen shops and one Sunday afternoon he was playing golf at a local golf club. The thought suddenly occurred to him, "Is this it? Is this all there is?" He told me it led to his eventually becoming a Christian minister.

Is the low tide of depression and disappointment washing up on your beach? Are you weary and emotionally drained? Are you also haunted by the question, "Is this it? Is this all there is?" Let me remind you that there is more, much more. Paul's prayer is that Christians might have an eye-opener as to the hope of their calling. That hope is not, "hope so". That hope is that which we expect with confidence. That calling will involve taking over with Christ the running of God's vast creation one day. That fact is more real than any career that you could possibly imagine. Science can't tell you why the universe started and inform you of its ultimate goal. In Christ, though, you know its purpose and you are called to share in that purpose. Eyes have not seen, nor ears heard the things that God has prepared for those that love Him. Isaiah gave us a glimpse of it all in his prophesy when he wrote, "And He will destroy on this mountain the surface of the covering cast over all the people, and the veil that is spread over all nations. He will swallow up death for ever, and the Lord God will wipe tears from all faces ...... for the Lord has spoken" (Isaiah 25: 7-8). See, then, in the midst of your busy circumstances, the hope of your calling.

February *twenty-first*

"That you may know ... what are the riches of the glory of His inheritance in the saints"
(Ephesians 1:18)

God's people are His inheritance. They are very precious to Him. He has spent an enormous amount upon them. They cost Him the cross. He has spent a lot of time perfecting their redeemed character. Malachi the prophet spoke of it succinctly when he wrote, "They shall be mine, says the Lord of Hosts, on the day that I make them my jewels, and I will spare them as a man spares his own son who serves Him".

If I cut a believer dead and put out untruths about that believer then the idea that they are God's inheritance is still only words in my experience. It has not percolated through and become a reality to me, yet. If it were a reality then I would be afraid to injure a child of God.

Let the Holy Spirit enlighten you to the fact that you, as part of the church, are part of God's gift to His Son. And you are not a poor inheritance, either. God sees you in Christ. His estimate of you is consistent with His estimate of Christ. You and I are part of the body of Christ, we are His bride. This is the glory of God's inheritance in His people; it consists of who and what they are in Christ. If our eyes were truly open to this truth would it not profoundly affect the way we behave every day?

February *twenty-second*

"And what is the exceeding greatness of His power toward us who believe"
(Ephesians 1:19)

Here is power. Here is His power. Here is great power. Here is exceeding great power. According to the Greek word employed it is power beyond the furtherest cast of thought.

Are you afraid? Are you feeling insecure? Do some people treat you so badly you almost feel like asking them would it be all right if you breathed? Are you feeling inadequate for the tasks you face? Do the forces of evil around you seem to be too great for you? Are you tempted to quit?

Stop then, for a moment, and contemplate the power of God. When the eaglet first flies the mother bird flies in behind and creates air currents that give the young one lift. That's what it means to be borne on eagles' wings. The Hebrew word for "bear" means "to lift". God will bear you on eagles' wings. You will mount up on His supporting power. Of course we fail. Of course we are inadequate to soar. But with this kind of power available we can be invincible. No wonder Paul prays that our spiritual eyes will be opened to be made aware of the awesome power at hand. Language fails to fully describe it. Let's hope it doesn't take a storm like the one the disciples had to go through to make us realise its effectiveness. There is no greater power.

February *twenty-third*

"Which He worked in Christ when He raised Him from the dead"
(Ephesians 1:20)

The power now available to us is, of course, resurrection power. Ray Steadman in his book "Riches in Christ" (Discovery Foundation, 1976) gives a very concise summary, in practical terms of what this resurrection power means. He points out that it takes no notice of obstacles, "For Jesus rose from the dead paying no attention to the stone, to the decrees of Ceasar, to the criticisms of the Jewish priests, nor to the guard in front of the tomb. It leaves problems to God and goes on. Resurrection power requires no outside support. It doesn't rely upon someone else, nor upon something else. It doesn't need a vote of confidence. It doesn't need statements of support from anybody. It can operate completely alone, if necessary. It doesn't make a noise or a display. It doesn't seek publicity. It quietly brings life out of death".

Have you found in your Christian life that you do not need to know key men and women to succeed? All you need to know is the one who holds the key. And He holds the key to this resurrection power. It doesn't mean you won't have heartache in this life or disappointment, even tears. The Lord Jesus had all of these but God raised Him from the dead by resurrection power. That same power is available to you, today.

February *twenty-fourth*

> *"... and seated Him at His right hand in the heavenly places"*
> (Ephesians 1:20)

Christ's victory over death is not only seen in His resurrecton. It is seen in His exaltation to a position of power and authority. The phrase "and seated Him at His right hand in heavenly places" does not mean that Christ sits all the time in any particular place. The phrase denotes that the Lord Jesus has been raised to the very highest position of power and authority. It has parallels in the ancient near Eastern world when a king was often represented as seated next to the deity of a particular city or nation. Occupying a place an the deity's right-hand meant that the ruler exercised power on behalf of the deity. So Christ is on God's right hand, a place of favour, of power and of victory.

From a Roman cross to a darkened tomb to the highest position is a long way. I have stood and gazed at the stars, betimes, or even on the beauty of a flower and ached. I know there is a hand behind it. There to the right of that hand is my Saviour who died for me. The power that put Him there is mine and yours to face what we must face today. Encouraging, isn't it?

February *twenty-fifth*

"Far above all principality and power and might and dominion"
(Ephesians 1:21)

There were false teachers about. They were causing trouble among Christians by grossly over-estimating the position of angels. They taught that angelic powers were controlling the heavenly realm and with it the persons access to the presence of God. One way of placating them was a subduing of the body to gain visionary experience of the heavenly dimension. This led, they said, to gaining full salvation. They taught that these angels had worship due to them.

Around Ephesus, (as Acts 19: 11-41 shows) there was a huge emphasis on magic and spiritual powers and it was the great centre for the worship of Diana, the primary goddess in Ephesus. Astrological beliefs were associated with the worship of Diana. It is difficult to define the precise meaning of principalities, powers, might and dominion but this verse is teaching that whatever powers exist they are all subject to the Lord Jesus. At the beginning of a new millennium with the huge rise of the interest in the occult and New Age teaching all around us, just concentrate on the word "all" in today's verse. There are no exceptions.

February *twenty-sixth*

"... amd every name that is named, not only in this age, but also in that which is to come"
(Ephesians 1:17)

On my desk lies a copy of the Oxford Dictionary of World Religions. It has eight thousand entries offering detail on the main religions, sects and cults, spiritual leaders, religious texts, beliefs and festivals around the globe. When I apply today's text to this book I find it very enlightening.

Our Lord Jesus is not only superior to every kind of power that exists, He is superior to every name that is named. Multitudes of teachers of religion and gods of men surround us in history and in our present day. You could begin a detailed study of them and never finish it in a lifetime. This Name, though, towers above every one of them. There are numerous names of gods that people call upon that we will never know. It doesn't matter. Christ is superior to all of them. And in a future age? That will bring nothing new. The victory of Christ's exaltation and superiority over every name will continue into the coming age, too.

Let's honour that Name. Let's never be ashamed of it and always seek to uplift it. Let's suffer for its sake, if necessary. Let's lean on its power. No matter who tries to make it equal to others let's resist such efforts. His name is not just higher, it's the highest.

February *twenty-seventh*

> *"And put all things under His feet"*
> (Ephesians 1:22)

These words are among the most difficult in all of Ephesians to interpret. Professor F. F. Bruce (The New International Commentary on the New Testament, Erdman's, Page 274-275, 1984) brings a hugely helpful comment to the questions they raise. He points out that in Psalm 110: 1 we read, "Sit at my right hand till I make your enemies your footstool". He says it is probable that the clause immediately following "sit at my right hand" was not remote from Paul's mind when he refers to Christ as being exalted to the Father's right hand.

Insofar as "principalities and powers, might and dominion and every name that is named" are hostile then they will experience being put down by force and placed under Christ's victory. The church, on the other hand, is also subjected to Him. He is supreme Head over the church, but it is a supremacy of love and force is not involved at any stage.

Isn't it superb to be under the supremacy of Christ by love rather than having to bow by force?

February *twenty-eighth*

> *"Which is His body, the fullness of Him who fills all in all"*
> (Ephesians 1:23)

Some think this verse means that just as the head is not complete without a body, so the church is that which makes Christ complete. They teach that each member of the church is needed to manifest Christ's fullness.

On balance the most accurate interpretation seems to be that the phrase means that the church is that which Christ fills. As a dawn sunlight fills the morning, so Christ fills His church. Note He fills "all in all". No matter what the church goes through, no matter what it faces whether in sorrow or pleasure, in persecution or revival, in times of war or in times of peace; He fills all in all. It also implies that Christ fills all of the universe in all respects. By Him all things consist. If He were to pull out the whole thing would fall apart.

I don't know where you are today. I don't know what you face but you have all of Christ in all you face. All in all. So don't be afraid.

February *twenty-ninth*

> **"To the praise of His glory"**
> (Ephesians 1:24)

As we come to the end of our meditations on this incredible chapter, it might be wise if we lifted our head to look at the amazing view before us. When mountain climbing it is rather easy to keep our's head down, or give so much attention to finding the right path to the top that we miss the splendour of the mountain range around us. We wouldn't want to get so much into the geology of mountains that we miss the magnificent vistas the mountain affords. Would we?

It's so easy to get into the detail of this part of Scripture and miss the wonder of the person of our Lord Jesus in all of this. Just lift your eyes to the summit of this great chapter and you will see your Saviour exalted in His resurrection to a place where He is above every conceivable thing. No wonder He said to Mary on that resurrection morning, "Do not cling to Me, for I have not yet ascended to My Father; but go to my brethren and say to them, 'I am ascending to my Father and Your Father, and to My God and your God'". He was saying, "Don't hold me back, Mary, I am on my way to that highest place where the very power that will take Me there will be the very power that will work in you". Selah.

MARCH

Mountains have their ravines and their summits, they plunge and rise. In Ephesians chapter two Paul shows very clearly that by nature we plunge into incredible depths because of sin. We are, by nature, alienated from God and without hope in the world. In the ravine of sin it is very dark indeed.

Grace, though, lifts us to incredible heights. In fact, by grace, God has "raised us up with Christ" and "seated us in heavenly realms."

For the Christian alienation from God is a thing of the past and through Christ both Jew and Gentile have access to the Father by one Spirit. Through March our theme of readings will be the incredible journey from darkness to light, from the kingdom of darkness to the kingdom of God's dear Son. To move from miry clay to having your feet set upon a rock is quite a transformation.

March *first*

> *"And you ... who were dead ..."*
> (Ephesians 2:1)

The contrast of what we are in Christ to what we were naturally is now highlighted. It is a devastating analysis of the human condition. Millions of people simply don't believe it and are blinded to the power of Christ and what His grace can do for them.

This verse is telling us that no matter how gifted, no matter how intellectually bright, no matter how well mannered and kind, no matter how vigorous in sport or business or politics or whatever, people who do not know Christ are spiritually dead. They are naturally alive, yes, but they have no spiritual life in their souls. "The natural man" says 1 Corinthians 2: 14 "does not receive the things of the Spirit of God for they are foolishness to him: nor can he know them because they are spiritually discerned". "She who lives in pleasure is dead while she lives", says 1 Timothy 5: 6.

Don't you think this realisation of devastating truth ought to give us compassion for those outside of Christ? The stained-glass windows of a great cathedral do not look much from the outside. You need to be inside to get people to catch their glory. So it is that those who are without Christ need to have the eyes of their understanding opened by the Spirit of God to see the beauties and glories of knowing and living for Jesus Christ. The Scripture puts it very succinctly when it says "The dead shall hear and live". It seems an impossible situation that the dead could ever hear but spiritually speaking that is exactly what happens when a person is led to Christ. In the meantime try and remember what it was like to be in the dark even though you are now in the light. Have pity.

March *second*

> *"In trespasses and sins ..."*
> (Ephesians 2:1)

The whole gamut of human evil is summed up in two words. To trespass is to deviate from the right path or to cross a known boundary. To sin is to "miss the mark", "to fall short of a standard".

The world would call this analysis very simplistic but in the final analysis it is absolutely accurate. I remember chatting to a former member of the British Cabinet and he told me how that at a Cabinet meeting one day the then British Prime Minister was discussing a huge problem facing the nation. The Cabinet discussed the problem in depth and then the Prime Minister suddenly looked up and admitted that the real reason for the problem was original sin.

No matter how high our ideals, no matter how well intentioned we are, we have a bias toward trespasses and sins. That's why we need to be born again. Remember that this verse is not describing a particular decadent part of human society. This verse is describing it all! It is a Biblical diagnosis of fallen society everywhere. It is a universal truth.

Let's not be afraid to use this diagnosis as we move amongst people. They will call sin everything but sin and trespass everything but trespass. Let our witness expose it for what it is for how can people know they need a Saviour if they don't know they have something to be saved from?

March *third*

> *"In which you once walked according to the course of this world"*
> (Ephesians 2:1)

In our world men, women and young people live as if this world were the only world that exists. They live as if this world, in its present phase, were going on forever.

Whatever you do, please to not live "according to the age" or according to "the present phase of this world". Why? Because it is not permanent. A scientist will tell you it is not permanent. Yet you don't even need scientists to prove it to you: you only have to look around. In the world of popular music, how long does a "hit" last? In the fashion world, how long does the current fashion last? In the world of architecture how long does an era last? In a world of empires, or world super powers, how long is it before they pass? It does not matter if you are speaking of the power of the Roman Empire or a modern day power: all decline, one day. Nothing is permanent, not even this earth on which we stand.

The spirit of our age and the course it takes is unconcerned about God or His purposes. It lives alienated from God. Paul is telling the Ephesian Christians that they once walked according to the course of this world and he is warning them not to yield to the temptation to go back. The things of God are permanent. The things of this world are temporary. Choose the eternal, always.

March *fourth*

> *"According to the prince of the power of the air"*
> (Ephesians 2:1)

" **T**he power of the air" is a very difficult phrase to understand. If you dip into various commentaries on the subject it is obvious that the phrase has caused a lot of discussion. Perhaps it simply means "the power of the unseen world". The air is all around us but we do not see it. It is invisible. Yet, it is extremely powerful. It pervades our environment, entirely.

Satan and his demons are invisible to us, yet there is no part of this earth in which their power is not felt. Satan is called "The Prince" of this kingdom of evil, unseen but real. Paul is saying to the Ephesian Christians that they once obeyed Satan, walking according to his dictate.

Are you afraid of Satan and his powers, Christian? You need not be. At Calvary Christ "disarmed principalities and powers" (Colossians 2:15) and "He made a public spectacle of them, triumphing over them". "The God of peace will crush Satan under your feet shortly", says Romans 16: 20.

When I was a lad my mother used to tell me that if I was tempted I should pray a simple prayer. I should simply say, "Lord Jesus, come close to me, now". Try it.

March *fifth*

> *"The spirit who now works in the children of disobedience"*
> (Ephesians 2:1)

If there is evil and greed, jealousy and envy, strife and violence, or sin of any kind you can be sure that the devil is at the back of it. He challenges every single law and force which God has brought about for the good of the human race. It has been well said that obedience to the wrong ruler means being in a state of disobedience to the right one. Across the world it is very obvious that Satan is the ruler of the spirit which works in disobedient people.

The spirit or mood of disobedient people is so depressing. The musician denies the God who created his music. The artist denies the God who created

54

the beauty he is painting. The scientist is amazed by the cell he is studying but denies the God who made its intricacy. "Do you think there is a God behind it all?", I asked the man-in-charge after a planetarium showing of the glory of the universe. "We are not allowed to answer religious questions", he replied!

Now, Christian, that you have been liberated by Christ from such a spirit of disobedience make sure, when the opposition arises, that you speak up for your Lord. Be obedient to your heavenly calling.

March *sixth*

> *"Among whom also we all once conducted ourselves in the lusts of our flesh, fulfilling the desires of the flesh and of the mind, and were by nature children of wrath, just as the others"*
>
> (Ephesians 2:3)

If we are motivated by the desires of the flesh and mind that our fallen nature has produced, is it any wonder we would be the object of God's wrath? There would be something wrong if God's wrath didn't rest on such a life.

We must always remember, though, that God's wrath is not like ours. It is not bad temper, it is not spite, nor malice, nor animosity, nor revenge. God's wrath is not arbitrary and is never subject to mood or whim. It is righteous and constantly hostile to evil. It is a settled refusal to compromise with it and the resolve to condemn it.

Today's verse shows that we are not all the children of God by natural birth. We are born "in Adam" with an inherited nature tainted by the fall. It does not mean that mankind does not have dignity for we have not altogether lost the divine image but it does mean that "outside of Christ" we are condemned under the wrath of God. If left to ourselves this is our natural condition.

Paul's diagnosis is an unpopular diagnosis and devastating. A look around the world today, despite all its education and legislation shows how Paul's diagnosis is absolutely accurate. That's why the world needs the Gospel. Are you telling it out?

March *seventh*

> **"But God"**
> (Ephesians 2:4)

Abraham lied and was thrown out of Egypt but God restored him and he became the father of the faithful. Jacob conned and manipulated his way but God met with him and transformed him into Israel, meaning a Prince with God. Joseph was the object of unremitting jealousy from his brothers and ended up an obscure slave but God made him Prime Minister of Egypt. Ruth was a stranger to the commonwealth of Israel, she had, socially, the lowest position in the land as a gleaner but God brought her into a position where, from her womb, down the centuries came the Saviour of the world. Elijah sat by a dried brook with neither water nor food but God sent the widow of Zarephath to give him her last meal. Then her bin of flour was not used up nor her jar of oil did not run dry until the day the Lord sent rain on the earth.

Then there was David ..... but God! And Esther ..... but God! And Job .... but God! And James and John .... but God! And Peter ...... but God! And Paul ...... but God! And the Ephesian Christians ...... but God! And you .... I care not how difficult your circumstances, how dark your day, how frightening the threats against you, it may all seem impossible but not so impossible that these two words cannot be applied to what you face at this hour ..... but God! Say them over to yourself. Tuck them into your heart and wait and see what they represent unravel before your eyes.

March *eighth*

> **"Who is rich in mercy"**
> (Ephesians 2:4)

God's wrath is something we should praise Him for. What if God were not consistently against evil? If He did not have the attribute of wrath where would we be? The wrath of God has been called "the law of an inevitable consequence". We should be very glad it is there.

Obviously we deserved wrath but then God moved to alleviate our misery. What moved Him? His mercy. Mercy is the outward manifestation of pity: it assumes need on the part of him or her who receives it and assumes resources adequate to meet the need on the part of him who shows it. Our need is the removal of the penalty we deserve, namely God's wrath and its consequences. Incredible, isn't it, that the very God whose wrath we deserve shows us pity and through faith in Christ's Calvary work the penalty is removed? Wrath and mercy met at Calvary and we go free. What if God had been stinting in His mercy? In mercy, though, He is rich. "The Lord is merciful", wrote David, "And gracious, slow to anger and abounding in mercy". If anyone should know David was that person. Take heart.

March *ninth*

"Because of His great love with which He loved us"
(Ephesians 2:4)

God's alleviation of our misery was motivated by His mercy but His mercy arose out of His love. Just as God is "rich in mercy", He is "great" in love.

My friend Douglas Gresham is fond of saying that love is not a feeling, love is what you do. God's love is certainly not passive, it is active. God loved us but He did something about it. When Adam went wrong, God went after him. He came after us, too. His love loves the unlovable. He didn't address us from the clouds. He didn't preach to us from a pulpit. He didn't just hand us some literature and tell us to read it. He was incarnated. He became one of us. Christ was known as a man of sorrows. He was acquainted with grief. He died out of His great love for us.

There are many comforts, I find, in the Christian life. God's love, though, is my supreme comfort. All through my life this incredible truth has kept breaking through my doubts, my fears, my worries, my times of deep anxiety and my times of deep joy. God loved the world: that's good. Christ loved the church: that's great. But it is as an individual I am loved of God, too. "The Son of God .... who loved me and gave Himself for me", says Galatians 2: 20. This applies to every moment of every day. If I were to swim in the ocean of God's love for ten million years I would never come to the shore. Why? Because there is no shore.

March *tenth*

> *"Even when we were dead in trespasses, made us alive together with Christ (by grace you have been saved)"*
> (Ephesians 2:5)

When a person becomes a Christian they immediately identify with Christ's death. Because a crucified person does not have any plans of their own, the new Christian dies to self and is "brought from death to life 'with Christ'". The new Christian also dies to his or her old life. "Do not", writes Paul, "present your members as instruments of unrighteousness to sin but present yourselves to God as being alive from the dead and your members as instruments of righteousness to God" (Romans 6: 13).

Today's verse, though, touches on another sequel. It is to be "made alive" (or "raised") with Christ from being dead through trespasses. This is not physical resurrection. It is, though, a spiritual resurrection. We read in John's gospel that "the dead shall hear and live". Can you imagine walking up to a dead person and speaking something to them and they rise up and walk? Imagine, then, someone completely dead spiritually though physically alive. Dead in trespasses. Dead to God. Dead to Christ. Dead to the Holy Spirit. Dead to the Scriptures and not interested in anything to do with the Gospel. And then? Then, suddenly, they hear the Word of Life, believe it and are made alive in Christ or co-resurrected with Christ! Impossible? It happens every day, as Paul asserts, by the grace of God.

So, keep on speaking of your Saviour and the good news of the Gospel. That spiritually dead one could be raised to spiritual life this very day through the Holy Spirit backing your word of witness. I read of one man who heard the Gospel preached in England and was converted in the United States seventy years later when he suddenly remembered the sermon!

March *eleventh*

> *"And raised us up together and made us sit together in the heavenly places in Christ Jesus"*
> (Ephesians 2:6)

Professor Bruce (Bruce, Page 287) gives a very succinct summary of this fascinating verse. He writes, "It can best be understood as a statement of God's purpose for His people - a purpose which is so sure of fulfilment that it can be spoken of as having already taken place. 'Whom He justified them he also glorified'" (Romans 8:30).

In Revelation 3:21 God promises the overcomer that He will "Grant him to sit with Me on my throne, as I myself overcame and sat down with My Father on His throne". Yet, if I am in Christ, that is, incorporated in Him, my true home is where Christ is. My citizenship is in Heaven. My life is hid with Christ in God. My name is on Heaven's register, my interests have been promoted there. If Christ is there, that is where my heart is. One day I'll be there physically. This verse assures me of that.

Meanwhile? Let me live a life that shows that my primary citizenship is in Heaven. Let its standards guide me and its language mark me. Let its glories make all other glories fade.

March *twelfth*

"That in the ages to come He might show the exceeding riches of His grace in His kindness towards us in Christ Jesus"
(Ephesians 2:7)

A principal of Ridley Hall, Cambridge, retired and an outstanding portrait of him was unveiled. He made a speech with a rather endearing comment. He said that in future he believed that people looking at the picture would not ask, "Who is that man?" but rather "Who painted the portrait?"!

Today's verse is telling us that it will take eternity, age succeeding age, to fully display all that God has done in His people through grace. The phrase is without limitation, it means for all of the future God will show the exceeeding riches of His grace in His kindness towards us in Christ Jesus.

Is God's grace extravagant? It certainly is. To capture its extravagance Paul speaks not just of God's grace, but of the riches of His grace, and not just the riches of His grace but the exceeding or surpassing richness of His grace. That grace is yours for all you face today, tomorrow and forever. So quit worrying.

March *thirteenth*

> *"For by grace
> you have been
> saved through
> faith"*
> (Ephesians 2:8)

The unsurpassed grace of God has brought us salvation. We have been saved from the wrath of God, made alive in Christ and are on our way to an eternity of service for Him where there will be no sickness, no sorrow and no death. "You have been saved", writes Paul, summing all our blessings up in one of the greatest foundation words of the Christian gospel.

This salvation is through faith. What is faith? It is the evidence of things not seen. The maxim of human experience says, "Seeing is believing" but for the child of God the reverse is true, "Believing is seeing". Of course to have faith three things have got to happen. Someone must make a promise. There must be a very good reason for believing the integrity of the person making the promise. Then there follows a comfortable assurance that it will be so!

The promises of God are faith's nature food. There is nothing God loves more than for you to bring before Him promises He has made and claim them as yours. You have been saved through faith; now move on in your Christian experience and let faith lift you out of the ranks of mediocrity. Let faith be the master principle of your life. It flourishes in any place, any circumstance, and at any time. Live by faith and see mountains fall before you.

March *fourteenth*

> *"And that not of
> yourselves; it is the
> gift of God, not of
> works, lest anyone
> should boast"*
> (Ephesians 2:9)

Lest anyone should boast; would they? Would they what? Man, written large, is very large indeed. Look at the world of sports, the world of business, the world of the arts, the world of design and fashion. Listen to people talk. Seldom is God ever mentioned. Man couldn't produce even a little alpine flower and you would think he was at the back of creation!

"We have the Rockies", "We have the Alps", "We have the Himalayas", "We have Table Mountain", "We have the Remarkables": travel around the world and you would think nations created their mountain ranges! If on some television programme covering the sheer beauty of the natural world a commentator said, "What a God to have created this!", there would probably be questions in Congress or Parliament!

If man thought he could gain status or privilege with God by some human accomplishment of his, how he would boast about it. Across the world the cry seems to be, "Glory to man in the highest - see what he has done!". It is not that man is incompetent, it is that his competence is a gift from God and has no part in his salvation. "Let him who glories, glory in this, that he understands and knows Me, that I am the Lord, exercising loving-kindness, judgment and righteousness in the earth, for in these I delight", says the Lord (Jeremiah 9: 24). Somewhere today in your busy life, "glory" in your conversation about the Lord. It brings Him delight.

March *fifteenth*

> *"For we are his workmanship, created in Christ Jesus for good works, which God prepared beforehand that we should walk in them"*
> (Ephesians 2:10)

So now that we are saved and works have nothing to do with it, does that mean our Christian life has nothing to do with works? The opposite is the case. Salvation is certainly not from works but it is most certainly for works.

For me, I read destiny in these words. The great Creator has brought about a new creation, for every believer is a new creation in Christ, a masterpiece of His workmanship. Long before they were born the Lord had works he wanted them to do for Him. I sometimes think about Samson. Did not the Angel of the Lord appear to his mother before Samson was even conceived and tell her that Samson would "begin" to deliver Israel out of the hand of the Philistines? For all his faults that is exactly what Samson did before he died.

The very man who wrote today's text also wrote that "It pleased God, who separated me from my mother's womb and called me through His grace, to reveal His son in me that I might preach Him among the Gentiles".

If God had a destiny for the people who appear on the pages of Scripture does He not have a destiny for you to fulfil? A destiny among pots and pans and school runs. A destiny in a computer programming or sales targets? A destiny in raising little children or managing a company? A destiny on your farm or in your factory? A destiny in the school class you teach or the hospital where you work as a nurse? Of course He has. One of the most wonderful things about being a Christian is that as you go forward in the will of God you will find yourself in a ministry which God has prepared beforehand that you should fulfil. Be patient, you'll see.

March *sixteenth*

"Therefore remember that you, once Gentiles in the flesh - who are called Uncircumcision by what is called the Circumcision made in the flesh by hands"
(Ephesians 2:11)

The Ephesians lived at a time when the divisions between Jews and Gentiles were absolute. God had called Israel to special privileges, and circumcision distinguished them from other people. Yet, they had twisted their privileges into favouritism and turned their differences into a barrier.

They saw Gentiles as an object of contempt. They did not even consider it lawful to help a Gentile mother in her hour of sorest need for that would be to bring another Gentile into the world.

As far as the Jew was concerned there were only those of the Circumcision and those of the Uncircumcision. There was no unity between them nor could there ever be.

That is the way it was until Jesus came with His Gospel. The Gospel is the only message that overcame that huge obstacle to unity. A Jew who trusted Christ as his or her Messiah and a Gentile who did the same became one in Christ. They were not a Gentile Christian or a Jewish Christian. They were simply Christians. When certain Judeans began to teach in the early church that "unless you are circumcised according to the custom of Moses you cannot be saved", Paul and Barnabas had no small dissention and dispute with them. A very important gathering of apostles and elders was called at Jersualem to discuss this question. At the Coucil of Jerusalem Peter speaking of Gentiles put it perfectly when he said, "But we believe that through the grace of our Lord Jesus Christ we shall be saved in the same manner as they."

It is no different today. Spread the Gospel and it will unite divided people like nothing else will. Look at New Testament times. Look at the diversity! We read, for example, of a slave and a slave owner, a business woman and a centurion, a jail governor and a formerly spirit possessed girl, a Pharisee and a doctor, a tent maker and an orator: it is an inspiring story of the power of the Gospel to reach people at all kinds of levels of society. Its power is just as great, today.

March *seventeenth*

> *"That at that time you were without Christ, being aliens from the commonwealth of Israel and strangers from the covenants of promise, having no hope and without God in the world"*
> (Ephesians 2:12)

Have you ever come across someone who has forgotten, or tries to forget their origins? They have risen to wealth, position and influence but don't want to be reminded of poorer, leaner, narrower times. It is an unhealthy state.

Christians too need to remember their former state in order to help them to constantly focus the change the Lord Jesus has accomplished in their lives. This remembering brings out praise and gratitude and a desire to live out an obedient, thankful life for God.

Gentiles, Paul emphasises, were deprived of five elements. They had no relation to Christ, they had no part in God's purposes with Israel, they were excluded from covenants like those God had made with Abraham and David, they were without hope, they worshipped other gods, but were without God in the sphere in which they lived. Without the Lord Jesus, of course, they would have continued in this state.

I feel the communion service is a particularly good place to think about what you once were and what you now are in Christ. Next time you attend one meditate on this question: Where would I be now and what would have become of me without the Lord Jesus? You'll find it a humbling, cleansing, inspiring meditation. Of course it would do no harm to meditate on this question at some time in every day, wouldn't it?

March *eighteenth*

> *"But now in Christ Jesus you who once were far off have been made near by the blood of Christ"*
> (Ephesians 2:13)

Let's approach the great Temple in Jerusalem in Christ's time. There are very clear divisions in its structure. There were four successive walled courts. The first was the Court of the Gentiles. It was not holy ground and non-Jews could enter it. Here buying and selling took place. A stone wall surrounded it and on the wall stones, three cubits high, were placed inscriptions in Greek and Latin. They read, "No stranger is to enter within the balustrade around the temple and enclosure. Whoever is caught will be responsible to himself for his death which will ensue".

Following this court was the inner court, the Court of the People, the temple precinct. It was holy ground. Here Jews could enter. Then there was the Court of the Priest, and of course the "Holiest of All" where no Priest could enter except the High Priest and he only once a year on the Day of Atonement. The furtherest away were the Gentiles who could not get into God's presence at all.

"It is finished", Christ cried at Calvary. His blood had been shed. His life had been poured out. The price of our atonement paid. And the curtain in the temple ripped from the top to the bottom. The way into God's presence was now open through a new and living way. The ritual was finished and the believer in Jesus with full assurance of faith can now draw near.

Do we, though, avail ourselves of this priceless privilege? We have been made near but do we draw near daily, coming boldly to the throne of grace to obtain help in time of need? Could it be Christian, that you have not because you ask not? Come on, even at this very minute, draw near and ask.

March *nineteenth*

> *"For He Himself is our peace, who has made both one"*
> (Ephesians 2:14)

If two estranged groups are to be united and the "far" brought "near" then peace is going to have to be made between the two groups. That peace must have a source. Up until now in each of the three preceding sections of this great letter to the Ephesians God has been to the fore in the thought pattern. Now in this section, Christ becomes central to the thought pattern before us. Some think this section may have been a hymn used by early Christians which theologians call a "Christological hymn", that is the Lord Jesus is the great theme of the hymn.

Peace, here, is a cessation of hostilities, an overcoming of alienation and a laying down and a removal of a soured relationship for a new unity of heart and purpose. How? It's all in a person. In our text Christ is not just the giver of peace or the proclaimer of peace or the peacemaker but He is our peace. Peace is a person.

Have you found Christ to be exactly that in your life, Christian? You feel animosity to someone and then you think of your Saviour and immediately your attitude changes. Your disturbing thoughts go because of Him. You feel ambition overwhelming you, the desire to "succeed" eats into your decision making and then you think of Him who made Himself of no reputation and you surrender your ambitions to Him and balance returns to your lifestyle. Worry over the future gnaws at the vitals of your life and then you realise that in Christ although all things that happen to you are not good they all work together for good. Result? Peace. No wonder our Lord Jesus is called the Prince of Peace. At all levels of your life and mine, all has changed "since Jesus came to stay". Right?

March *twentieth*

> *"And has broken down the middle wall of division between us"*
> (Ephesians 2:14)

Shortly before his escape from Elba, Napoleon Bonaparte granted a rare interview to a young Englishman called Charles Standish. Standish wrote about the interview in a letter to his cousin Peregine Townley.

The interview was first published in the Daily Telegraph on Saturday, April 24th 1999. It stated that Standish was asked by Napoleon if he had ever been in the army or navy and Standish replied that he hadn't. Napoleon asked him why and he told him that being of a different persuasion from the established Church of England, promotion was not open to him.

"You are a Catholic and I too", replied Napoleon, "we are the same, then. But what stupidity. What weakness for a great nation like yours". Napoleon poured questions on the subject of laws enforced against Roman Catholics in England. He was obviously fascinated by the subject and then be began to tell Standish his views on religion. "I, I tolerate all", he said, "I have made churches of Protestants, Jews and Catholics". He told of building a mosque for the Turks who "believed him to be a true son of the Prophet".

It was the last interview with the tyrant but it shows clearly how ambition in Napoleon's heart led him to "play religion to suit a political purpose". How different Paul's teaching and attitude! Napoleon ravaged and plundered across Europe driven by his ambitions and ultimately united nothing. The Lord Jesus stooped to conquer on a cross and of His kingdom there will be no end. The middle wall of partition between Jews and Gentiles was broken by Calvary's work and now out of every tongue and tribe and nation you will find people who are all one in Christ Jesus. Away with political religion! Let's preach, live, breathe Christ and Him crucified, buried, risen and coming again.

March *twenty-first*

"Having abolished in His flesh the enmity, that is the law of commandments contained in ordinances, so as to create in Himself one new man from the two, thus making peace"
(Ephesians 2:15)

One thing the law of God did above everything else was to reveal the character of God and the standard of righteousness He required. When it was written down as a written code it threatened death to those who disobeyed it and sacrifices for sin by Israelites could not enable them to obtain the righteousness required.

The Old Covenant and the New Covenant are very different. The Lord Jesus by His death bore the "curse of the law", the judgment that it threatened to those who disobeyed. Its rules and regulations of sacrifices, dietary laws and ritual cleanness and uncleanness are abolished. Circumcision and festivals which divided Jew and Gentile are gone. The regulations of the ceremonial law and the frightening condemnation of the moral law were abolished by Christ's victorious death at Calvary.

You remember the woman taken in adultery? The religious authorities asked Christ, "Now Moses in the law commanded us that such should be stoned. What do you say?" How could the Lord set the woman free, which He subsequently did, and uphold the law at the same time? Because in a few weeks He would climb Calvary's hill and be executed in the woman's place. He met the law's demands and on repenting toward God and faith in Christ the woman was forgiven. And so, Christian, are you. Is it any wonder that Calvary is the central point where past and future meet? We glory in the cross.

March *twenty-second*

"And that He might reconcile them both to God in one body through the cross, thereby putting to death the enmity"
(Ephesians 2:16)

The story is told of a mother and father who were estranged. Love had gone between them. They could not, it would seem, be reconciled. Then their daughter took very ill. The child was taken to hospital and the authorities could see that though the child loved her mother she also deeply loved her father and was pining for him. They asked that the father visit his daughter.

Eventually he came to the hospital and there was his wife sitting at the side of the bed. The "body language" between them said it all. The enmity, hostility, aggravation and even detestation between them was obvious. Then, suddenly, their daughter with one hand took her mother's hand and her father's with her other hand and brought them together over her body. Her head then fell in death.

Do you think that the mother and father continued with their hostility? Do you think they continued to be estranged? No. They were reconciled to each other through the death of their daughter.

So on Calvary our Lord Jesus reached out and "touched" His Father and reached out and "touched" you and me. On a response to His call to repentance and faith we are reconciled to God. Just as Jew and Gentile are reconciled in Christ in one body and the enmity "put to death" between them, so it is for all who are reconciled to God through the death of His Son.

March *twenty-third*

"And He came and preached peace to you who were afar off and to those who were near"
(Ephesians 2:17)

Christ is our peace (v. 14), Christ made peace (v.15) and our text for today tells us that He preached peace. The very first words the Lord Jesus said when He re-appeared to His disciples after His death were "Peace be with you". What kind of peace is Paul talking of in the text? He is speaking of peace with God. Christ brings peace between Jew and Gentile, of course. But He also brings peace with God for each group.

How can I ever tell whose eye will fall on these lines that I am writing? Maybe you would give anything to have peace with God. You don't need to give anything. All that is required has already been given in the death of the Lord Jesus. God's wrath against your sin was poured out on the Saviour. He died as your substitute. Rest in His finished work and you will have peace with God, immediately. The peace of God is conditional on praying with a grateful heart (see Philippians 4: 7) but peace with God on conversion is immediate and eternal. Once you were at war with Him, but trusting Christ you are now at peace with Him. Devil, demon, circumstance, sickness, threat, disaster, you name it, nothing, no nothing can destroy this peace that you possess.

If you are a Christian go and tell someone today that this peace is available. You'd be surprised at the millions of people in the world who are totally ignorant of its availability in Christ.

March *twenty-fourth*

"For in Him we both have access by one spirit to the Father"
(Ephesians 2:18)

The more I read this letter to the Ephesians the more I am staggered at its incredible claims. We never read the phrase 'on the other hand' in the Bible. This is no letter or religious chicanery where "we'll not emphasise this if you don't emphasise that". Here is no diplomatic "ducking and diving" desperately seeking to watch the sensibilities of various religious groupings. Paul simply says that through Christ and through Christ alone Jew and Gentile have access to the Father. Preach that today and you will have fierce opposition even from members of the "professing church"! Has it not always been so? Right from the very beginning sincere followers of the Lord Jesus dedicated to declaring Him as the only way to God have faced persecution and even martyrdom. In certain areas of the world you could be torn limb from limb for teaching that it is "through Him" people have access by one Spirit to the Father.

Whatever men may say, religious or otherwise, it is through Him we have access to the Father. We have not just an audience with the Father, we have constant access. Think of it. People who have access to a President, a King or a Queen are counted privileged. Christian, you have access to God the Father. Now. At this very moment. Use it!

March *twenty-fifth*

> *"No longer strangers and foreigners"*
> (Ephesians 2:19)

Have you ever entered a room or a gathering of any kind and you know no-one? What do you do? Where do you sit or stand? To whom do you talk? You were maybe invited by the organisation to come along but when you arrive you find yourself to be a stranger. In this world the rule often is that it's not what you know but who you know. And you know nobody. Think of refugees crossing a border into another country. The familiar streets of their home town or village are gone. The haunts of childhood, the relationships of a lifetime are left far behind. Now they face unfamiliar streets, villages, towns and cities. The language around them is foreign. The culture is foreign. The lifestyle is foreign. The very food is foreign. We once were strangers and foreigners, aliens in a foreign land. Now in Christ, everything has changed. We have a new identity, a new status, a new privilege; we belong.

I shall always remember Dick Lucas tell the story at the Keswick Convention of being in a shop in Keswick that week when a Jewish father and his little boy entered the premises. They were both distinguished by the clothes they were wearing. Somehow the child got separated from his father and in his distress cried, "Abba! Abba!". Dick stood and worshipped. We are no more strangers and pilgrims but children of the Father. Enjoy your relationship.

March *twenty-sixth*

*"But fellow citizens
with the saints
and the household
of God.."*
(Ephesians 2:19)

This is a beautiful metaphor of what it means to be a Christian. It is important to remember the background to the metaphor. The Christian church had a Jewish base. Jesus was a Jew. The Apostles were Jews. The first Gentiles who became Christians were brought into a church predominantly full of Jews who had become Christians. What was their ethos? I am reading a book at the moment by Rabbi Julia Neuberger called "On Being Jewish". It contains fascinating material and brings out in detail the traditions and practices of a Jewish family. Julia, now Chancellor of the University of Ulster, writes of the special meals on Friday evenings at her grandmothers at the beginning of the Sabbath. She tells how she hurried back from school with a deep desire to change into something more respectable than her school uniform. It "was a sign of a weekly sense of the holy .... there was something special, separate about the Friday evening en famille that made me respond both to my close family and to the wider net. It is a sense I have never lost, a sense of wonder at the end of the week, at the day of rest, that is, I believe, quintessentially Jewish" ("On Being Jewish". Heinemann: London 1995, Page 21).

We must remember in a crisis that arose in the early church that Peter and others would not even eat with Gentiles who had become Christians! Now Paul sums up his views on the matter. Gentiles who had become believers, if the Christian community is viewed as a city, are citizens, not resident aliens, with those who first hoped in a Messiah (see Romans 9: 25-26). If the Christian community is viewed as a household, Gentiles who had become believers are full members, sons and daughters. For a former Pharisee to write as he does here shows what an incredible change the Lord Jesus brings when He enters a life. Is that unity of spirit displayed in your life, Christian?

March *twenty-seventh*

"Having built on the foundation of the apostles and prophets"
(Ephesians 2:20)

As we walk through Ephesians on "highest ground" our privileges and status as believers becomes clearer and clearer; we are citizens of God's kingdom and we are members of God's family. But there is more! In today's text we are seen as a new building.

For nearly a thousand years Israel's focal point of identity as the people of God had been a temple. Would there be a new temple? There was a new people, a new international society. Would it have a geographically localised centre? What would be its focus of unity?

It would not be a material building but a spiritual one made up of God's people and God would dwell in it. He lives in His people. Just think of it: He whom the heaven of heavens cannot contain! Remember, the highest heaven that exists is but a created heaven that He was pleased to make. "There are not two things, self-existent and equally eternal, God on the one hand and some place for God to be on the other", comments Professor David Gooding. That very God now lives in His people, in my heart and personality and yours!

Part of the foundation of the building is the apostles and prophets. It would appear that Paul is not referring to Old Testament prophets but New Testament ones and to the New Testament apostles, Paul, James, the twelve and one or two others.

The New Testament Scriptures are the foundation documents of the church and cannot be tampered with. If a foundation is tampered with once it has been laid there will be serious repercussions. Beware of those who claim to be apostles and prophets today who would add to, take from, dilute or modify the New Testament foundation truths. To use a modern idiom, if there's trouble on the 48th floor of a building the first thing to be checked is the foundation.

March *twenty-eighth*

"Jesus Christ Himself being the chief corner stone"
(Ephesians 2:20)

All the measurements of a building are taken from the corner stone. Everything in the building relates to it. It helps to hold the building steady. It sets and keeps it in line. The corner stone is cut out beforehand and when it is eventually put in place it shows whether the building has been carried out to the architect's specifications. It is the most important stone in the building.

So it is in the life of the Christian church, local or universal. Members need to constantly realign all that they do with the Lord Jesus. If they are not in close touch with Him and living for His glory then it will affect the unity of the Church and its growth. When the Lord Jesus was set between the two broken-hearted disciples on the road to Emmaus, what happened? As He talked they felt their hearts burn within them. The same spiritual condition pervaded the early church which was soon turning the world upside down. Tell me, are you closely aligned with the Lord Jesus? If you are it will show to the blessing of all around you.

March *twenty-ninth*

> *"In whom the whole building, being joined together grows into a holy temple in the Lord"*
> (Ephesians 2:21)

As a child at the services of the CSSM in Newcastle in County Down I used to sit with dozens of other children by the sea every morning and sing the beautiful CSSM choruses. One of my favourites as a lad went like this:

"We are building day by day
As the moments pass away
A temple that the world cannot see
Every victory won by grace
Will be sure to find a place
In that building for eternity".

The chorus is a very good encapsulation of the truth of today's text. The church is made up of people who are joined together in Christ. All around us barriers are raised against the truth. In the world there are barriers between nations and classes and communities and families and tribes and religions. In Christ, though, there are absolutely no barriers or divisions either of race or social position or cultural differences. Identity is very important to human beings but, I ask, what is the Christian's identity? Simply this - that they are joined to the Lord Jesus. Christians may raise barriers between each other but it is a barrier of their own making; the reality is that each new Christian is added as a stone to the building. Nothing in the universe can change their position. And, whether they like it or not, they are joined to every other believer on the face of the earth in a joining which cannot be broken. Black and white, male and female, rich and poor, educated and uneducated, this tribe or that tribe, this culture or the other: they are all "in that building for eternity".

March *thirtieth*

"In whom you are also being built together for a habitation of God in the Spirit"
(Ephesians 2:22)

This verse tells us that God lives in His people "in the Spirit". What, then, does the Holy Spirit do in the life of each believer? Many things. Here are some of them. He becomes the controlling influence of God within us (Romans 8: 9). He enables us to acknowledge God is our Father (Galatians 4: 6; Ephesians 2: 18). He teaches us to pray (Ephesians 6: 18; Jude 20). He is our guide (John 16; 13). He constantly works to make us more like Jesus (2 Corinthians 3: 18). He gives us the capacity for supernatural love (Colossians 1: 18; Romans 15: 30). He leads us and helps us (John 14: 16; Galatians 5: 18; Acts 16: 6). He empowers us for service (Acts 1: 8). He renews us (Titus 3: 5). He provides us with special gifts and fruit (1 Corinthians 12; Galatians 5: 22). He can be grieved (Isaiah 63: 10; Ephesians 4: 30). He stays with us forever (John 14: 16).

What is happening through the power of the Holy Spirit worldwide? Worldwide 3,500 new churches are opening every week. Christianity is growing at the rate of 70,000 persons every day: in China alone it is growing by an average of 28,000 every day. In Africa the church is growing by 20,000 every day, on average. More Muslims in Iran have come to Christ since 1980 than in the previous one thousand years combined. In Islamic Indonesia the percentage of Christians is so high the Government won't print the statistic - which is probably nearing 25% of the population. After seventy years of oppression in the Soviet Union people who are officially Christians number one hundred million, five times the number in the Communist party and 36% of the population (statistics from the International Foreign Mission Association in co-operation with the U.S. Centre for World Mission and reprinted in AD 2000 and beyond - November/December 1990). What a temple! What a mighty Spirit!

March *thirty-first*

"The Prince of the power of the air"
(Ephesians 2:2,3)

Let's think further of Satan's power. He is violent (Mark 5: 3; Revelation 2: 10; Matthew 11: 12). He is a liar (John 8: 44) and attempts to counterfeit the works of God (2 Thessalonians 2: 9). He attacks God's purposes for men and women (Genesis 3: 1-19). He is a deceiver (Genesis 3: 13; Luke 4: 10) who attempts to cast doubt on God's trustworthiness (Genesis 3: 1, 5). He assaults human minds with doubts, fear and propaganda (Genesis 3: 1-5; Matthew 16: 22-23; Mark 5: 36; Acts 9: 26; 1 John 4: 18). He assaults the human spirit with lust, pride and hatred (Ephesians 2: 2,3; Galatians 5: 19-21). He assaults human institutions with structural evil (Revelation 2: 13). Satan manipulates nations, (Daniel 10), city councils (1 Thessalonians 2: 18), rioting mobs (John 8: 44, 59), military forces (Job 1: 17) physical sickness (Job 2: 7) and the elements (Job 1: 19). He is persistent (Revelation 12).

We must, then, never under-estimate Satan. He is dirty fighter. He will use the most surprising people to do his work. Yet the glorious fact is that he can be defeated. Resist him and he will flee from you. The Name of Jesus will overcome him but all other names he brushes aside.

APRIL

I t must have been amazing to view Mount Sinai in the
days when the Children of Israel arrived there in the
third month after their departure from Egypt. It was
there that the Lord revealed Himself to Moses and gave the
ten commandments and other laws. The people had to keep
their distance or die.

In all that happened at Mount Sinai, though, there was
nothing about the new body that would be formed one day
which would reveal the "manifold wisdom of God". A new
body comprising of people from every tongue and nation.
Indeed in the generations to come, through the times of
the prophets and the judges and even the early Roman
occupation of Israel there was not a word about this body,
not even in all religious literature of any or every tradition.
The church of Jesus Christ was a great mystery. It was
revealed through the Gospel and to Paul the huge privilege
was given to preach its message. Our April readings are a
meditation on this great mystery and the love which
surpasses knowledge that has made such a body possible.
Here too is a power that can do more than we could ever
ask or think.

April *first*

"And power"
(Ephesians 1:21)

Our Lord Jesus has been raised far above all principalities and powers and might and dominion. Those powers include the power of demons. We have thought about the power of Satan; what about the power of his demons? What do the Scriptures say about them? Here are some pointers:

They are spirits without bodies (Ephesians 6: 12). They are numerous and organised (Matthew 12: 24; Mark 5: 8-9). They were once in fellowship with God (Jude v. 6). They recognised Jesus as God's Son (Matthew 8: 29; Mark 1:23, 24). They oppose God's people and attempt to destroy them. (Ephesians 6: 12; 1 Peter 5: 8).

They tremble before God (James 2: 19). They torment unbelievers (Mathew 12: 43-45). They possess supernatural powers (Revelation 16: 14). They can possess or control human beings and animals (Mark 5: 13; Luke 8: 2). They teach false doctrine and one day will be judged and condemned (1 Tim 4: 1; 2 Peter 2: 4).

Obviously Satan employs his demons to do his work but there is available to us the whole armour of God that we may be able to stand against the wiles of the devil. Put it on and see those demons flee.

April *second*

"For this reason I, Paul, the prisoner of Jesus Christ."
(Ephesians 3:1)

This section of Ephesians (3: 1-13) is a fascinating digression. The original intention of the thought begun in today's text ("for this reason") is not completed. Paul picks it up in 3: 14 and shows that his intention is to pray for his Gentile readers who have become Christians. He is about to tell them his intentions but abruptly digresses in order to explain the unique role he had in God's purposes for them. He further defines himself.

What, then, is Paul's self designation? He sees himself as "a prisoner of Jesus Christ". Was he not a prisoner of the emperor Nero? He certainly was. Paul had been accused of treason against the Emperor and had dramatically appealed to Caesar when before Porcius Festus at Caesarea: "I stand at Caesar's judgment seat, where I ought to be judged. To the Jews I have done no wrong, as you very well know. For if I am an offender, or have committed anything worthy of death, I do not object to dying; but if there is nothing in these things of which these men accuse me, no-one can deliver me to them. I appeal to Caesar" (Acts 25: 11-12).

Paul had been committed to trial before Nero but nowhere does he ever refer to himself as Caesar's prisoner. Paul did not see Caesar as the one who was directing his affairs; Caesar did not have the final say about his life. Yes, he was under the care of the personal bodyguard of the Emperor, chained day and night to a soldier. Yes, he was under house arrest awaiting trial. Through it all, though, he believed that the Lord Jesus was in control of his life. He believed that his Lord opened and shut the doors of his life and ultimately gave the orders as to what happened to him. Paul believed himself to be under the Lordship of Christ, not Caesar. His physical imprisonment was seen as a direct consequence of his spiritual captivity and absolute allegiance to Jesus Christ. Essentially Christ had laid hold of Paul; the Romans, the Jews and others laying hold of him was purely part of the over-riding sovereignty of God's purpose for his life.

Say, Christian, are your circumstances and mine not in the same hands? Relax, the Lord is in control. He will guide you all the way.

April *third*

"For you Gentiles" (Ephesians 3:1)

Many years before his imprisonment Ananias had been told by the Lord to go and visit Saul of Tarsus; "Go", said the Lord, "for he is a chosen vessel of mine to bear my name before Gentiles".

Paul had been free for many years to teach and preach God's Word across continents. Now he had been confined for some time to testifying before Gentile kings and governors and he was now waiting to testify before the Roman Emperor. "For you Gentiles", was one of the most unique ministries for Christ this world has ever known. Think of the vast distances Paul travelled, the abuse he took, the beatings he endured, the shipwrecks he survived.

Think of his great public preaching at Athens, his work at Corinth, his help in establishing the church at Philippi. Now, though, the ministry "for you Gentiles" had narrowed in its focus. God was now leading Paul to define the Gospel for the leaders of his day.

Has God narrowed your circumstances? Are you not as free to move about for Him as you once did? Just remember what happens to you is not haphazard. When God began to focus Paul's ministry in a new direction by changing his circumstances the heart of the Empire was touched. Who can tell what God will do with you in your village, town, city or nation or among other nations even though your circumstances have narrowed? Paul was not as free in his movements but he was just as effective.

April *fourth*

"For you Gentiles"
(Ephesians 3:1)

Let's stay with this little phrase for another day's meditation. It was the Lord's will for Paul to be under house arrest in Rome but the situation which took him there was because he thought Gentiles had the same access to God as Jews did. Back at Jerusalem the real reason why the Jews charged Paul with treason against the Emperor was because he was saying to the Jews that the Gentiles could have equal standing with the Jews before God. It was when Paul got in his testimony to saying that the Lord had told him to "depart for I will send you far from here to the Gentiles" that "they listened to him until this word and then they raised their voices and said, 'Away with such a fellow from the earth for he is not fit to live!'"

The plain fact is that if Paul had remained a Jew who had become a Christian with a mission to the Jews he would not have been in prison! Even if he had stayed with the "law imposing" Jews who had become Christians who wouldn't even eat with the Gentiles who had become Christians he wouldn't have had to suffer like he did. How very easy it is as a Christian to stay in your own quarter with your own folk in your own comfort zone. Thank God Paul reached out to us Gentiles. Paul's ministry still refreshes. His writing still inspires with its vast reach. Tempted, are you, to stay in your comfort zone? Look what you are missing!

April *fifth*

"If indeed you had heard of the dispensation of the grace of God which was given to me for you"
(Ephesians 3:2)

Paul tells us that he was given God's favour to dispense something, to administer it. He will tell us in his next phrase what his special privilege was and what he had stewardship over. He saw himself as having a very special responsibility in life, he knew his was a very special ministry.

And you? Do you not have a stewardship too? Has the Lord not given to you gifts and talents, money and possessions which are only on loan? You will remember the story the Saviour told of the steward, as recorded in Luke 16, who was soon going to be out of his job. He made himself some friends while he still had his job who were there for him when his job was over. He was commended, not for the way he made his friends but for the fact that he was shrewd enough to have them at all! Jesus urged us to "make friends" for ourselves while serving Him on earth with what he has given us so that when we arrive in the eternal state we will have friends to go to.

Tell me, how are you getting on with your stewardship? You may tell me you haven't seen anyone directly won for Christ. You may be very discouraged. Let me tell you about some folk I know who bought a castle in Austria for Christian work. They were hugely used by God and many young folks were converted to Christ. They wondered at the unusual blessing they were experiencing in their work in that Austrian castle. Then they discovered that the man who had built the castle had written a prayer on the flyleaf of his Bible asking God to use the castle to His glory. He had died persecuted for the Gospel's sake. He never saw his prayer answered in his lifetime. Then my friends discovered a fascinating fact. They discovered that the prayer on the Bible was 700 years old! Got it?

April *sixth*

"How that by revelation he made known to me the mystery (as I wrote before in a few words, by which, when you read, you may understand my knowledge in the mystery of Christ)"
(Ephesians 3:3-4)

The wonderful thing Paul was given stewardship over was a great mystery which was made known to him by revelation. He was "given the insight" by God himself. The Gospel he preached, he once wrote, was "not according to man for I neither received it from man, nor was I taught it but it came through the revelation of Jesus Christ". Fourteen years after his conversion when he compared notes with the other apostles, he comments, "they added nothing to me". He tells how Christ appeared to him and told him what had gone on in the Upper Room! Can you imagine how the apostles felt when a former persecutor and murderer of Christians not only understood the deepest doctrines of the Christian faith but even knew about the events they had passed through!

The Lord Jesus specially commissioned Paul to pass on the revelation he had received. Earlier in the letter to the Ephesians (1: 9-10) he had written about it and comments in today's verse that anyone reading about it would plainly see that he had a clear understanding of what this great mystery was: it was the mystery of Christ and of His church. The revelation showed the significance of Christ at the heart of it all.

A few hours ago I was watching a BBC television series on the planet. I listened as brilliant men and women spoke about the mystery of the universe and watched as incredibly powerful telescopes probed the far reaches of space. Nobody but nobody said a word about the Lord Jesus. Yet, at the very heart of the vastness of space is Jesus Christ whether scientists like to acknowledge it or not. At the very heart of the mysteries of life and death is Jesus Chirst. Whatever problem you have, no matter where you turn, the Lord Jesus is the final solution to it. Realise this now open-secret and see the difference it will make to your life.

April *seventh*

> **"Which in other ages was not made known to the sons of men"**
> (Ephesians 3:5)

The great mystery revealed to Paul was that in Jesus Christ a new body was going to be formed: the body of Christ. Nowhere in the Old Testament will you find any reference whatsoever to the body of Christ. So through all the history of Israel from Abraham to Malachi themes of forgiveness and redemption arise, themes of God's love and compassion, kindness and wrath, guidance and intervention flow across the centuries. Nowhere, though, is there any mention of the body of Christ. Not even in the great prophesy of Isaiah where you will find lots of wonderful things about the person of Christ.

Outside of Israel in the writing of civilisations that rose and fell through history there is not a line ever written about the body of Christ. The Rosetta Stone found near Rosetta on the River Nile was the key which unlocks the mysteries of ancient Egyptian writing but there is not a line about the body of Christ; the code of Hammurabi, the famous King of Babylon has nothing about the body of Christ either. Think of all the times that passed from Alexander the Great to the rise of the Romans and in all the millions of words spoken and written this mystery lay hidden.

Even when Jesus lived out his amazing ministry on earth he never mentioned it. He simply said that after His ascension the Holy Spirit would come and lead His disciples into all truth. And did He? What the Lord promised was fulfilled. So there was a purpose in history, there was a progression, there was a progress of revelation. God was bringing about something new.

So, when liberals say that this view of the progress of history was only Paul's view, they were wrong. Why, even angels glorify what God has done in history through Christ. Even the very devil himself didn't know that through Christ the church of Chirst would be formed. Isn't it great to know that there are some things the devil doesn't know?

April *eighth*

"That the Gentiles should be fellow heirs"
(Ephesians 3:6)

What is this? Me, an heir? But I am a Gentile! Wasn't the covenant made with Abraham? God "brought him outside and said, 'look now toward Heaven, and count the stars if you are able to number them ..... so shall your descendants be' ". Where then do Gentiles like me come in? How on earth do I ever get into that wonderful convenant?

The answer is that the promise of future inheritance was made to Abraham and his descendants. In Matthew chapter one a long genealogy given. It begins with Abraham and moves across forty-two generations from Abraham to David. It then moves from David to the Babylonian captivity and from the captivity to a carpenter in Nazareth called Joseph "The husband of Mary of whom was born Jesus who was called Christ". Christ is a direct descendant of Abraham and is able to incorporate men and women, boys and girls into Himself.

The inheritance was promised to Abraham and his descendants. Christ is a descendant and because I am in Him I am an heir! I am no longer myself by myself. I am in Christ and an heir to incalculable spiritual wealth. I am not "in Aristotle" or "in Karl Marx" or "in Gandhi" or "in Mohammed" or "in Confucius": I am "in Christ". Not in "a denomination" or "in a sect" or "in a school of theology, old or new" but "in Christ" and "in Christ" forever! That's what I call an inheritance of inheritances.

April *ninth*

"Of the same body"
(Ephesians 3:6)

This new body, it really is something, isn't it? It is one body in the Lord. It is the same body, not many bodies. I know that all kinds of forces try to divide it but God does not see it as divided. If He did then all that Paul is writing about here is farcical.

I well remember the last meal I had hosted by Dr. and Mrs. Rupert Rea. We, who were guests, did not know that Brenda, Rupert's wife had but seven months to live. The conversation was fascinating and my last memory is of the turn it took. At that meal was Mr. Anthony Cordle who has done wonderful work for Christ over his life amongst "movers and shakers" in our society. He began speaking of his experience of what I will term "church institutions" are like at a very high level. It had often left him cold and uninspired. Then he began to speak of what he felt Christianity was really about. His "yardstick" was whether or not a person was truly following Jesus. He spoke of one of the greatest "personal" evangelists he had ever known. He was a very quiet man who did not raise his voice. Yet, when he spoke, people listened and their tears even flowed. Their consciences were touched, their hearts were moved and many, many conversions took place. He was, Anthony said, a true follower of Jesus, not merely of church institutions.

I was at Brenda's memorial service recently and my abiding memory of her was the animated conversation we had together that afternoon at the Templeton Hotel in Templepatrick. Brenda was one of those followers of Jesus Anthony spoke of and now shares His glory.

If you are a true follower of Jesus Christ then you are part of the body of Christ and we are promised that the gates of Hell will not prevail against it. Death itself cannot close over it. Brenda would want me to tell you that it is so. The church of Christ is indestructible and, in the eyes of God is absolutely indivisible. Let's remember that it isn't "labels" that will impress the unbeliever; labels will only add to their confusion. True following of Jesus Christ, though, will touch them like nothing else will.

April *tenth*

> "*And partakers of His promise in Christ through the Gospel*"
> (Ephesians 3:6)

The mystery had been revealed to Paul but it wasn't for keeping, was it? Gentiles became partakers of God's promise in Christ through the Gospel. Paul, as he had already emphasised had to "dispense" it, he had to get it out to others. He did this through the Gospel.

Jesus spoke of reaching others, too. He put it in terms of fishing. He said to His disciples that He would make them to become fishers of men. It was a process. They wouldn't become fishermen for Christ in an hour or two. It would require much learning. All fish are not the same. Their habits are different, their behaviour varies. The bait used to catch them will also have to vary. A study of the various ways of fish will be required and much patience will be necessary.

Imagine a modern day fisherman. Here he is in his brand new wading boots. On his head is his "tweed" hat and various flies are pinned to it. He wears his "fishing fleece" with its various useful pockets. On his back is a dirty and useful fishing bag. Here are various rods, state-of-the-art rods, too. He even has his sandwiches packed.

But where is he sitting? He is sitting in his bathroom on the edge of his bath. The bath is full of water. He is comfortable. He looks good. He has been there for hours. He could stay there for days but he would always have the same result. He would never catch any fish. Why? Because there aren't any there.

Don't you think a lot of evangelism is just like that comfrotable fisherman?

April *eleventh*

"Of which I became a minister according to the gift of the grace of God given to me by the effective working of His power"
(Ephesians 3:7)

God's grace will never take you to a place where His power cannot keep you. That is an irrefutable fact. If He calls you to do something, no matter where, no matter how difficult, no matter how daunting, He will give you the power you need to see it through.

Today's verse explains how that by the grace of God Paul received a ministry that was entrusted to Him. As we have already seen it was a very unique ministry, particularly as it related to the Gentiles and their leaders. It appeared before kings and commoners and was even now waiting to go before the Emperor for Jesus' sake. God's grace, though, didn't take him where God's power couldn't keep him.

Take note, Christian, of the problems this man faced. "Five times", he once wrote, "I received from the Jews thirty-nine lashes. Three times I was beaten with rods, once I was stoned, three times I was shipwrecked, a night and a day I have spent in the deep. I have been on frequent journeys, in dangers from rivers, danger from robbers, dangers from my countrymen, dangers from the Gentiles, dangers in the city, dangers in the wilderness, dangers on the sea, dangers among false brethren: I have been in labour and hardship through many sleepless nights, in hunger and thirst, often without food, in cold and exposure. Apart from such external things, there is the daily pressure upon me of concern for all the churches".

All the way through his tumultuous ministry God's power was effective. It never, ever, failed him. Nor will it ever fail you. You may this very day have to face something daunting. It may not be what Paul faced but it is just as real to you as Paul's circumstances were to him. Come on, lift up your head, relax those shoulders, get out of that door and into your day with all that it holds. You have all of God's power at your back. Go for it!

April *twelfth*

"To me, who am less than the least of all saints this grace was given"
(Ephesians 3:7)

"Come on", say the critics of today's verse, "this is false modesty. This is artificial. This is huge exaggeration. This is not true self-evaluation". They are wrong. This is exactly the Apostle Paul's view of himself. Notice the tense he uses: not "who was" but "who am less than the least of all saints". He was always aware that he had once persecuted Christians and was amazed that he had been chosen by God to now herald the message of the very Christ he had opposed.

It is important, though, that we do not allow this verse to lead us into unbalanced thinking. Paul once wrote, "For I consider that I am not at all inferior to the most eminent apostle. Even though I am untrained in speech, yet I am not in knowledge. But we have been thoroughly made manifest among you in all things" (2 Corinthians 11: 5).

Paul is saying that he is what he is by the grace of God. He never forgot where he had come from and although he was hugely gifted and mightily used it was all because of the Lord's gifting, grace and power. Have you been promoted recently? Have you enjoyed success? Don't get carried away. Remember you are what you are and you have what you have because of God's goodness. Give Him the glory.

April *thirteenth*

> *"That I should
> preach among
> the Gentiles the
> unsearchable riches
> of Christ"*
> (Ephesians 3:8)

Unsearchable? The only other occurrence of this adjective in the New Testament is when Paul writes: "Oh, the depth of the riches both of the wisdom and knowledge of God! How unsearchable are His judgments and His ways past finding out!" (Romans 11: 33).

We must not think, surely, that the riches of Christ are inaccessible. In our meditations on this amazing passage we have found the riches of His grace, the riches of His redemption, the riches of His inheritance, the riches of His power, the riches of His mercy, the riches of His love and kindness greatly accessible. I find these riches are accessible every day of my life. Walter Liefeld has put it very well when he says that the word "unsearchable" riches here emphasises "uniqueness rather than inaccessibility" (Liefield, p. 84). They certainly are unique. No riches like them can ever be found.

We shall be forever discovering more aspects of the uniqueness of all the riches that are available in the Lord Jesus. They will never be exhausted, they will never fail. Go after these riches! Meditate on them! Enjoy them! Exult in them! Live for them!

When I was a lad my mother had very little money. Being a widow she knew the blast of being in need. Yet as a child I remember her trusting in the promise of the beautiful text which states, "My God shall supply all your need according to His riches in glory by Christ Jesus" (Philippians 4: 19). I have proved in my life, as she did, that such trust is not misplaced. Have you? Let me repeat: these riches may be unique but they are accessible! Go draw from them today.

April *fourteenth*

> *"To preach the
> unsearchable riches
> of Christ"*
> (Ephesians 3:8)

Continuing with this text for a second day I would like to give a personal testimony in today's meditation. In my lifetime I have had the privilege of speaking and testifying for Christ in all kinds of places. I recall vividly speaking at a public evangelistic service as a twelve year old boy. Virtually every week of my life since then I have been involved in public witness for the Saviour. It has been a privilege I do not deserve but a privilege which has brought me immense joy.

I have to smile when I think of some of the varied places the Lord has called me to preach and teach His word. From a farm barn, with my congregation sitting on straw bales to satellite radio. From a Korean tennis stadium to a Scottish football stadium. In universities and schools, in prisons and homes and churches. From public Bible classes to children's services. From Thurso to Sidmouth, from Glasgow to New York, from Ballywillwill to Bucharest, from Aughnacloy to Oakland, from London to Hong Kong, from Invercargill to Inverness, it has been an honour to speak of the Lord Jesus.

As I look back I have found there is no theme greater, no privilege higher, and nothing more satisfying than preaching the unsearchable, inexhaustible, unfathomable, inimitable but accessible riches of Christ. I have never found them to be unsuitable, they have never made me blush with embarrassment, they have never failed to touch some life listening or watching. They are always in some way inspiring, comforting and assuring. I do not boast in my travels but I do boast in the incredible riches that I have carried with me across the world.

Is there someone reading this meditation and you are wondering how best to make your life count? I would say to you to give up affluence for influence and success for significance by preaching the unsearchable riches of Christ. And, as the man said, only use words when necessary.

April *fifteenth*

> *"And make all people see what is the fellowship (stewardship or administration) of that mystery"*
> (Ephesians 3:9)

What the Gospel is about is not limited, of course, to Gentiles. Paul might have a special ministry to Gentiles but dispensing of the wonderful good news is for "all people". Today's text emphasises the contrast of spiritual light and darkness.

The good news, the gospel of Christ, when presented "enlightens" people. Satan holds people in great spiritual darkness lest the light of the glorious gospel should shine in. Only God can open their eyes and He does this through the Gospel. Slip the Gospel into your conversation. Let people hear it and you will be amazed what God will do with it. Think of it: somebody who started out today in rank spiritual darkness could end the day enlightened and be eternally saved by God using a word from you about the good news of the Gospel. It was once a mystery but it is now plain and clearly revealed. How can you ever know its power to enlighten if you never share it? Be God's eye-opener to somebody today.

I once knew a man in the city where I live and he was so ignorant of the Gospel he went to a hillside and built a little altar and tried to sacrifice some pigeons to appease God. The pigeons escaped and he was deeply frustrated until a fellow foundry-worker witnessed to him and he became a greatly loved Christian. I remember reading in the first part of Sir Dirk Bogarde's autobiography, "A Postillion Struck by Lightening" that he once built a small altar by a Glasgow burn and prayed to God and reckoned he got no answer. He has lived his life and in all of his writings there is not a word of the Gospel comforting him, reaching him, saving him. Remember, Christian, please remember that there are people all around you in deep spiritual need. Tell them of Jesus. Selah.

April *sixteenth*

"Which from the beginning of the ages has been hidden in God who created all things through Jesus Christ; to the intent that now the manifold wisdom of God might be known by the Church to the principalities and powers in the heavenly places"
(Ephesians 3:9-10)

Christianity is effective in declaring the unsearchable riches of Christ: it is effective in enlightening people regarding God's plan for the world but we are now told that it is effective in demonstrating a very unique and wonderful thing; the manifold wisdom of God.

There is a vast difference between knowledge and wisdom. A gifted artist or scientist or anybody in any profession or walk of life could have a lot of knowledge but that person needs wisdom in how to apply it. Wisdom is the capacity and power to make use of knowledge.

What is the wisdom of God? It is the attribute by which He arranges His purposes and plans and arranges the means which bring out the results of those purposes and plans. God's wisdom is manifold. The word "manifold" means "many-coloured", as used of Joseph's "coat of many colours".

As history unfolds we see God's wisdom at work bringing about the creation of His church like the weaving of a huge tapestry. Jew and Gentile, slave and free, rich and poor, are all one in Christ Jesus.

I don't know if the principalities and powers mentioned in today's text are the good ones like angels or the evil ones like demons but I do know that both are well aware of the incredible wisdom of God. The Devil and his hoards "see and tremble" and angels worship. As the church moves forward it displays to watching principalities and powers the "many coloured" wisdom of God. Just remember that the next time your local church meets: it is part of a universal communication.

April *seventeenth*

> *"According to the eternal purpose which he accomplished in Christ Jesus our Lord"*
> (Ephesians 3:11)

History is "His story". God's eternal purpose concerns His church, uniting and reconciling people internationally through the Lord Jesus. The plan was conceived by God, kept hidden through the ages and then realised through the life, death, burial and resurrection of Christ and the proclaiming of His Gospel.

As a new millennium breaks upon the world a lot has been writtten about world history over the last two thousand years. Secular history though concentrates on the leaders. If you read the secular history of the Roman Empire you would find it concentrates on the Emperors. They thought they were the important people. Christians are hardly mentioned. Read on and you will find that eras are chronicled around politicians, generals, presidents, kings and queens and captains of industry, scientists, media people, film stars, playwrights, novelists and sports people. Few Christians have a big profile. Wars and peace treaties roll endlessly through the centuries. Christians seem to be the insignificant people of history.

Are they? Not as far as God is concerned. Paul puts it very succinctly in another letter: "As unknown, yet well known: as dying and behold we live: as chastened and yet not killed: as sorrowful yet always rejoicing: as poor yet making rich: as having nothing yet possessing all things" (2 Corinthians 6: 9-10).

Are you discouraged? A missionary on arriving back in his native land saw a VIP feted at the dockside with a welcoming party. He felt so lonely, unrecognised, even jealous. Then a voice whispered, "But you are not home yet". Neither are you, Christian. Don't let the world around you mould you into a limited view of history. God is building a temple that "the world" cannot see. It will outlast all the glitz of this present age.

April *eighteenth*

> *"In whom we have boldness and access with confidence through faith in Him. Therefore I ask that you do not lose heart at my tribulations for you, which is your glory"*
> (Ephesians 3:13)

It is very easy in life to forget the big wider picture of what God is doing. It is easy to get thoroughly discouraged by the nitty-gritty of everyday hassle. Americans have a phrase for it. They say "When you are up to your ears in alligators it is hard to remember that the original intention was to drain the swamp!"

Over the past weeks we have been meditating on some of the greatest doctrinal truth in the Scriptures. I confess while writing this book my mind has soared, even reeled at these great themes. Here is the very secret of what the whole understanding of history is all about. Still, life is real and problems in life bring a multitude of pressures.

What is the practical application of all the doctrine we have learned? The practical answer comes from a man chained to a soldier and under house arrest in Rome. It is that we approach God with boldness and confidence through faith in the Lord Jesus, our Mediator. In classical Greek this "boldness" meant freedom of speech, the democratic right to say everything one wished to say. It is freedom of access with confidence based on Christ's faithfulness, of course, and not our faith.

You can meet with God at any time. You have as much right in His presence as the greatest Christian who ever lived. Draw near to God and He will draw near to you. The pressures around you might be horrendous but you can without fear hold communion and fellowship with God. Today's verse may seem an anti-climax to the great peaks of doctrine we have scaled in the opening section of Ephesians. It is no such thing. It is what it is all about; getting you and I into the presence of God with confidence to obtain help in time of need and to have the deepest fellowship possible with Him.

April *nineteenth*

> *"Therefore I ask you that you do not lose heart at my tribulations for you, which is your glory"*
> (Ephesians 3:13)

Here we have a fascinating perspective of how Paul viewed his imprisonment. He told the Ephesian Christians that they should not be discouraged by the fact that he was in prison. Now, I ask, how could he have such a view of what would appear to be a very discouraging circumstance?

The answer was that he knew he was in prison for faithfully standing up for their right to hear the Gospel and to be equal in Christ before God as any other. He was fighting for them and if it entailed imprisonment, so be it. He was as deeply involved in their interests in wanting to face Nero on their behalf as ever he was while ministering to them when he was at liberty. He mediated grace, now he was mediating glory. His sufferings would bring them glory.

Maybe you will be caused to suffer in some way for the Christian faith in your local area. Paul suffered for the Christian's freedom, you might have to suffer in order that the Christians in your area might be free. Their glory might be bought by your facing the foe on their behalf. Is it worth it? Ask Paul and he will tell you that it is eternally worth it.

April *twentieth*

> *"For this reason I bow my knees to the Father of our Lord Jesus Christ"*
> (Ephesians 3:14)

Did Paul always kneel when he prayed? We don't know. Nowhere in Scripture is there any command that we must kneel to pray. Jesus fell on His face to pray. The publican and Pharisees stood to pray. The phrase surely means reverence in prayer. There should be no presumption, no taking everything for granted, no cheek, no glib familiarity.

We are to come boldy to God in prayer and are to enjoy confidence in our access. All the time, though, there should be reverence and godly fear. Not craven fear but being humbly aware of our great privilege.

Of course the phrase "bow my knees" implies worship. Daniel's three friends refused to bow down before Nebuchadnezzar's image of gold. They simply would not worship anything or anyone but the Lord. Daniel on hearing the edict that whoever petitioned any god or man for thirty days except King Darius would be cast into the den of lions deliberately "knelt down on his knees three times that day and prayed and gave thanks before God as was his custom since early days". Bowing down was an act of worship to these men.

We are told that the devil took the Lord Jesus up on an exceedingly high mountain and showed Him all the kingdoms of the world and their glory. "All these I will give you if you will fall down and worship me", he said. Notice He didn't say, "If you will sing hymns to me", or "If you will say certain words of petition to me". He said, "Fall down and worship Me". Christ refused saying, "Away with you, Satan! For it is written, 'You shall worship the Lord your God and Him only you shall serve'".

When Paul said he bowed his knees to the God and Father of our Lord Jesus Christ it had powerful meaning for the Ephesian Christians. Millions bowed to the goddess Diana. Her temple was in Ephesus. In our day may we never bow to any god by heart or knee but bow only to the God and Father of our Lord Jesus Christ. We worship Him, alone.

April *twenty-first*

> *"From whom the whole family in heaven and earth is named"*
> (Ephesians 3:15)

Paul is about to pray a big prayer for the members of the church with its huge role both here on earth and before the principalities and powers. So Paul writes of the bigness of the God to whom he is about to pray. In fact he begins his prayer with the bigness of God and he ends his prayer with the bigness of God. (See 3: 20-21). What is the scope of His influence? The scope of His influence "as Father extends over every grouping in the cosmos because he is Christ and Lord of them all", says A. T. Lincoln (Lincoln, Page 204).

Every grouping in the cosmos? Think of the animal family across the earth. Millions upon millions of animals owe their origin to God. Think of billions of human beings who also owe their origin to God. Think of the groupings of trees, flowers, of the whole family of botany. God brought them all into being. Think of the stars, the present Hubble telescope in space showing up millions more. They were created by the word of His power and He calls them all by name. Think of the millions of angels created by God. Every grouping has God as their origin.

When you worship and bring a petition to Him you are before an awesome being. Yet He listens to you. He cares about your home and your family and your job and your future. He has the very hairs of your head numbered. "Then those who feared the Lord", says Malachi, "spoke one to another and the Lord listened and heard them; so a book of remembrance was written before Him for those who feared the Lord and who meditate on His Name" (Malachi 3: 16).This is your God!

April *twenty-second*

"According to the riches of His glory"
(Ephesians 3:16)

The word "riches" is a word which occurs quite often in this wonderful letter. There is mention of "the riches of His grace" (1: 7), "the riches of the glory of His inheritance in the saints" (1: 8), "the exceeding riches of His grace and His kindness" (2: 7), and "the unsearchable riches of Christ" (3: 8).

Paul is about to mention that he has asked God for something very special for the Christians in Corinth. He is convinced that God has the resources to give it to them. Those resources are described in this beautiful phrase, "According to the riches of His glory". What does the term mean?

In Romans 6: 4 we read of Christ being raised from the dead by "the glory of the Father". Obviously the word glory can be synonymous with the word power. The measure of God's giving is measured by the inexhaustible wealth of His power. The "limit" set is the "limit" of His power and that is limitless!

If you were to take a glass of water from the River Nile it would be diminished by that glass of water. If you were to draw from the power available to you from God He will not be diminished in the slightest. There is more available where that power just given comes from and it is the very same power as raised Christ from the dead! The nations are as "a drop in the bucket", compared to our God. The world itself is but His footstool. The great men and women of earth are powerful but our God "brings" the princes to nothing: "He makes the judges (rulers) of the earth as vanity". The unfathomable depths of space are mentally numbing; "Lift up your eyes on high", said Isaiah, "and see who has created these things, who brings out their hosts by number; He calls them all by name, by the greatness of His might and the strength of His power: not one is missing". It is "according to the riches" of that power you can overcome whatever obstacles are in your way today.

April *twenty-third*

> *"According to the riches of His glory"*
> (Ephesians 3:16)

Recently, at our church, we had a visit from Dr. Os Guinness, the social scientist and distinguished Christian writer. He spoke to us most helpfully on the famous incident where Moses asked God to show him His glory. Os pointed out that the word "glory" as used by Moses, meant "weight". God's glory is not a light thing, it is substantive. Moses was asking God to show him as much of His glory as a person could see and live. That glory was not only synonymous with the word "power" it was also synonymous with the word "weight".

Paul is about to ask that God give His people something they desperately need but he knows that the rich source of what they need is substantive, it has weight, eternal weight. Let me tell you a story from the life of Dr. Guinness that is an inspiring example of that source of work.

In 1815 Daniel O'Connell (he of O'Connell Street, Dublin, Ireland) shot and killed a man in a duel. His widow, the 18 year old Jane D'Estere, mother of two children, fled in her distress to the little town of Ecclefechan on the Scottish-English border. Going down one day to a local river Jane contemplated suicide. Suddenly she looked up and there was a ploughboy, about her own age, beginning his work in the field across the river. He set about his work with such skill and meticulous attention to detail that Jane became absorbed in watching him as he with pride turned his furrows. He was well known for whistling Christian hymns at his work.

Jane, on the edge of death jolted into life. Why, she mused, should she descend into self-pity? Her two little children were entirely dependent upon her. If the young ploughman was dedicated with such relish to his responsibility, she should return to Dublin and her responsibilities. Chastened yet inspired Jane returned to Ireland and some weeks later came to faith.

Fourteen years later Jane married Captain John Guinness, the youngest son of Arthur Guinness, the famous Dublin brewer. She prayed consistently for her family down through a dozen generations and if you trace Jane's line through the illustrious Guinness family, a fascinating group of outstanding Christian ministers and missionaries and leaders emerge.

One of them is my good friend Dr. Os Guinness who is now impacting leaders across the world for Christ in the wonderful work he does with The Trinity Forum. Os is Jane's great-great grandson! All work done for the glory of God is significant. I often wonder did the whistling ploughboy of Ecclefechan ever realise just how significant his work was?

April *twenty-fourth*

"That He would grant you, according to the riches of His glory, to be strengthened with might through His spirit in the inner man"
(Ephesians 3:16)

Paul wants something and he knows God has the resource to give it to him. God's resources are called "the riches of His glory". He is speaking of God's glorious wealth. And what does Paul want? He wants the Christians to have something very special. In fact this prayer is something unequalled. No matter how long you live, no matter what book you read, no matter what speaker you hear and no matter where you go, you will find nothing to equal this prayer. It is highest ground. It is one of the greatest mountain peaks in Scripture. The things Paul asks for are just incredible.

All the things he asks for, though, are spiritual. He does not even ask that he get out of prison, though he must have wanted to, dearly. Food, clothes and money are not his priorities. The priority with the unconverted is the seen while the priority for the Christian is the unseen. The Christian method is to build up resistance to all the pressures and problems of life in the inner being. When we become Christians a new nature is put in us (called the "new being"). Here is a new realm which is spiritual and unseen. It is not temporal or physical or vanishing but something which is of God. We are made partakers of the Divine nature. The "outward being" perishes but the "inner being" is being strengthened day by day.

Who does the strengthening? The Holy Spirit. Do we not have the Holy Spirit already? We certainly do. He has already been given to the church and to each believer in it. We do not have to ask for the Holy Spirit to be given to us but we certainly do need to ask for His strengthening as we face the tasks of our lives. I do not know what task you face today but whatever it is you can be strengthened with might (i.e. power) in your inner being by the Holy Spirit. Ask for it and you will get it.

April *twenty-fifth*

> *"That Christ may
> dwell in your hearts
> through faith"*
> (Ephesians 3:17)

What is "the heart" in Scripture? It is understood as being the centre of a person's personality, the seat of all their thinking and feeling and decision making. Does Christ not live in a Christian's heart on conversion? Yes. What then does Paul mean by praying that "Christ may dwell in your hearts by faith?" Is He not there, already?

The answer to this question is found in the word Paul chooses for "dwell". In Greek there are two similar verbs. One means to "inhabit" a place as a stranger and the other means "to settle down" somewhere. It is the latter verb that Paul chooses. It is quite obvious that many a Christian is in a relationship with Christ and they are not controlled by Him. Is that possible? Just read Revelation 3: 20. It states, "Behold, I stand at the door and knock. If anyone hears My voice and opens the door, I will come in to him and dine with him, and he with Me". These words were written to the church at Laodecia which was full of Christians who were in a very poor spiritual condition.

Be very careful with the phrase "asking Jesus into your heart". From our text it is obvious that you can be in the body of Christ, be a believer in the Lord Jesus Christ and not have Christ at the very centre of all that you do. Charles Hodge said, "The indwelling of Christ is a thing of degrees". Jesus distinctly promised that "he who loves Me will be loved by My Father and I will love him and manifest Myself to him" (John 14: 21).

So, as your Christian life proceeds the Lord Jesus will make Himself known to you more and more if He is allowed to dwell in your heart. Let him "settle down" in your heart to such an extent that He will increasingly dominate and shape the whole orientation of your life. Let the deepest longing of your heart be that the Lord Jesus will be more real to you than the breath you breathe.

April *twenty-sixth*

> *"That you being
> rooted and grounded
> in love"*
> (Ephesians 3:17)

Of all virtues in the Christian life love is supreme. Paul shows how important it is by linking two metaphors. Here is a great tree and the wind gets up and it stands firm. Why? Because it has a labyrinth of roots which go very deep and wide. Here is a fine building and the same winds test it and it stands. Why? Because it has a good and firm foundation.

The Christian's roots are in the soil of love and love is the foundation of their lives. What drove Paul to go through all his trials and tribulations many of which he could have avoided? Love. What led Mary to pour her best perfume at Christ's feet? Love. What motivated the widow to give her last "mite"? Love. What led Mary Magdalene to the tomb of Christ on that resurrection morning? Love. What made Nicodemus and Joseph of Arimathea take their lives in their hands before the Romans and beg for the body of Jesus? Love. What makes you teach those restless little children the Scriptures every Sunday? Love. What makes you give of your time and help and advice to the sick, the bereaved, the hurting, the confused, the disappointed, the lonely? Love.

Though you have the gift of all prophesy and understand all mysteries and all knowledge. Though you have all faith so that you could remove mountains. If you do not have love, you are nothing. Love is the power, the motivating force of all true Christians. This love is poured into people's hearts by the Spirit of God (Romans 5: 5). Never, ever forget that the nutrient of all your service for Christ is love, the very stability of your ongoing Christian living is love. Nothing more and nothing less.

April *twenty-seventh*

"That you .... may be able to comprehend with all the saints what is the width and length and depth and height and to know the love of Christ which surpasses knowledge"
(Ephesians 3:18)

Paul tells us of his great ambition: it is to know the love of Christ. He emphasises, though, that it is a love that is not to be known all by himself. The comprehension of Christ's love which Paul desires for Christians is not an isolated contemplation. It is a shared insight amongst the whole international body of Christians. Note the little phrase "with all the saints".

One of the loveliest things in Christian experience is to listen to Christians sharing their insight into what Christ's love means to them. Every single one of them has their own personal experience of the love of Christ. Scientists, bankers, farmers, air hostesses, teachers, doctors, managers, computer analysts, factory workers, street cleaners, kings, queens, presidents, writers, home makers, high school students, shop attendants, soldiers, leaders .... all across the world Christ's love has invaded lives and when people share it together, the fellowship is beyond words.

Franklin Graham tells the story of being in an African refugee camp one day when he heard a little child singing. She had nothing but the clothes she sat in. She had lost everything in the genocide in her country, including her family. A guard stood by. Franklin asked him what she was singing. He leaned down and listened and replied, "She is singing, 'Yes, Jesus loves me, the Bible tells me so'". Selah.

April *twenty-eighth*

"That you may be able to comprehend with all the saints what is the width and length and depth and height - to know the love of Christ which passes knowledge: that you may be filled with all the fullnes of God"
(Ephesians 3:18-19)

What does it mean "to comprehend" the love of Christ. It means to take a firm mental grasp of it, to lay hold of it with your mind. Dr. Martyn Lloyd-Jones illustrated this truth beautifully in his Bible class one morning at Westminster Chapel. He said that Isaac Watts' great hymn began with the words, "When I survey the wondrous cross". He described how that you and I might be staying somewhere in the country and somebody tells us of a beautiful view which can be had from a nearby mountain. It requires, though, a two hour climb. So you set out and make the effort and at last you stand and gaze at the tremendous panoramic view. You drink it all in, feasting your eyes on it; you survey it. You don't just glance at it.

This, the Doctor points out, is the idea behind comprehending the love of Christ. You can go up to highest ground and "survey" that love. It will involve mental activity. It will involve thinking about it, looking across all aspects of it. It will mean meditating. It will involve analysing and considering it. It will mean studying it.

Paul's prayer is that we will make the effort. This love of Christ is not just a feeling. It is something to be comprehended. The truth is the more we comprehend it the more our hearts will rise in love to Christ who first loved us and gave Himself for us.

April *twenty-ninth*

> *"To know ... the love of Christ"*
> (Ephesians 3:19)

What is the difference between "comprehending" and "knowing"? Comprehending has to do with the mind. Knowing has to do with personal experience. I marvel at God's love. As I comprehend it I find it is not just affection and not just friendship, it is a love that loves the unlovable. Its breadth, depth, height and length are just thrilling. I look in the Scriptures and I see from Adam in the Garden of Eden to John on the Isle of Patmos that God's love is awesome. I see that God loved the world. I see that Christ loved the church. It is all stupendous.

There is, though, another side to all this. I am also aware that Christ loves me. He tells me so, personally. This love is something I experience constantly in my everyday life. The Son of God loved me and gave Himself for me.

If Paul prays that I will know the love of Christ why does he then say it surpasses knowledge? Can I know the unknowable? What does this paradox mean? It means that the more I know of Christ's love, the more there is to know. To know Christ's love, I will know more of Christ's love and the great thing is that its horizon will stretch before me forever. Nothing will ever be able to separate me from it, either in the present or in the future. Nothing! The children are right when they sing, "Jesus' love is very wonderful. It's so wide you can't get over it. It's so low you can't get under it. It's so high you can't get over it. Oh! Wonderful love".

April *thirtieth*

> *"That you may be filled with all the fullness of God"*
> (Ephesians 3:19)

This request seems, on the face of it, to be unrealistic. How can I be filled with the fullness of God? If this were possible would I not lose my masculinity? Would a woman filled with the fullness of God lose her femininity? Would people filled with the fullness of God be an awesomely frightening people to meet? The answer to this question is answered by asking another: was Christ? We read that in Him "dwells all the fullness of the Godhead bodily" (Colossians 3: 9).

Did He lose his humanity? No. Were others afraid to bring their children to Him for a blessing? Never. Did Nicodemus or Mary Magdalene or blind Bartimaeus find Him unapproachable? Certainly not.

All that God is was expressed in what Christ was in bodily form while on earth. He was the express image of God's person. So Paul is praying that Christians will express in their lives and personalities the attributes and characteristics of God.

It's like the story that is told of the little boy who was walking along carrying his jigsaw puzzle. Crowds were on the street and a man rushing for his train accidentally bumped into the lad and knocked the jigsaw box out of his hand. Its contents spilt all across the busy pedestrian pavement. The man turned in his tracks and got down on his knees and started picking up the scattered pieces of the jigsaw. People walked all around him and almost over him. Suddenly, the lad, helping him, looked up at the man and said, "Is your name Jesus?"

MAY

When the Lord Jesus taught His amazing Sermon on the Mount the crowds were amazed by His teaching. He taught them as one who had authority and not as their teachers of the law. After two thousand years we are just as amazed at what the Sermon contains. Here is the great Christian counter-culture; it is a call to be different. True revival has always come when the Church has taken the Sermon on the Mount seriously and when its members have started to live out its implications in their lives.

In the section of Ephesians we shall study in our meditations for May, Paul lays the same emphasis on the importance of the implications of following Christ in our everyday lives. He particularly deals with the importance of unity in the body of Christ and he also warns of those who would create havoc amongst God's people. He urges us to grow to maturity. There is no clash with the Sermon on the Mount whatsoever. Here is a further exposition of the standard the Lord requires of all who would follow Him.

May *first*

> *"Now to Him who is able to do exceeding abundantly, above all that we ask or think"*
>
> (Ephesians 3:20)

Paul has asked for stupendously staggering things in his prayer for Christians. He has asked that they be given the strengthening of the Holy Spirit, the ruling presence of Christ, the rooting of their lives in love, the knowledge of Christ's love, the fullness of God Himself. The requests on "highest ground" are just mind-bending. Is it at all possible? Is it realistic? As Stuart Briscoe once asked, "Is it like putting a 747 in a Volkswagen?!"

Paul shows that it is all possible because of God's ability. Are you downhearted? Are you ready to scream or flee? Has some tiny-minded person tramped all over your dreams? Do they want you to keep to the realm of the possible while you dream of the seemingly impossible? Did not Gabriel say to Mary, "With God nothing shall be impossible". Did not another angel say to Sarah, "Is there anythig too hard for the Lord?"

Meditate then, despairing Christian, on the seven stages of one of the greatest doxologies ever written:

(1) "Now to Him who is able to do". He is not a passive God. He does things. When Adam strayed he went after him! He is able to do.

(2) He is able to do what we ask. He listens to our requests and answers them with a "No", a "Yes" or a "Wait".

(3) He is able to do what we think. Sometimes we think things and don't ask for them. God, though, reads our thoughts and delivers on our unspoken desires. He is full of surprises.

(4) He is able to do all that we ask or think. You can never say, "That is beyond God".

(5) He is able to do more than we ask or think. He is beyond us!

(6) He is able to do exceeding abundantly above all that we ask or think. He is able to do more than more!

To sum up: It is no secret what God can do! You have read about it in today's verse. So, believe it!

May *second*

"According to the power that works in us, to Him be glory in the church by Christ Jesus throughout all ages, world without end. Amen"
(Ephesians 3:20-21)

As this great section of the Ephesian letter ends Paul's mind soars. He has told us of the riches of God's grace, mercy and wisdom. He has told us of God's abilities and purposes. Now he reminds us once more of the resource of God's omnipotent power to deliver all answers to prayer. This power is already at work in us. It doesn't hover! Just remember as you face your day or turn over to sleep tonight that the power that raised Jesus from the dead is the very same power at work in you. The power that brought Jew and Gentile together to form the church and make them one is the power at work in you. You don't need to manipulate your life or grovel to men and women of influence: there is power at work in your life which is as limitless as the love that makes it available.

Paul, overwhelmed by the depths of the truths he is teaching and the blessings poured out on the church of Christ now gives homage and worship and adoration to the God who brought it all about. He wants glory to be given to God in all generations of history and in all eternity. It is a beautiful way to draw all he has been teaching together. The church is composed of those who do not deserve God's grace and love. Those very same people can bring God glory in all generations. The Christ, who is the head of the church also brings glory to God. So, together, through all eternity the church and its Head bring glory to God. Pathetic, isn't it, that men and women rise in the church who want to give glory to themeslves? Perish the thought. Who cares who gets the praise as long as God gets the glory.

May *third*

"I therefore, the prisoner of the Lord, beseech you to lead a life worthy of the calling with which you were called"
(Ephesians 4:1)

Are you and I worthy of all the spiritual blessings we have in Christ? Are they given to us because of something good we did or something honourable? No. In fact when we were without strength Christ died for us. We are not worthy of one thing we have received at the Lord's hand. Who am I that a king should die for? And the King of all Kings at that.

We are not worthy of it all but there is one thing we can do: we can live out our Christian calling in a worthy way. If God shows me mercy then I should show others mercy. If God showers me with grace, then I too should be gracious. If Christ is my peace then I should work for peace in all that I do. If I am part of the indivisible church of Christ then I should reflect that truth in my dealings with all Christians wherever I find them. If I have a calling from God in Christ then surely I should reflect the dignity of such a calling. I should not be moaning of the work the Lord has given me to do. I should not complain that my circumstances are too narrow or, on the other hand, that my responsibilities are too great. I should not spend my time wishing I were someone else.

Every single Christian is called of God. When I sin I bring dishonour on my calling. How? When David sinned, he who had been called to be Israel's king, found that the Lord had sent his prophet Nathan to him. The message was haunting. "I anointed you king over Israel and I delivered you from the hand of Saul", said the Lord through Nathan, "I gave you your Master's house and your Master's wives into your keeping and gave you the house of Israel and Judah. And if that had been too little I would have given you more". I don't know any more haunting words in the Old Testament, do you? The Lord chastened David for his unworthy walk, "Because", he said, "by this deed you have given great occasion to the enemies of the Lord to blaspheme". Our walk can dishonour our calling. No wonder Paul beseeches us to lead a life worthy of the calling with which we are called.

May *fourth*

> *"With all lowliness and gentleness, with longsuffering, bearing with one another in love"*
> (Ephesians 4:1)

Paul believes that five qualities should dominate and characterise every life lived worthily for Christ. Let's do a short study of those five qualities.

"Lowliness". This word literally means "lowliness of mind" and is the opposite of haughtiness. In the Greco-Roman world the word was associated with contemptible servility but in the Christian world it is a vital quality for all Christians. How is it best characterised? Jesus took a little child and set him in the midst of the disciples who were arguing about who should be the greatest.

Notice that he did not tell them to be childish but He did tell them to be child-like: such is the secret of humility.

"Gentleness". Here is a quality which involves courtesy, considerateness, and the waiving of one's rights in seeking the common good. It is the opposite of self-aggression and self-advertisement. "Nothing", said Chrysostom, "will sew a veil to divide the church as love of power".

"Longsuffering". We are apt to throw our "heads up" at the slightest aggravation. Long temper in contrast to short temper is the best way. Patience will enable us to endure annoyances and tolerate others' exasperating behaviour. "But my temper is over in a second", said the lady. "So is the shot of a gun", replied her listener.

"Bearing with one another". To live above with the saints we love, that certainly will be glory. To live below with the saints we know is quite another story. Bearing with others means fully accepting them in their uniqueness, including their weaknesses and faults. It is to allow them worth and space.

"In love". This is the crowning quality. There will be inevitable clashes of attitudes, character and actions in any Christian church. Love will win. Here is the binding quality. ""Put on love which is the bond of perfection".

Do these five qualities dominate our lives?

May *fifth*

> *"Endeavouring to keep the unity of the Spirit in the bond of peace"*
> (Ephesians 4:3)

The church of Jesus Christ is indivisible. That is a fact. It simply cannot be divided. It is the body of Christ and Christ is its Head. How then can we endeavour (literally "be eager") to keep the unity of something which the Spirit of God has already united?

The answer is that we are, as John Stott puts it, to "preserve in actual concrete relationships of love that unity which God has created and which neither man nor demon can destroy" (Stott, P.152). He makes the analogy of a family which has disintegrated as a family. Relationships have all broken down between mother and father and sons and daughters. Divorce has come. Nobody rings anybody any more. Are they still one family? In God's sight, yes. Would we then try to excuse the tragedy of the disunity by appealing to how the family is in God's sight? No. We would urge them to 'maintain the unity of the family by means of the bond of peace' and to demonstrate their family unity by repenting and getting reconciled to one another.

I always remember a story I heard when ministering God's Word in New Zealand. A certain Christian had got into real problems with his local church. He eventually left them and was away from them for a considerable length of time. Then came repentance and reconciliation and he said he would be returning to their services on a certain Sunday. Word got out and when he and his family arrived in the church car park they found the entire church membership out at the front of the building waiting to welcome them back. Now that really impressed the neighbours more than a lot of preaching about unity, didn't it?

May *sixth*

"There is one body"
(Ephesians 4:4)

The church is the body of Christ. When Paul says there is only one body he is obviously referring to the great mystical, unseen body made up of all believers. Why does he refer to it as one body? Simply because there can only be one. Just as a human body can only have one body, so the great mystical, unseen church of Christ can only be one body. It consists of all believers from the past and in the present. The sad thing is you could be on the membership roll of a visible local church and not be in the mystical, invisible one. To be a member of the latter you have to have a new birth experience.

In the body of Christ, as in a human one, no one part dominates. The foot doesn't tell the ear it has no need of it. The brain does not despise the little finger or vice versa. There is diversity in unity. There is no standardisation or strict uniformity. An eye is not a foot and a finger is not a nose.

In a body if one part gets hurt then the rest of the body does not say,"We don't care about you". In a body the less good looking parts are not despised by the more attractive, are they? They all work together for the good of the whole. And let's not forget - if one member of the body is honoured, then all the rest are honoured with it.

Be glad, Christian, that you belong to the body of Christ and learn to never despise even its humblest member.

May *seventh*

> *"There is ... one Spirit"*
> (Ephesians 4:4)

There are many evil spirits. The man of Gadara whom the Saviour healed said his name was "Legion: for we are many". Many evil spirits inhabited the poor man. How many evil spirits are there? We don't know: there could be millions operating in the world. But there is only one Holy Spirit. He brings about the unity of the mystical body of Christ. How? By giving life to it.

Every person who is a member of the body of Christ has to be born into it by the regenerating work of the Spirit of God. The Holy Spirit convicts a person of their need of Christ. He draws a person out after Christ and the person puts faith in the Saviour and is born again. Let's acknowledge the Holy Spirit and His unifying work. The Holy Spirit is not an influence. He is a person and must never be called "it". Don't you think we often seem to demote Him from His place as God, the Holy Spirit? Without Him the body of Christ would have no unity. He keeps it alive and enables it to act.

The Holy Spirit then baptises the person who has trusted the Saviour into the body of Christ. A baby when born needs air in its lungs. It is all very well that the baby has been put into the air but if air is not put into the baby it will die. So, the Holy Spirit puts us into Christ and Christ into us. Like the famous day when C. S. Lewis set out in a sidecar with his brother Warren for Whipsnead Zoo in London. He later spoke of how that when he set off for the zoo he did not believe Jesus was the Son of God but that when he got to the zoo he did! "The wind blows where it wishes, and you hear the sound of it, but cannot tell where it comes from and where it goes. So is everyone who is born of the Spirit."

On conversion the Holy Spirit gives us power. Power to discern truth from error. Power to discern new directions. Power to serve others. Power to endure threats and physical abuse. Power to die. (On average in excess of 330,000 Christians die as a result of their beliefs each year). The Holy Spirit also brings about what the Bible calls "fruits". Over the world you will find people displaying those fruits, seven in number. They are love, joy, peace, longsuffering, gentleness, goodness, faith, meekness and temperance. Let's always give the one Spirit His place.

May *eighth*

> *"Just as you are called into one hope of your calling"*
> (Ephesians 4:4)

What does hope do? It lifts your day. It gives you an air of expectancy. It refuels your life after bad decisions. Without it no student would finish a university course, no artist would finish his painting, no entrepreneur would complete his business deal, no marriage would survive. In spiritual things hope is what I call the fresh air of spiritual survival.

This one body of Christ, with the one Holy Spirit invigorating it, is moving toward a great day. The Lord will come for His church and she will move into her place in the New Heaven and the New Earth. God is not hard-up for ideas as to what to do with His church in eternity to come, is He? She will certainly not sit around singing hymns for ever, will she? There will be a universe to run. A universe in which there will be no sin and every tear will be wiped away. The church will go into her future inheritance. We shall reign with Christ as "kings and priests to God" forever.

This Christian hope is not "hope so", is it? It is a hope that is an anchor of the soul which already enters Heaven itself. What does that mean? Sometimes a great sailing ship would sit outside a harbour in stormy weather and could find no hold for its anchor. It would then put the anchor in a small boat and the small boat would go into the harbour and put it down in calmer waters. So our anchor is placed in Christ who is there at the Father's right hand in Heaven. We shall soon enter that safe harbour. That is our hope. Have a good day!

May *ninth*

> *"There is ... one Lord"*
> (Ephesians 4:5)

Sundar Singh, as I stated on February 10th, was once asked by an agnostic professor of comparative religions in a Hindu College what he found in Christianity which he did not find in his old religion. "I have Christ", he replied. "Yes, I know", said the Professor showing a little impatience, "but what particular principle or doctrine have you found that you did not have before?" "The particular thing I have found", he replied, "is Christ" ('The Christ of the Indian Road' by Stanley Jones, 1926, Hodder and Stoughton, p. 64).

Christianity is Christ. Take Him away and it crumbles. Show a failure in Him and the whole thing is a farce. Divorce him from Christian teaching and it will make a vital difference. It would not be valid. There is only one Lord. Jesus was more than a teacher giving advice. He said, as recorded by Luke (6:40): "Why do you call Me, 'Lord, Lord' and do not do what I tell you?" He was the Master of His disciples showing commandments to be obeyed. "Not everyone who says to me, 'Lord, Lord' shall enter the Kingdom of Heaven", he warned, "but he who does the will of my Father in Heaven. Many will say to me in that day, 'Lord, Lord, have we not prophesied in your Name, cast out demons in your Name, and done many wonders in your Name?' And then I will declare to them, I never knew you; depart from me you who practise lawlessness!"

Notice Christ did not object to being addressed as Lord. He knew it was true, He accepted it as exactly appropriate. What He did object to was being called Lord, glibly.

"You call Me Teacher and Lord", He told His disciples, "you say well, for so I am. If I then your Lord and Teacher, have washed your feet, you ought also to wash one another's feet". They spoke of Him as Teacher first and Lord second. In speaking to them about Himself Christ reversed the order. Why? Because if we come to Christ first as Lord and determine to obey Him whenever He teaches us our attitude to His teaching will be different, won't it? There will be no "maybe I will obey" or "maybe I won't".

Do the claims of Christ make Him a tyrant? Certainly not. After making his statement Christ washed their feet in loving service to them. He then sent them out, and us too, to humble Christian service to others.

May *tenth*

> *"There is ... one faith"*
> (Ephesians 4:5)

Where are my roots? Are my roots in the great evangelical awakening of the 19th century? Are my roots in John Wesley or Martin Luther? Are they in the apostles? Are they in Isaiah? Are they in David? No. My roots go back to one evening when God took Abraham out, pointed him to the stars and told him He would give him, through the generations, as many children as there were stars. And what did Abraham do? He believed God. And what happened? "It was accounted to him for righteousness" (Romans 4: 8). Abraham was justified by faith and became the "father of the faithful" (See Galatians 3).

And now? "To him", writes Paul, "who does not work but believes on Him who justifies the ungodly, his faith is accounted to him for righteousness". It is this justifying faith that Paul is referring to when he says there is only "one faith".

Paul's great subject is unity. So he is now teaching there is only one means of salvation, faith in Christ's finished work at Calvary; all who are in the one body come into it through the one faith, justifying faith. "Therefore know", writes Paul in Galatians, "that only those who are of faith are sons of Abraham. And the Scripture, foreseeing that God would justify the nations by faith, preached the Gospel to Abraham beforehand saying, 'In you all the nations shall be blessed'. So then those who are of faith are blessed with believing Abraham .... that the blessing of Abraham might come upon the Gentiles in Christ Jesus that we might receive the promise of the Spirit through faith".

It is beyond me, indeed has been beyond me all my life, why people would ever want to add their own works to such a simple plan of salvation based on a mighty finished work. Why? If the Scriptures are so plain about salvation through the one faith and one faith alone why do people feel they have to earn salvation? If you are trying to earn it, stop this very moment and put your faith in Christ alone for salvation. With Zinzendorf we sing:

"Jesus, Thy robe of righteousness
My beauty is, my glorious dress,
Midst flaming worlds, in this arrayed
With joy shall I lift up my head.

Bold shall I stand in that great day,
For who ought to my charge shall lay?
Fully through Thee absolved I am
From sin and fear, from guilt and shame".

May *eleventh*

"There is ... one baptism"
(Ephesians 4:5)

For Paul to use baptism as something that promotes unity seems a contradiction in terms. Few things cause more argument and division than a discussion of the subject of baptism. I have seen bitter tears shed over it within my lifetime. There are those who believe that the baptism of babies brings regeneration, makes them Christians. There are those who hold, as I do, that baptism is for converted people who have exercised justifying faith. Others hold that it is not the mode that is essential as long as the person has become a Christian. Some teach, falsely, that you cannot be saved without being baptised.

I suggest that the baptism mentioned in today's verse is not water baptism. "For by one Spirit we were all baptised into one body - whether Jews or Greeks, whether slaves or free - and have all been made to drink into one Spirit", says 1 Corinthians 12: 13. All converted people have this experience. "For as many of you as were baptised into Christ", writes Paul, "have put on Christ. There is neither Jew nor Greek, there is neither slave nor free, there is neither male nor female, for you are all one in Christ Jesus. And if you are Christ's, then you are Abraham's seed, and heirs according to the promise" (Galatians 3: 29). Now there's unity for you! There are people in the body of Christ from whom you may differ in many ways; ways of culture, ways of lifestyle, ways of language, ways of education, ways of environment. It makes no difference whatsoever to the unity we enjoy. We have all been baptised into Christ by the Holy Spirit and that one baptism unites us as no political or economic unity ever could. I have met believers in lowly and humble places and in high and exalted places. I have met them in newsrooms and boardrooms and back rooms. All are such that the Lord Jesus means more to them than life itself. The connecting link is that they have all experienced the same baptism which took them out of the Kingdom of darkness and placed them into the Kingdom of God's dear Son.

May *twelfth*

> *"There is ... one God and Father of all, who is above all, and through all, and in you all"*
> (Ephesians 4:6)

"Monotheism brings tension", said the Professor on the television programme I was watching on the subject of the Romans and religion. Yes, the Romans were very tolerant of other religions. Monotheism always brings a problem, she argued. Monotheism? The belief that there is only one God.

In Roman times you could worship Jupiter, and I could worship Mars and we could get along fine. Let me say, though, that there was only one God and that all the rest were the work of the Devil and see what would happen! Yes, the apostle did teach that there were three persons in the Trinity but he also taught that there was only one Godhead. It is a "Tri-unity".

It has been pointed out that there are three great themes here. The first is transcendence. The second is pervasiveness. The third is imminence. Transcendence? It means that God is separate from and above His creation. Christians are not pantheists believing that God is the trees or the stars or the sky. They do not believe that everything is God. They do not worship creation but the Creator. There is one God and Father of all. This, of couse, in the context of Paul's argument is true of the Church. With regard to salvation, the Father thought of it, the Lord Jesus brought it, and the Holy Spirit wrought it. The mighty Creator of the church is "above all" (transcendent), He is "through all" (pervasive) and "in all" (imminent).

Pervasive? This means that He is spread right through the Church. From Africa to America, from the UK to China He pervades what He has created, working through each member.

Imminent? This means that God is present in His church. An unconverted person entering a church gathering can suddenly be aware if God is present among His people (See 1 Corinthians 14: 24-25). We speak of having a sense of God's presence. We are right. Such a transcendent, pervasive God can come right among His people in palpable imminence. It is appropriate that Paul should bring the theme of unity to a climax in showing us the great unifying Heavenly Father we have.

May *thirteenth*

"But to each of us grace was given according to the measure of Christ's gift"
(Ephesians 4:7)

There is a change, here, in Paul's emphasis. He has been speaking of unity. Yes, there is one body, one spirit, one hope, one Lord, one faith, one baptism, one God and Father of all. How, though, does Christ bring unity and maturity? The amazing thing is He does it through individuality. Paul now turns from the third person used in verses 4-6 to the first person, from 'all of us' to 'each of us'.

There is no question that each one of us has been given a gift (charisma). The ability to use the gift given to each one of us is called in today's text the "grace" given to each. Our Lord Jesus apportions gifts and grace is given to use them.

I well remember being in the Soviet Union in the 1960s, as a university student. I was staggered by the boring standardisation of things under the Communist regime. I am afraid there sometimes seems to be a "spiritual Communism" abroad, an attempt to have Christians in a standarised uniformity. As Communism was colourless, so is any attempt to standardise Christians.

None of us are the same. There was the impulsive Peter, the enquiring Philip, the cautious Thomas, the guileless Nathaniel, the devoted Mary Magdalene, the brave Joseph of Arimathea, the humble Ananias, the big-hearted Lydia, the diplomatic Aquila and Priscilla, the faithful Luke, the fiery James and John. Page after page of Scripture is full of people who were very different in temperament, background and experience. The Lord reached and saved them all. To each of them, as to each of us, no matter how different, He gave a gift and the grace to use it. You do not get one without the other. Rejoice in people's gifts; don't be jealous of them. Don't try to standardise Christians. Christians did just that with an evangelist in Belgium, once, and he turned away from his Christian service and eventually committed suicide. His name? Vincent van Gogh. Now if Vincent could have painted like that, how could he not have preached?

May *fourteenth*

One of the shortest parables ever told by the Lord Jesus was stated in the following words: "When a strong man, fully armed, guards his own palace, his goods are in peace. But when a stronger than he comes upon him and overcomes him, he takes from him all his armour in which he trusted and divides his spoils".

In those few shorts words you have what the Lord Jesus did. Satan, the strong one, had taken captive the souls of mankind by the million. He guarded them carefully from Adam on trying to fool people that even talking to God was a waste of time. This was, for the most part, a silent planet toward God. Then the Saviour came and, amazingly, people started to talk to God Incarnate. They couldn't believe God was like this: the devil's lie was exposed. The stronger than Satan eventually overcame him at Calvary and rose again. What happened then is described perfectly in today's text: "When He ascended on high he led captivity captive and gave gifts to men". In terms of the parable the stronger overcame the strong and divided his spoils.

Think of it like this. Here is a gifted young musician but Satan leads him away from God. His talents are spent on himself and the world. Then he hears the Gospel, trusts the Saviour and what happens? His talents held by the strong are now released by the stronger and used to God's glory and to untold blessing among people in his generation. Here is a gifted writer and she writes of transient things of time and sense. She is converted and she starts writing for Chirst. Her writing now has eternal repercussions. So Christ, in His risen power, is constantly dividing the spoils of His victory. To each Christian a charisma, a grace gift is given. Are you using yours to His glory or your own?

May *fifteenth*

"Now this, 'He ascended' - what does it mean but that He also first descended into the lower parts of the earth? He who descended is also the One who ascended far above all the heavens, that He might fill all things"
(Ephesians 4:10)

Christ's ascension obviously implies that there was first a descension. What then does this descension into the lower parts of the earth mean? The phrase is used of a mother's womb in Psalm 139 v. 15 by King David. He writes, "When I was made in secret and skillfully wrought in the lowest parts of the earth". When people are born they enter into life on earth. The Psalmist's phrase for this is "The lowest parts of the earth". Some folk think, then, that the descension means Christ's incarnation.

The expression is used in Psalm 63: 9; "But those who seek my life, to destroy it, shall go into the lower parts of the earth". Some think this may mean the grave so our text refers to the burial of Christ. Others think the phrase means Hades and teach that Christ went down into Hades, the abode of the dead, and preached to people there who had been destroyed in the flood at the time of Noah and set them free. They base it on 1 Peter 3: 19. Still others think that Christ went to Hades and set at liberty the saints of the Old Testament who had been held in captivity ever since their death.

The best explanation I have read in all these matters is that given by Dr. Martyn-LLoyd Jones in the book "Christian Unity" (Banner of Truth Trust, Page 158-159). I commend it to you. He says: "We have no evidence for saying that our Lord ever preached in Hell. It is a supposition, mere speculation and a theory. There is nothing in Scripture to substantiate it, not a word to suggest He liberated people who had been held captives. There is no indication whatsoever that our Lord finally conquered the devil and His powers in Hell after death: indeed we are told, positively, that that work was done upon the cross". He concludes "That what we are dealing with is nothing but a graphic and pictorial manner of describing our Lord's coming down to earth". As the Heavens are the highest part so the earth is the "lower parts".

It was down to earth He came, down to the death of the cross. It is because of its victory He is now ascended far above all the Heavens, beyond all that can be conceived in terms of created reality. He is higher than the highest. Isn't it wonderful to have a friend like Jesus?

May *sixteenth*

*"And He Himself
gave some to be
apostles"*
(Ephesians 4: 11)

We now move to the character of the gifts the ascended Lord has given to His church. There are at least twenty distinct gifts mentioned in the New Testament and five are mentioned here. The first listed is "some to be apostles". John Stott helpfully points out that there are three meanings to the word "apostle" in the New Testament (Stott, P. 16). Once it "seems to be applied to every individual Christian, when Jesus said, 'A servant is not greater than His Master; nor is he who is sent (apostolos) greater than he who sent him" (John 13: 16). So every Christian is both a servant and an apostle. The verb "apostello" means to "send" and all Christian people are sent out into the world as Christ's ambassadors and witnesses. Does this meaning apply to our text? No, simply because it says "He Himself gave some to be apostles".

The second meaning is that "there were 'apostles of the churches'" (2 Corinthians 8: 23; Philippans 2: 25), "messengers sent out by a church either as missionaries or on some other errand".

The third main meaning is that there were "apostles of Christ". These consisted of the Twelve, including Matthias who replaced Judas, Paul, James the Lord's brother and possibly one or two others. Notice the qualification of these apostles. They were personally chosen and authorised by the Lord Jesus and had to be eyewitnesses of the risen Lord (Carefully read Acts 1: 21, 22; 10: 40-41; 1 Corinthians 9: 1; 15: 8-9). In this sense there are no apostles today. Such apostles can have no successors as the original apostles saw the risen Christ. Their authority is preserved for us today in the New Testament Scriptures.

Sometimes I preach in the Blackdown Hills of Somerset where a man became a legend in his lifetime. In 1859 he came to the Blackdowns on the wave of the 1859 Revival and found ignorance, superstition, squalor and crime. Through his amazing ministry in those hills George Brealey left a work of God which continues to this day. Enlightenment, faith, godliness and good works came to the hills as a result of his preaching and teaching. Some called him "The apostle of the Blackdown Hills". In the light of our study today I find such a description perfectly scriptural, don't you? Are you an apostle, in that sense, to your village, town, city or community. I hope you will be.

May *seventeenth*

*"He Himself gave ...
some prophets"*
(Ephesians 4: 11)

"Do not listen to the words of the prophets who prophesy to you. They make you worthless: they speak a vision of their own heart, not from the mouth of the Lord", said the Lord through His prophet Jeremiah (23: 16).

So in the primary sense a prophet was a person who was a mouthpiece or a spokesman of God, a vehicle of His direct revelation. As with apostles, so with prophets, a very definite distinction needs to be made. Biblical prophets or "canonical" prophets, whose words are in the cannon of Scripture, are no longer with us today. If they were then every time they prophesied we would need to add words to the Bible. To do that would bring the wrath of God on our heads (See Revelation 22: 18-19). What is more, every time they prophesied the whole Christian population would be called to obey them. It is a very serious thing to come in to people's lives and make a prophesy concerning their future.

I trust I am healthily sceptical of those who claim "prophetic utterances" for individual Christians or congregations today and would always want to test what they say with given Scripture. The most powerful guidance regarding the future I have ever known has come from Scripture or someone expounding Scripture into my situation. It could be that the person who applies Scripture into the great issues of our day locally or internationally is the one with a "prophetic gift". The prophets and apostles who were the foundation of the church of Jesus Christ are now gone to their reward. Our work is to preserve and expound the precious truth they gave to us: not add to it.

May *eighteenth*

*"He Himself gave ...
some evangelists"*
(Ephesians 4: 11)

The gift of an evangelist is a very special gift. Again it is emphasised that not everybody has this gift. Everyone who is a Christian is called to be a witness for Christ. Indeed, how can you possibly be evangelical without being evangelistic? Yet, the gift of the evangelist is not given to every Christian.

The Bible highlights Philip particularly as a Christian who was an evangelist (See Acts 21: 8). Greatly used of God in Samaria (see Acts 8) he is led by God to "go towards the south along the road which goes down from Jerusalem to Gaza". It was desert country. I sometimes try to imagine what it must have been like for Philip that day. Can you imagine another Christian meeting him on the road to Gaza and saying, "Where are you going today, Philip?" "I am going towards the south." "Where?" "Ultimately I don't know." "What about the great revival in Samaria?" "The Lord told me to come here." "And you don't know where you are ultimately heading?" "No, I am just obeying." "Strange people, evangelists," you can almost hear the Christian thinking.

Soon, though, a chariot appears and in it a man of Ethiopia, a man of great authority under Candace, the Queen of the Ethiopians who had charge of all her treasury. The Ethiopian is reading the Scriptures and nearing the verse which speaks of Jesus when suddenly the Spirit says to Philip, "Go near and overtake this chariot". Philip runs to overtake the chariot and heard the man reading the prophesy of Isaiah. "Do you understand what you are reading?" asks Philip. "How can I, unless someone guides me?", answered the Ethiopian.

I sometimes like to reflect that if Philip hadn't obeyed the Spirit's call to run he would have arrived at the wrong verse! Soon Philip led the Ethiopian to Christ. It wasn't Samaria that day for Philip; God wanted to reach Ethiopia. Lesson? Whatever your gift, when the Lord prompts you to go somewhere and use it - go!

May *nineteenth*

"He Himself gave ...
some pastors"
(Ephesians 4: 11)

The pastor's gift is to shepherd God's flock. A pastor nurtures and cares for them, oversees their activities and guides them. One of the most powerful illustrations I have ever encountered of what a pastor should be was a portrayal in a painting of what he shouldn't be.

I stood gazing at the painting, transfixed. It was entitled, "The Hireling" and it had been painted by Holman Hunt. Beneath the painting was a letter in a glass case. The letter had been written by Holman Hunt and it explained the meaning behind this painting. The young man, for example, he had painted sitting on the grass bank talking to a girl was a hireling brought in for a day to look after the flock. He was sitting chatting to the girl with a death's-head moth in his hand which was, in Victorian days, a bad omen. He didn't care for the flock.

While he discussed superstition two sheep were in the corn. The sheep were as good as dead for corn causes a sheep's stomach to be blown. Some other sheep were standing on marshy ground where, noted Hunt, the little marshmallow flower grows. The hireling has some sheep on the wrong ground and they will get foot-rot and die. Only two sheep are lying down and they are sick. Sheep normally only lie down when they feel secure, so all the rest of the sheep in the painting are standing.

Hunt explained that his painting was representative of what he felt the state of the church was in his day. He felt that many Christian leaders were hirelings and while they spoke of superstitious nonsense in the pulpits of his day, their flocks were eating the wrong food, were on the wrong ground, many were sick, others were frightened and quite a few were in danger of perishing. I went home, chastened.

May *twentieth*

"He Himself gave ... some teachers"
(Ephesians 4: 11)

Preaching in an English city I spent a few hours trying to encourage a gentle and dedicated pastor who was facing huge difficulties in his work. Prostitutes were not helping things by plying their immoral trade from the front gate of his church building; three of their number in the city had been murdered by a serial killer in recent days. The housing estate around him was infested with drug dealing. It was so inspiring to see him going on bravely teaching the Scriptures in such a situation. I greatly admired what he was doing.

Is it worth it to teach God's Word? Of course it is. "Don't just chase money in life", a Professor once warned a class he was teaching, "go after more wonderful things". One of his students forgot all about the warning and for fifteen years chased success. One night watching his big TV screen in his big house in Detroit he was amazed to discover his former teacher talking about dying. The man was wasting away with a debilitating disease.

Overwhelmed with compassion and guilt that he had not kept in touch, the student, now a famous sports commentator rang his old teacher the next day. He then flew to see him and was deeply moved by what he found. The man was an inspiration.

"If you haven't learned how to die you haven't learned how to live", he quipped. He was full of new discoveries and excitement despite his huge problems. The commentator flew to see his former teacher every Tuesday for five months until the teacher's death. The rekindled relationship turned into a final "class". Its agenda? Lessons on how to live.

The pupil, Mitch Albon, turned what he learned from the dying professor, Morrie Schwartz, into a book called, you've guessed it, "Tuesdays with Morrie". The slim volume has sold one million copies (Little, Brown and Company, 1997).

Mitch Albon's book is not a Christian book but it does illustrate the power of a teacher. If a teacher teaches God's Word have you any idea of the repercussions? My wife has a little plaque on our kitchen wall. It reads: "To teach is to touch a life for ever". Margaret's right.

May *twenty-first*

"For the equipping of the saints for the work of the ministry"
(Ephesians 4:12)

"But the manifestation of the Spirit is given to each one for the profit of all", says 1 Corinthians 12: 7. Nowhere but nowhere is a gift given to an individual so that that gift stifles other gifts in the church.

All the gifts mentioned in our study of this section of Ephesians are service-gifts. They are given so that members of the body might be equipped to serve other people.

Nowhere was this more deeply emphasised than in an experience I had once at the Keswick Convention in England. I was preaching that year with one of the great founders of Tear Fund (The Evangelical Alliance Relief Fund) George Hoffman. George and I were close and I was always fascinated by the great work he and his colleagues did across the world helping to raise millions of pounds for the poor. That summer at Keswick young people were giving George their very "jumpers" for folk in Bosnia.

As we walked towards the tent that evening I told George of the frustration I sometimes felt as a Bible teacher spending the most of my life in preaching and teaching when sometimes I longed to go and spend my life helping the poor.

He stopped in his tracks and earnestly emphasised to me that the Lord had called me to my work. He emphasised that some of the young people to whom I was ministering would one day go to the needy areas of the world. He urged me to keep on preaching. He was right. Now I find after years of teaching young people the Word of God that some of them are scattered over the earth serving the Master.

Sadly that summer was the last time I ever saw George. He was killed in a car accident a few weeks later. I still remember his cheerful smile and encouraging words and remember his helpful comments which are encapsulated in today's text. I am sure that those who are called to teaching and preaching often feel the frustration I have felt in that it can be theoretical and not very practical. I urge you, if that is your gift, not to get downhearted. You are, under God, equipping folk for service and that service before it is through could touch the very ends of the earth.

May *twenty-second*

"For the edifying of the body of Christ"
(Ephesians 4:12)

There can be no more important truth in the whole area of gifting than the emphasis in today's text. The emphasis is that if the body of Christ is not "edified" or "built up" by my using of any gift God has given me then I had better not use my gift at all. The great passage on love in 1 Corinthians 13 comes between two chapters on gifts. Why? Because if I am not motivated by love when I use my spiritual gift no one will benefit.. No-one will be built up in their faith, or equipped for service. I will have become as a resounding gong. How many of those resounding gongs have you heard at gatherings of the church? People who go on and on and are saying nothing that edifies you!

Let today's text search us deeply. Every time you and I use the gift God has given us, what exactly is our motivation? Do we ask, "Will this build these people up?". How many hours are wasted on men and women trying to build their own empires within the church? Such behaviour will all come to nothing. They build that which when touched by the refining fire will prove to be wood, hay and stubble and not gold, silver and precious stones. Interestingly, Paul uses the word "To edify" fifteen times.

Moses, for example, left the glory of Egypt to edify or build up the people of God. The last glimpse we get of him in Scripture is standing by a transfigured

Christ on the mountainside. Though the Children of Israel broke his heart at times and often drove him to distraction, he coveted them for God. His motivation was not his own glory but the greater glory of God. He achieved his goal. After all, you get what you go in for. In your service for God within the Christian church always use your gift for the edifying of the body of Christ and one day you will be glad as you stand by the risen Saviour in His day of glory. Earth's glories fade and die but God's glory and the sharing of it is forever.

May *twenty-third*

> *"Till we all come to the unity of the faith and the knowledge of the Son of God, to a perfect man, to the measure of the stature of the fullness of Christ"*
> (Ephesians 4:13)

The image is of a little child growing up. Who of us have not seen it? The baby becomes a toddler and the toddler the young child. "My", we say, "you've grown in a year!" The young child becomes the awkward teenager and we say, "You've just shot up". The teenager becomes the young adult, then mature adulthood is reached with a permanent height and stature.

One day the body of Christ will reach full maturity. All of us will reach the full stature that God has set for us. This, of course, does not mean that as we are on our way that all of us are all the same, does it? The feet are not the same as the hands, the eye as the ear. We don't all speak the same, walk the same, react the same. Our personalities are very different. There is unity with diversity. One day, though, every part of the body will be fully grown.

The life of the body is the blood, reaching even the most distant parts of the body. It is the same blood carrying the same life. So the fullness of Christ, the Head of the church is in every part of His body. It is in the knowledge of the Son of God that this maturity is reached. Get to know the Lord more and you will grow in spiritual maturity. And there must be no disunity about the faith of the Son of God. He is the Son of the living God and the doctrine concerning His person and work is absolute. You are not even in the body if you do not believe that. It is the unity of the faith of the Son of God and personal faith in the Son of God that will bring you to spiritual maturity. It is guaranteed.

May *twenty-fourth*

*"That we should
no longer be
children, tossed to
and fro and carried
about with every
wind of doctrine"*
(Ephesians 4:14)

It's a long journey from infancy to adult maturity. We begin as babies, not as adults. When I was a lad a speaker came to speak at our Scripture Union meeting and his first phrase was that he had an advantage. I listened in immediately! "I was born young!", he said. His sense of humour "tickled" me then and I still smile at it, yet! The truth is that some adults in the Christian church forget that fact when it comes to spiritual things. They forget that when people are converted they are spiritual babies to begin with and they don't become spiritual adults overnight, do they?

The little child with its changing temperament, its whims, its hilarious comments on the most mature adult subjects about which it really has no knowledge, its ignorance of dangerous situations are all very real. There are the extremes of childhood, of course. Children deeply dislike discipline. I distinctly remember falling out with my mother and hiding behind the sofa and saying I would never, ever come out again not in ten million years! Then she made me some delicious food and soon I came out from behind the sofa, said I was sorry, gave her a kiss and tucked into that delicious food!

It is so easy as a spiritual infant to be tossed to and fro, to be carried around in all directions, by every wind of doctrine or theological fad. Winds change direction suddenly and spiritual infants can be carried around in all directions. This is all due to a lack of knowledge and having no standard with which to judge things.

If, in life, you are confronted with various teachings how can you tell what is right? Knowledge is so necessary. Spiritual babies need the good Word of God to grow by. It will give them the standard by which to judge various teachings they come across. It will save them from huge instability. Of all the gifts listed in the church surely that of the teacher is one of the most vital. Keep going, teachers, and may those of us who listen to you teach the precious things of God know that your work will steady us when every wind of doctrine begins to blow.

May *twenty-fifth*

"By the trickery of men, in the cunning craftiness by which they lie in wait to deceive"
(Ephesians 4:14)

At this time in my life I have the privilege of broadcasting with Trans World Radio. It is an international Gospel network, broadcasting in more than 140 languages from twelve primary transmitting locations around the world. They have a staff of over 1,200 dedicated people and work in more than thirty countries.

Today the number of Christians in China is estimated at 40-50 million. It is encouraging to see such encouraging figures but there are some saddening trends as well. In Trans World Radio's Chinese Ministry International "Bulletin Voice" recently two letters were published reflecting problems created by heresies in China. Erroneous teachings have caused divisions and dissentions. Some have left the church.

The first letter states: "In 1995 two evil people claiming to be angels came. They called themselves Eastern Lightening. They have caused a majority of the people in the churches in this area and in our church to stumble, and they still have not got up. The preachers have forsaken their work and the churches are desolate. These people said that the gate of grace had been closed now and there was no need to proclaim the Gospel any more, and that we just needed to wait for God's coming and for salvation. They also said that those who followed them would be angels. In our church even those who had been Christians for many years have followed their teachings and are not loving any longer, nor do they spread the Gospel any more."

The second letter states: "Our church is made up of a group of older people. At first we did not know much, but we all made up for it with zeal and love. Then a few women came to the district, claiming to be God's servant girls coming to water us with God's ways. At first their teachings were quite moving. They said that only following them was the way of truth, while the rest were all heresies. They said all money should be donated to them to take away for preaching the Gospel. They also interpreted the poor in the Bible as servant girls - themselves, and that we were to share with them what we had. The believers at church gradually lost their love for others, and instead gossiped about this and that. The church was a mess. So they just divided up the church and nobody was to communicate with each other". I find these letters extremely disturbing, don't you? Let's be very careful to be on the lookout for the trickery and cunning craftiness of which today's text warns us.

May *twenty-sixth*

> *"But speaking the
> truth in love"*
> (Ephesians 4:15)

I recall having a meal with a pastor once in Eastern Europe. He was telling me of a huge gathering of Christians he had visited once. All day long he had listened to their preaching and turning to me, he said with a smile that at the end of it all they had certainly told out what they were against but they had not told out what they were for!

It is very easy to become a "heresy ferret" always ferreting away wherever you go, listening and looking for heresy. It can make you an extremely hard individual. As always the Bible is so balanced. How do we speak the truth? According to today's text, it must be "in love". It is so easy to win a battle for truth and lose the war not by what you say but by the way you say it. The way you say it can make it most unattractive. How often, too, we profess the truth but negate it by the way we live. Truth becomes very hard when it is not softened by love. Love, on the other hand, becomes very soft if it is not strengthened by truth. There will be times when we are called upon to strongly criticise a view that someone holds. Christians are not called upon to say that there is a certain amount of right and truth in everything. There isn't. We need, though, when criticising, to watch how we criticise. Recently I read comments between two major figures of faith in past history. To be honest their communication was downright disgusting. The firstfruit of the Spirit is love. Steep your defence of truth in it!

May *twenty-seventh*

> *"May grow up in
> all things"*
> (Ephesians 4:15)

Holding and standing for the truth as it is in Jesus is the imperative of Christians everywhere. The problem of error is constantly around them and as they stand firm against it they are called upon to make progress at the same time. They are not to get in a rut but are all called on to move towards a goal of Christian maturity. To grow up "in all things" is to grow up in every respect.

Isn't it pathetic how so many people never seem to mature? A friend of mine was at a function one day where an older member of the British Royal family was speaking. My friend was thrilled with what she heard and was even inspired by it. As she crossed the car park after the function a lady who was accompanying her was fuming. What about? You would be surprised to learn that she said, "It isn't fair. Did you notice that she hadn't got any wrinkles!".

Amazing, isn't it, that all the lady could see in what had been a truly fascinating and instructive morning was a lack of wrinkles of which she was jealous? Some people remain so immature, so self-centred, so childish in their thinking. They simply never grow up.

Paul's wish is that we might grow up in "all things". Are there areas of your life which could do with maturing? I'm afraid there are all too many in mine. It would have eased huge burdens in my life if I had learned to "grow up" quicker. I would have saved myself a lot of bitter heartache. How about you?

May *twenty-eighth*

"May grow up in all things into Him who is the Head - Christ - from whom the whole body, joined and knit together by what every joint supplies, according to the effective working by which every part does its share, causes growth of the body for the edifying of itself in love"
(Ephesians 4:15-16)

Two beautiful truths are emphasised in the first part of today's texts. As the Lord Jesus is the Head of the church, He supplies everything that is needed for the church's growth. At the same time it is the measure of His full stature that is the goal of the church's growth. In other words the Lord Jesus supplies me with what is needed to become more and more like Him! Christ is, then, both the source and the goal of Christian maturity.

As Christ gives the supply of life to His body, the church, so each part is enabled to function together. In a joint in the human body there is a "cup" on one bone into which there fits a ball at the end of another. The surfaces are smooth and there is absolutely no friction. Each bone is brought and held together and the human body functions.

The body of Christ is composed of many parts all joined together and to every part God gives all that it needs in supply. Some need more than others but all get what they need.

I emphasise this to you, Christian. Do you have a needed supply of tact, of wisdom, of grace for a certain task the Lord has called you to do at this time? He will give you today exactly what you need. No more, no less, just enough. As we all function in the body, doing the will of God, the body of Christ will grow, edified in love. The challenge is, though, if part of the body is poisoned does it affect the rest of the growth of the body? It certainly does. Let me remember the privilege of being a part of the body of Christ and make sure that what I do does not hold up its growth.

May *twenty-ninth*

> *"This I say, therefore, and testify in the Lord, that you should no longer walk as the rest of the Gentiles walk"*
> (Ephesians 4:16)

When God spoke to Abraham He asked him to do something. He asked Abraham to "walk before Him". He did not ask him to crawl or fawn before Him but to walk. Man is different to animals and not just anatomically.

When a woman who had an infirmity eighteen years came into the synagogue one Sabbath Jesus immediately healed her. Her infirmity meant that she was "bent over and could in no way raise herself up". Immediately she was made straight. The ruler of the synagogue was very angry. She could have been healed on another day, he insisted. Our Lord Jesus insisted to the ruler that the woman, who was "a daughter of Abraham" should be healed on the Sabbath of all days. As Abraham was told to walk before God, a woman of his race should surely walk too. And was not the Sabbath all about being freed from slavery? Was not the stance of a slave that of being bent over? "And remember", said God to Moses, "that you were a slave in the land of Egypt and that the Lord your God brought you out from there by a mighty hand and an outstretched arm: therefore the Lord your God commanded you to keep the Sabbath." The Sabbath was a celebration of straightening people up to walk! The synagogue ruler had forgotten that.

The Lord has straightened you and me up too, has He not? In His Name Paul calls us to make sure that when we walk we do not walk like Gentiles do. The three questions that Gentiles ask, said Jesus, are "What shall we eat? ..... What shall we drink? ... What shall we wear?" After these things the Gentiles seek. We are not to be like them but rather we are to "seek first the Kingdom of God and His righteousness and all these things will be added to us." Are you walking like a Gentile?

May *thirtieth*

"That you should no longer walk as the rest of the Gentiles walk, in the futility of the mind, having their understanding darkened, being alienated from the life of God, because of the ignorance that is in them, because of the hardening of their hearts; who, being past feeling, have given themselves over to licentiousness, to work all uncleaness with greediness"
(Ephesians 4:17-19)

The Gentile mind, outside of Christ, Paul emphasises, is deeply affected because the Gentile heart has hardened itself against the truth. The heart is the source of all loyalties. The Greek origin of "hardness" means "a kind of marble". There is obviously an inevitable consequence of this hardness. Here we have a very powerful analysis of a Godless mind set.

First, their minds are empty. They go after meaningless things. A look around you on any day will prove that! Their understanding is darkened. Since they refuse the light God would give them, spiritual darkness engulfs them and so affects their intellect. They are alienated from the life of God. This means they are spiritually dead, they are without God. They are also without spiritual knowledge, spiritual "ignorance is in them". They are "past feeling", that is, they are without moral sensitivity. This means they do not exercise any moral restraint and therefore pursue and give themselves over to sensuality, impurity and lust. Having experienced what such a pursuit brings they are never satisfied and therefore desire to have more and more; they "work all uncleanness with greediness".

In Romans 1 and Colossians 3 there are striking similarities to what appears in Ephesians 4. They make an interesting study. The interesting point I would like to emphasise in today's meditation is that while in Romans 1 Paul teaches that God gave them over to their sin, in Ephesians 4 he teaches that they choose to do so. Here you have the Biblical balance of God's sovereignty and man's responsibility.

Today's verses show, as an analysis of the godless mind that the Bible is more relevant than tomorrow's newspaper.

May *thirty-first*

"But you have not so learned Christ"
(Ephesians 4:20)

Here we are in the school of Christ and our education is awesome in its implications and influence. What we learn in Christ's school could not be more different from the principles learned in the school of paganism. Millions of students have enrolled in Christ's school since the days of Paul and no curriculum could be more life-changing. No matter what our background, occupation, profession, social status, possession of wealth or lack of it, this teacher welcomes us all. This education is suitable in any culture on the face of the earth.

In his work "In The School of Christ" (The Myrtlefield Trust, 1995) my friend Professor David Gooding has pointed out that when Christ taught His disciples in the Upper Room the atmosphere created by Christ in His school was very special. Here was a sympathetic, helpful and patient teacher even though He was the Almighty Ruler of the universe. The disciples reclined full length on their mats at the low table, supporting themselves on their left elbow and leaving their right hand and arm free to reach for food. "When one of the disciples who was reclining next to Jesus", writes the Professor, "wanted to ask him a question, he simply and naturally leaned back on Jesus' breast and looked up into His face (John 13: 35). Nor was any of them afraid to interrupt Him and tell Him, if he did not understand what He said (John 14: 5-10, 22-23). Once Peter even protested at something Jesus did. It was foolish of him, no doubt: but the fact that he was not afraid to do so, shows how completely at ease they felt in the presence of the Lord, and that in turn reveals what a gracious and approachable teacher He was". He still is.

JUNE

The Mount of Transfiguration must have been something else! Peter was so moved by what he saw he wanted to build three shelters for Moses, Elijah and Christ. The Scriptures tell us that Peter did not know what he was saying. His condition is perfectly understandable. How would we have reacted in such a circumstance? We would probably have wanted to stay on that mountain as long as possible or, at least, to savour such a transfiguration for a little while longer.

The Lord had other plans for Peter. He must leave that thrilling transfiguration scene and face the problems in the valleys below. He must even face death for the Lord's sake before he would be promoted to glory. In June's readings we shall dwell on the challenge Paul gives to living a truly Christian life in the "valleys" where bitterness, rage, anger, brawling, malice, obscenity, slander, greed, corruption, drunkenness and every kind of evil pervade. In the midst of all of this we are called to redeem the time because the days are evil. It is quite a challenge!

June *first*

"If indeed you have heard Him and been taught by Him"
(Ephesians 4: 21)

Heard Him? Yes, I've heard Him, haven't you? I heard him calling me in my childhood and know Him as my shepherd. Following Him, I soon learned that there is no voice like His. "Mary!", said the risen Christ in the garden. Up until she heard His voice she had supposed Him to be the gardener but on hearing His voice she turned to Him and said joyously,"Teacher!" How did she know it was He? He tells us that His sheep know His voice and they follow Him. That voice is immediately recognised by every Christian the world over. There is no mistaking it.

Been taught by Him? Certainly. In ten thousand ways. He has taught me through circumstances, allowing them to flush out the mediocre, the futile, the transient. He has taught me from His Word, a Word that is absolute, always relevant and which never passes away. He has taught me through nature around me. He has spread my table from His bounty every day of my life. He has shown me His glory in the sight of silvery stars set in the deep blackness of the night sky above me or in the intricacy of the forest floor beneath me. The bubbling of the mountain stream and the incredible outpouring of a skylark. He has taught me the range of His creative power.

A reader might respond to my joy in hearing Christ's voice and my pleasure in His teaching by saying they wish they could have the same experience. You can! How? Read the Scriptures, particularly John's Gospel to start with and all the while pray to God that He will enlighten you by His Holy Spirit. If you are sincere in your desire He will do just that. You doubt me? Then read Luke 11: 5-13.

June *second*

"As the truth is in Jesus"
(Ephesians 4: 21)

We have travelled a long way since January 1st in our meditations in this superb letter: we have sought together to scale highest ground. Now we reach a turning point where Paul turns to apply the great doctrines he has been teaching to everyday life.

Near to me there lives a Mr. Stelfox who is the only Ulsterman to have scaled Mount Everest. He would be the first to admit that life is very differently viewed after someone has had the experience. He is an architect and I listened to him present his ideas for a project in which I am involved. The chairman who is overseeing the project introduced the architect to us as the man who had scaled the highest mountain in the world. Mr. Stelfox is marked in public by his experience.

As we have scaled Christian doctrine together we too are going to be affected by what we have seen in our lifestyle and behaviour. Paul closes this magnificent section of his letter by saying that the whole content of Christian truth is summed up in Jesus. He embodies truth. He is the truth. The teaching of the Gentiles is blatantly false but the truth as it is in Jesus stands for ever true.

It has been said that the test of an individual's greatness is "what did he leave to grow?" By this test Jesus stands head and shoulders above all others. He, though, is the measure against which the church grows and His truth the standard by which it judges everything. Soon we shall see Him and, in the meantime, as we live out our lives for the truth as it is in Jesus, one word covers us. What word? It is found under a 150 year old oak in a church cemetery in rural Louisiana. Carved on the tombstone is only one word:"Waiting".

June *third*

> *"That you put off,*
> *concerning your*
> *former conduct, the*
> *old man"*
> (Ephesians 4: 22)

The first thing that learning the truth as it is in Jesus does for you is that it teaches you to "fling off" former false teaching and conduct. It is a filthy garment anyway. The former was a lifestyle dominated by sin. This life was corrupt, on its way to ruin, dominated by uncontrolled passions and full of deceit. It was, as the book of Romans teaches, rooted "in the flesh".

Let me ask you, Christian, a simple question. What did "the flesh" ever do for you? I know it brought pleasure, but how long did it last? I know it fed ego, boosted pride, and drove you to seek achievement as an end in itself. I know it filled your mouth with gossip. That gossip was sweet to your taste but as a result good reputations died and deep hurt was inflicted. "The flesh" promised much, gave its best gifts first but never warned you that the end result was emptiness. You had to find that out for yourself.

Now things are different. The filthy garment is seen for what it is, filthy. The old life is identified as heading in one direction only, destruction. So then what did "the flesh" ever do for you in terms of blessing? Did it ever give you any lasting peace or joy? Well then, if it didn't, why on earth do you want to put that filthy garment on again and be tempted to go back to that old lifestyle? You are now rooted in the Spirit so sow to the Spirit and you will reap the Spirit. If you sow to the flesh, you will reap just that. Its fruits shrivel and die.

June *fourth*

> *"And be renewed in*
> *the spirit of your*
> *mind"*
> (Ephesians 4: 23)

This verse is, categorically, not speaking of the work of the Holy Spirit. The Holy Spirit is never described in Scripture as being part of a human being any more than a tree or a mountain or a flower as being a part of God. The Spirit of God is transcendent and separate from us though He is, at the same time, dwelling in us.

Note the text: "it speaks of "the spirit of your mind". What does this mean? It means your perception, your outlook. This needs to be constantly renewed. As the old self, without God, was constantly being corrupted, so the new self is being constantly renewed. It all starts in the mind. Sow a thought, reap an action. Sow an action, reap a character. Sow a character, reap a destiny. Constant renewal of our minds will transform our lives. The truth, as it is in Jesus, informing our minds will transform our attitude to everything.

Is not history full of the influence of people's ideas springing from their minds? From Hitler's "Mien Kampf" to Marx's "Das Kapital" to "The thoughts of Charman Mao"? The other day I stood in Sir Walter Scott's house at Abbotsford and saw his famous collection of memorabilia. It is just a fascinating collection. There was Napoleon's pen case with his insignia on it. How many lost their lives because of the thoughts issuing from the orders written by the pen that lay in that case?

Let your outlook be constantly renewed by prayer and Bible study, by praise and worship. If Victor Hugo was right when he said, "Mightier than the tramping of a mighty army is an idea whose time has come", then what of the influence of a renewed mind? The power of truth liberates, enobles and refines.

June *fifth*

"And that you put on the new man which was created according to God, in righteousness and true holiness"
(Ephesians 4: 24)

I have always found the conversion of Augustine to Christ an intriguing story. He craved satisfaction and made four famous ventures to find it. First he tried the sensuous, the carnal. After momentary excitement he was left with a feeling of loathing and disgust. He then turned to the aesthetic, developing his taste for art, music, rhetoric and science. He still craved something infinitely more satisfying. He then tried philosophy but still could not find what he longed for. He then became religious but his pride shrunk the challenge of humility.

In time Augustine left his devout and praying mother, Monica, for Rome, eventually becoming a Professor of Rhetoric in Milan, his heart still crying for light in his dark and vacant soul.

Then, one day, he was given wise advice. He was urged to study Paul's Epistles. He decided to do this with his boyhood friend Alypius. They decided to begin with the Epistle to the Romans. One beautiful afternoon the pair sat in a lovely garden on the outskirts of Milan. Something read or said reminded Augustine of his squandered years. He took himself off to a corner of the garden and wept profusely. "So", he wrote, "while I was weeping in the most bitter contrition of my heart, lo! I heard from a neighbouring house a voice of a boy or girl - I knew not which - chanting repeatedly the words, 'Take up and read! Take up and read!'"

He went back to Alypius, seized the sacred scroll and his eyes fell on the following powerful words: "Not in revelry and drunkenness, not in licentiousness and lewdness, not in strife and envy. But put on the Lord Jesus Christ and make no provision for the flesh, to fulfil its lusts".

"No further would I read, nor was there any need", wrote Augustine, "For at once with the end of the sentence, as though the light of eternity had been poured into my heart, all the darkness of doubt vanished away".

"Put on the Lord Jesus Christ", urges Paul in Romans. "Put on the new self!", urges Paul in Ephesians. The new self is, in essence, the saving life of Christ lived out in our lives. The new self was created, our text says, "According to God" which means that it was created "In the image of God". So, put on that new Christ-like self today. Saying a daily "yes" to Christ is saying a daily "no" to Satan.

June *sixth*

"Therefore put away lying, each one speak truth with his neighbour for we are members one of another"
(Ephesians 4: 25)

One day a minister spotted a group of several boys out in the church car park gathered around an irresistibly cute little puppy. They were making quite a commotion. The minister walked over to them and asked:

"Well boys, what's going on here?"

"We found this puppy", said one of the boys, "and all of us want to keep it. So we're having a contest. The one who can tell the biggest lie wins the puppy".

"Shame on you", said the minister, "I can't believe you would do such a thing, deliberately telling lies. Why? When I was your age I never told a lie".

The boys fidgeted and looked at each other rather nervously. Finally one boy said: "Ok, Mister, you win the dog!".

Lies, there isn't one of us who has not stretched the truth and told a barefaced lie. Few things are as essential to God's character as truth. Lying is inconsistent with God's character. The Bible tells us that God cannot lie and of the six things God hates, listed in the book of Proverbs, lying is one of them. Fellowship is built on trust and trust is built on truth. Falsehood and lies undermine fellowship and truth strengthens it. Husbands and wives need truth between them and parents and children need the same. In today's text Paul emphasises that fellowship in the body of Christ depends on truth being spoken between members.

If you are into telling lies then be sure your sin will find you out. A woman went into a shop to buy a chicken. The man lifted one out of the ice barrel and weighed it. "Five pounds", he said. "I would like a bigger one", said the woman. He took out the same chicken and put it on the scales, adding pressure and said, "Seven pounds". "That's fine", said the lady, "I'll take both of them!" So, put away lying.

June *seventh*

> *"Be angry and do not sin: do not let the sun go down on your wrath, nor give place to the devil"*
> (Ephesians 4: 26)

There is such a thing as Christian anger. If God gets angry at sin, so should His people. Wholesale abortion, the constant rise in the occurrences of rape, the exploitation of the weak by drug dealers, the exploitation of the poor by the wealthy, "ethnic cleansing" and genocide by governments, the sexual abuse of children, the cruelty of "walk away husbands" or wives, all of these sins and others too should arouse the Christian's anger. Not to be angry at such sin would be a sin. Christians are clearly encouraged by this text to be angry. There are, though, to be three qualifications to our anger. All of them restrict it. First we are to be angry but in our anger we are commanded not to sin. God's anger, of course, is very real but it is never vindictive, never spiteful and always righteous. Human anger often behaves irrationally with stamping of feet and slamming of doors. God's anger is never irrational. Be careful that your anger does not lead you to sin. The second restriction on our anger is that we must never "nurse it to keep it warm". "Let not the sun go down on your wrath", certainly doesn't mean that we are to be angry until sunset: that would give the folks in Greenland a wider scope for anger! It simply means that it is better if you never go to bed angry. Don't let it smoulder overnight. Make it brief.

The third restriction is that in our anger we are to give no opportunity to the devil. You can be sure that the devil is always waiting to exploit our anger. Give him a "toehold" in your anger and he will soon crash in upon you and push you into revenge, hatred and even violence (See 1 Timothy 3: 7; 2 Timothy 2: 26; 1 Peter 5: 8) . The devil lurks around angry people. Be on your guard!

June *eighth*

> *"Let him who stole, steal no longer, but rather let him labour, working with his hands what is good, that he may have something to give him who has need"*
> (Ephesians 4: 28)

There was once a group of thieves who were not into growing their own crops but who were into stealing other people's crops. They were called Midianites. Every year for seven years they came up and denuded Israel of its food.

One day an angel was found sitting at the foot of an oak tree watching a humble farmer threshing wheat in a winepress. It was not the normal place to thresh wheat. This was done in the open air so that the wheat and the chaff could be separated as the farmer winnowed it. To appear in the open air threshing wheat would have cost you your life at the hands of the Midianites.

"The Lord is with you, you mighty man of valour", said the angel to the farmer. The farmer, whose name was Gideon, was not impressed He saw himself as insignificant. The message was then given to him that the Lord was with him and that he would defeat the Midianites as one man.

What was his secret? The answer was that an army marches on its stomach as does a nation. Gideon, by working with his hands, defied the enemy and restored the food supply line to his family. That is why he was chosen to lead the nation. Even when one of the Midianites dreamt that a loaf of bread had rolled down a hill and flattened his tent, his fellow soldier told him "this is nothing else but the sword of Gideon the son of Joash, a man of Israel; for into his hand God has delivered Midian and the whole camp" (See Judges 7: 9-15). Even the enemy knew what Gideon represented. He, of course, eventually saved Israel under God.

It is very easy to have a Midianite lifestyle. You can evade taxes, dodge customs, clock into work late and out early, in your employer's time. You can steal another man's wife or husband, boy or girlfriend, you can rob God of His dues. The Midianites are not dead, by any means. If you put on the new self, though, all that lifestyle is abhorrent. Now you stop sponging and start contributing. Now you stop stealing and start working, supporting yourself and your family and giving to those in need. I want to be a Gideon, don't you?

June *ninth* ~~Sunday~~

> *"Let no corrupt communication proceed out of your mouth, but what is good for necessary edification, that it may impart grace to the hearers"*
> (Ephesians 4: 29)

We can have falcons to land on our wrists, pigeons to carry out messages, dogs to fetch the newspaper and tigers to sit on benches. We can also train elephants to stand on rolling balls and killer whales to take trainers for a ride around a pool. I have even seen parrots who were trained to ride on roller skates! The tongue, though, cannot be tamed by any person.

The Bible teaches that the tongue is capable of terrible injury. It is verbal cyanide. It can assault and sear and destroy at will. "In the tongue is the power of life and death", says the book of Proverbs. The longer I live the more I am convinced that we seldom stop to think of the power of the things we say to each other.

James asks, "Does a spring send forth fresh water and bitter from the same opening?" (James 3: 11). Such a thing is impossible but the tongue can send out blessing and cursing from the same mouth!

Paul calls upon us to ensure that no corrupt communication proceeds out of our mouths. This means that we must quit unwholesome talk. This includes abusive language, obscenities and malicious gossip. Paul is not promoting silence but he is promoting control.

Instead of corrupt communication we are called to use edifying language. This means language which builds people up. I have to confess that I have often listened to Christians using sarcasm to each other and I detest it, don't you? Instead of building up each other's confidence, encouraging each other in their tasks, often all you hear is a series of "put-downs". Let your speech be up-building language that it may impart "grace to the hearers". The force of that word is "to do a favour" or "to confer a benefit". Don't send the person you have talked to away hurt and humiliated by your words but benefitted. Ask God to help you to find words according to the need of the moment to fit the occasion. Let's watch our tongue at all times. After all, our tongue can easily slip for it sits in a wet place!

June *tenth*

> *"And do not grieve
> the Holy Spirit of
> God by whom you
> were sealed for the
> day of redemption"*
> (Ephesians 4: 30)

It was Marcus Barth who said that the God who is proclaimed in Ephesians is not "an unmoved mover". The same God, the Holy Spirit, who indwells believers is the guarantee of the coming redemption of their bodies on a coming day. Paul is saying that it is possible to grieve and hurt that very same Spirit. To grieve in Greek means "to cause sorrow, pain or distress".

How is such a thing possible? By doing the things Paul has been telling us not to do. Lying grieves the Spirit. Sinful anger grieves the Spirit. Stealing in any form whatever grieves the Spirit. Misuse of language grieves the Spirit. The Spirit of God is the Holy Spirit and unholy behaviour grieves Him.

The other side of this serious commandment of Paul's is that if it is possible to grieve the Holy Spirit it is also possible to bring Him pleasure. As we put on the new self and the saving life of Christ empowers us, our lives can bring great pleasure to the Spirit of God. A kindly word, a neighbourly act, a helpful letter or E-mail. A positive attitude, a turning of the other cheek. An hour of our time to make a child's heart glad. A smile where a frown might have been. A giving up of our comfortable seats. A patience when the check-out machine has broken down. A longsuffering reaction when the computer hangs fire. A "walking away" when to stay would mean disaster or a staying when to "walk away" would mean the same. Such actions bring pleasure to others but meditate on the fact that they also bring immense pleasure to God the Holy Spirit. Do you enjoy bringing pleasure to other people? Remember too that the Holy Spirit is a person. He feels pain and enjoys pleasure.

June *eleventh*

> *"Let all bitterness,
> wrath, anger,
> clamour and evil
> speaking be put away
> from you with all
> malice"*
> (Ephesians 4: 31)

Here are the dangers of anger listed and emphasised very decisively. Each one is to be removed or put away from our lives. Let's think about them. "Bitterness": this is a harbouring of resentment about the past which makes a person angry. Millions of people are held by the clutches of bitterness. Are you all fouled up in your life by it? Let it go. Why let it ruin your life? It isn't worth it.

"Wrath": this is the initial explosion of rage. It can, of course, lash out. Always remember it is the second blow that makes a battle. "Anger": in this context it has been suggested that this could mean a gnawing hostility. Such a condition makes you a sullen person. Come on, then, Christian replace such wrath and anger with a cheerful spirit. "Clamour": this means anger that erupts in yelling and shouting which abuses and vilifies others. "Chill out", as teenagers say! "Put it away", says Paul.

"Malice": this means any attitude which intends to harm a person. The pattern of the intensification of anger is clear and sadly ends up in the summarising term used here by Paul which is sheer downright malice which means and even plots to harm others.

Let the searchlight of today's verse search our lives today. Let's ask the Lord's help to "put away" all these vices associated with ungodly anger. If you don't put them away you will be going around with an "anger bomb" ticking away in your life which when it explodes could bring huge devastation. All those angry people, where do they all come from?

June *twelfth*

> *"And be kind to one another, tenderhearted, forgiving one another, just as God in Christ also forgave you"*
> (Ephesians 4: 32)

If the former vices of ungodly anger listed by Paul disrupt and destroy harmony and relationships, the lovely qualities listed in today's text do the very opposite. In Chapter 2: 7 Paul has spoken of God's kindness towards us in Christ Jesus: truly if we have known the incredible kindness of God in our lives it would follow that we should be kind to one another. "Be kind" is as good a motto behind any day's busy activities as I know. Whatever you do today, wherever you go, be kind!

Tenderheartedness is not a human trait which has dominated the twentieth century and even in the last few months of it, as I write, war in the Balkans has dominated everyday headlines. Horrors long associated with the Holocaust are being repeated. To be tenderhearted is to show compassion. Are you a compassionate person? Do you care about the needs of others or are you coldhearted? You will, if you go on with such an attitude, become an isolated island to yourself in life. Keep a tender heart, not a hard one.

Just as we have known love and compassion from God so we have known His forgiveness. In the same way as you have known God's forgiveness in Christ so you should show forgiveness to others. Notice the motivating force for this forgiveness. The motivating force is not that you might have forgiveness but rather it is because you already have it. What if God had not forgiven you? What if He had continued to treat you and estimate you for ever on the basis of what you had done in the past? What if He pressed judgment for all eternity on you for your sins? The thought doesn't bear thinking about. Since, then, God forgives you in Christ, have a forgiving spirit to others.

June *thirteenth*

> *"Therefore be*
> *followers of God, as*
> *dear children"*
> (Ephesians 5: 1)

Paul is calling us to be, the word is, literally, "imitators" of God. Interestingly this is the only place in the New Testament where we are told explicitly to imitate God. In other places churches are to imitate other churches (See 1 Thessalonians 2: 14), Christians are called on to imitate Paul (See 1 Corinthians 4: 16; 10: 33, 11: 1; Philippians 3: 17, etc.) and to imitate the Lord Jesus (See 1 Thessalonians 1: 16) but nowhere else are we called on to imitate God.

Do children imitate their parents? Of course. If bad languge is used by children the reaction often is "who did they learn it from?" If bad habits emerge then relationships with their parents come under scrutiny. Paul has been emphasising in the first half of his letter the relationship believers have with God.They have become His children. We are not all born children of God, we become children of God through the new birth. Then we call God "Abba", "Dear Father" and we become his dearly loved children. Obviously we will bear a family resemblance. If there is no family resemblance in us then we must not be His children.

The question used by Charles Sheldon in his influential book, "In His Steps" was, "What would Jesus have done in this circumstance?" It is a very useful question. I don't know where your work or where your responsibilities will take you today or tomorrow. I don't know just how awkward or pressing your circumstances will be. Perhaps some huge decision bears down upon you and you are distraught as to how to act. Talk to your Heavenly Father about it. You are his dearly loved child. Ask for His help and then whatever you do, imitate Him. Imitate His kindness, His love, His compassion and His forgiveness. "You be holy" said the Lord to Israel, "for I the Lord your God am holy". As sure as I write these words people around you will soon say: "There is something different about you". They too may soon become His children as a result.

June *fourteenth* & *love.*

> *"And walk in love as Christ also has loved us and given Himself for us"*
> (Ephesians 5: 2)

If we would imitate God then we must know Him. How can we know him? Through the Lord Jesus. Track every move He made on earth and He reveals what God is like. When people who detested religion, as represented by the Pharisees, came across the Lord Jesus they were astonished at what they found. They found that He loved them and instead of coming to condemn the world He had come to save it! Their reaction was that they had never heard any man speak like this man. They basically said, "We never thought God was like this!" Christ could hardly eat His meals at times for sinful people who wanted to talk with Him and be where He was.

We are called as His followers to walk in love as Christ loved us and gave Himself for us. Such love stirs love. Those who are forgiven much love much in return. If anyone epitomises in Scripture the principle that the last shall be first and the first, last, Mary Magdalene is that person. She was forgiven much, for out of her life Christ cast seven demons. Mary loved much in return. A close study of her life will show you that she not only gave her whole time and substance to the Lord (Luke 8: 2-3) but more importantly she gave her whole heart. There she was standing by His cross and, famously, while it was still dark, by His tomb. Love? How could you define a love which said to the supposed gardener that if he knew where Christ was to tell her and, she added, "I will take Him away". How, logistically, was she ever going to do that? She was oblivious to her own strength which was so unequal to such a burden. For Mary, neither death nor life, nor angels, nor principalities, nor powers, nor things present, nor things to come, nor height, nor depth, nor any other creature could separate her from the love of God which was in Christ Jesus her Lord. What seemed to be her worst day, though, turned out to be her best. Great love inspired great love. Let it do the same for you.

June *fifteenth*

> *"An offering and a sacrifice to God for a sweet-smelling aroma"*
> (Ephesians 5: 2)

Is there not an implication in today's text? The Lord Jesus gave Himself up for us and willingly obeyed all that His Father asked Him to do. When faced with the darkness of Calvary He said, "Not what I will but what you will". His supremely unselfish behaviour was a sacrifice which brought great pleasure to God. The implication Paul brings in today's text surely is that as Christ's self-giving brought pleasure to God so does ours.

A helpful example of Christian self-giving being one of God's pleasures is given by Paul when he writes to the Christians at Philippi. He mentions that a fellow worker Epaphroditus, who for the work of Christ, "came close to death not regarding his life to supply what was lacking in you in your service toward me". The Philippian Christians could not give Paul immediate help because of his house arrest in Rome but Epaphroditus was willing to give up his very life, and very nearly had to, carrying the Philippians' gifts to Paul. Those gifts were, says Paul, a sweet smelling aroma, an acceptable sacrifice, well pleasing to God.

Meditate a moment on what Paul is saying. The aroma of this beautiful act of kindness by the Philippian Christians wafted right up into Heaven and God was well pleased with it. Anything we might perform for Christ's sake because we have been animated and moved by our love to Him, though we may think we are doing it only to that person or cause, is an act taken right out of that level and is something that God sees and blesses.

Walking into a room you suddenly smell the beautiful scent of fresh flowers in a corner. It is very pleasant. Your acts of kindness give a sweet smelling aroma to God.

June *sixteenth*

> *"But fornication and all uncleanness, or covetousness, let it not even be named among you, as is fitting for saints"*
> (Ephesians 5: 3)

The interesting question raised here is that if the vices listed by Paul should not be named among Christians is Paul breaking his own prohibition by naming them in today's verse!? The answer is that sexual sin should not become the object of interest in conversation. Paul is not asking us to refuse to call sin, sin. Any counsellor who wants to help a person caught in one of the vices named would need to talk about it if they were to help the person who wants to break free. The Bible does not shy away from calling these sins what they are in the lives of many characters through history who rise on its pages.

Paul turns from a discussion of self-sacrificial love to self-indulgence, particularly self-indulgent sexuality. "Fornication" is a broad word covering any sexual sin. "Impurity", covers all impurity and "covetousness" means "greed" and, in the context, sexual greed. The problem with sexual sin is that greed, or the desire to have more, grips and drives the person who gives in to it. There is no end to this desire if not controlled by the Lord. It is frightening that sexuality, created by God and not Hollywood, with all its beauty and joy of fulfilment is turned into something so rancid by sin. There is nothing so empty and lonely as sex without a promise. Remember that Samson left a prostitute at midnight. There was no true companionship, there. In such a situation there never is.

If such subjects become the objects of interest in conversation it can lead to the practice of the sins themselves. Such conversation is not fitting, is not appropriate, is not proper for people who are set-apart for the Lord.

June *seventeenth*

> *"Neither filthiness,*
> *nor foolish talking,*
> *nor coarse jesting,*
> *which are not*
> *fitting, but rather*
> *giving of thanks"*
> (Ephesians 5:4)

Paul now concentrates on naming the sins of the tongue. It is an interesting fact that if you go through the Ten Commandments you will see that the tongue can be involved in breaking every one of them. It is a microcosm of mischief. There is no part of life which the tongue cannot affect and there is no time of life when its influence cannot change the course of anyone's life. It is as potent and active when you are old as it is when you are young.

What sins does Paul highlight? He highlights "filthiness": this means obscenity, that which is disgraceful or shameful in speech. Linked with this is "foolish talking" and "coarse jesting". Foolish talk comes from a "fool", a person who is empty of understanding. Perhaps like Arabella Young. Arabella Young? Her epitaph read:

"Beneath this lump of clay
Lies Arabella Young
Who on the 23rd May
Began to hold her tongue"

"Coarse jesting?" This is speech full of double meaning, much loved in our day by millions of people. Let us also remember that dirty jokes and innuendo are not fitting for a follower of Christ.

What is the alternative to such language? It is the "giving of thanks". To meet a person whose language is full of thanksgiving is a very refreshing experience. The supreme attitude to carry through the day is an attitude of "in all things give thanks". Try it, today. People will be glad they met you.

June *eighteenth*

> *"For this you know, that no fornicator, unclean person, no covetous man, who is an idolator, has any inheritance in the Kingdom of Christ and God"*
> (Ephesians 5: 5)

The salient point in the solemn warning of this verse is that the person living a life of unrestrained sexual greed is an idolator. Idolatory is all about priorities. It is when we invest other things with the devotion and commitment that rightly belong to the Lord that we are guilty of practising idolatory. When God says, "You shall have no other gods before Me" we must not just look on His commandment as a relentless negative. The other side to this commandment is wonderfully positive. "You shall not have other gods", true, but the implication is that "You shall have Me!"

The hedonist in sexual matters looks on the Christian view as so restraining. They think of it as "Look what they are missing" and never stop to think of "Look what they have gained". To put God at the centre of life and treat sexuality as His gift, bounded by His wholesome laws, is to gain immeasurably over unrestrained sexual lust as the centre of life.

Today's verse is not warning believers that they can lose their salvation nor is it saying that if a believer ever falls into sexual sin that there is no place for that believer in the Kingdom. There is a place of repentance for such and also restoration.

Western society is often soaked with the god of unrestrained sexual greed. The media titillates with it. A lot of literature is sold by it. Films on television and in the cinema frequently draw huge audiences with it. Even language, as we have seen, is often riddled with it. The great Roman Empire that straddled the world around Paul seemed invincible. It was anything but invincible.

One of the huge cracks that split its foundations was unrestrained sexual greed in its leaders and in the life of its society. The foundation of the Kingdom of God and of His Christ, though, will never split. Those who worship the god of unrestrained sexual greed are outlawed within its boundaries.

June *nineteenth*

> *"Let no-one deceive you with empty words, for because of these things the wrath of God comes upon the sons of disobedience"*
> (Ephesians 5: 6)

If the wrath of God did not come upon those who deliberately and habitually disobey laws He sets around His gifts and who turn those gifts into gods, there would be something wrong. Would you expect Him to step back and care less about it all? It would be unworthy of God not to be angry. If He wasn't he would cease to be God.

Would I be angry if a drunk pervert killed one of my family? Would I say, "Who cares? Let him do what he likes". Of course I would be angry. I would cry out for justice to be brought on his head. If I didn't what kind of person would I be?

Taking this thought a little further I want to ask another question. What does the blood of millions of innocent Jews cry out for from the ground of Europe?

Put into ghettos, deported East, and from 1941 onwards subjected to the "final solution", their deaths amounted to at least six million. What if there were no anger from God against the perpetrators of the whole ghastly atrocity? I tell you I would repudiate Christianity if the fact of the reality of the wrath of God were untrue: it isn't untrue. Wrath is what all those unrepentant perpetrators will receive in the Final Judgment.

Many empty words are spoken against the whole concept of the wrath of God. The fact is that the very subject of the wrath of God has become taboo in much of society. Paul is telling us that we are not to let empty words deceive us. In truth no human being is entirely without awareness of judgment to come: it is imprinted on our conscience whether or not we are believers. Let us not play the subject down. God's wrath is not irrational or unjust. It is an attribute of God without which God would not be God: we should be very glad of it. It is not unworthy of Him.

June *twentieth*

"Therefore do not be partakers with them"
(Ephesians 5:7)

"Therefore": here is a prohibition. Christians are not to be "partakers" with the immoral. Does this mean a complete distancing from them in every single aspect of life? Are we to shun them on the street? Are we never to speak a kindly word to them? Must we never help them when they are bereaved? Are we not to feed them when they are hungry? Can we not give them a drink when they are thirsty? Must we refuse to help their children? Must they never enter our homes or we theirs?

If we were to follow such a line of action we would need to go out of this world altogether (See John 17: 15; 1 Corinthians 5: 9-10). If our Saviour on earth had followed such a line of conduct we would never have had Christ's encounters with Zacchaeus and the woman at the well or the adulteress in the Temple, would we? What if Christ had shunned the woman who approached him at the house of Simon the Pharisee? Make no mistake as to who she was. "Behold", writes Luke, "a woman in the city who was a sinner, when she knew that Jesus sat at the table in the Pharisee's home, brought an alabaster flask of fragrant oil and stood at His feet behind them weeping: and she began to wash his feet with her tears, and wipe them with the hair of her head: and she kissed his feet and anointed them with the fragrant oil".

Did the Saviour turn away from her? If He had Simon the Pharisee would have recognised Him as a person who, in his view, was on the moral high ground. The Saviour, though, reached out and forgave her sins and sent her on her way in peace. Simon despised the sin and the sinner. Jesus despised the sin but loved and saved the sinner.

No. We are not to "partake" with the immoral, that is to participate in their sin. We must not become partners in their immorality but we can certainly reach out to them with the good news, that they might repent and come to know the sinner's Saviour.

June *twenty-first*

"For you were once darknesss, but now you are light in the Lord. Walk as children of light. (For the fruit of the Spirit is in all goodness, righteousness and truth)"
(Ephesians 5:8-9)

Me? Light in the Lord? Really? The striking thing about what Paul was saying here is that a Christian was once darkness, not just in darkness. He is saying that a Christian is now light, not just in the light. Since my identity is being "in Christ" I am now identified with the light He is. The darkness Paul is speaking of concerns ignorance of the truth and error in sin and evil. Conversion has brought me to being light in the Lord.

Think about it, Christian, God has taken you from the dominion of darkness and now you have been brought into the Kingdom of His dear Son. What does it mean in practical terms? It has to do with ethics and behaviour. It is the pleasure of doing what is right. It is in being reliable, helpful, kind, and decent.

Paul describes what these Ephesians once were. He has commented that they were into craftiness and deception and lying (4:14, 25); now the Spirit would produce a harvest of goodness, righteousness and truth within their lives. I once came across a man who told me he reckoned that if you traced every single conversion that ever occurred you would find that some Christian had done a kind or good act that had crossed the path of those converted. It is a challenging premise. Jesus told us to let our light so shine that people would see our good works and glorify our Father in Heaven.

You might, of course, feel weakened at the thought of your being light in the moral darkness around you. Who am I in the face of such a task, you might ask? Think then of Gideon and his men on that famous night when they broke their pitchers and the light shone on the hill above a massive host of enemies in the valley below. Don't you think Gideon and his men felt weak? What the enemy saw, though, was the light, not their weak knees! The light was the thing. It was the light that routed them. Shine on, Christian, though you and your fellow Christians may be few in number. The light you are in Christ will have far reaching influence for good.

June *twenty-second*

A recent study concluded that all of us face between 300 and 17,000 decisions every day. There are, though, a lot of people who are so afraid of being wrong in their decisions that they never get anything significant done in their lives. Former President Reagan learned the need for decision-making early in his life. An aunt had taken him to a cobblers to have a pair of shoes made for him.

"Do you want a square toe or a round toe?", asked the cobbler. Reagan hummed and hawed. So the cobbler said, "Come back in a day or two and let me know what you want". A few days later the shoemaker saw Reagan on the street and asked what he had decided about the shoes. "I still haven't made up my mind", the boy answered. "Very well", said the cobbler. When Reagan received the shoes he was shocked to see that one shoe had a square toe and the other had a round toe! "Looking at those shoes every day taught me a lesson", said Reagan, years later. "If you don't make your own decisions somebody else will make them for you".

Today's text is a golden rule for decision-making. It has been translated "discovering what is pleasing to the Lord". The verb is calling us to test, to discern and approve what, in any given circumstances, is the right course of action. We are to ask, "What would please the Lord, here?". The Holy Spirit will guide us to the right decision. I have in my life, of late, cried to the Lord in my heart, even while having a conversation with someone, for guidance as to the right answer to give or phrase to use for my very next spoken sentence. From spoken word to moral or practical decisions, let what pleases the Lord dictate what we say and do. Let's not forget that the Scriptures give us a promise with such behaviour. The promise? When a man's ways please the Lord He makes even his enemies to be at peace with him.

June *twenty-third*

The Spirit of God, we have learned, produces a harvest of light. The Devil produces a harvest of darkness. Notice, though, that the harvest of darkness is described as being "unfruitful". In the Epistle of Jude we read of certain ungodly men who crept in amongst the Christians and who turned "the grace of God into licentiousness". They are described graphically as "clouds without water carried about by the winds; late autumn trees without fruit, twice dead, pulled up by the roots; raging waves of the sea, foaming up their own shame; wandering stars for whom is reserved the blackness of darkness for ever".

The Lord Jesus told the story of the sower who went out to sow and of his seed falling among thorns. "They", He said, "are the ones who hear the word, and the cares of this world, the deceitfulness of riches, and the desires for other things entering in, choke the word and it becomes unfruitful".

Imagine spending your life and pouring all its energy into that which has nothing to show for it all. Yes, "works" are produced but they are utterly futile and sterile. Such are the unfruitful works of darkness.

The "fruit of the Spirit" though, is anything but sterile. Recently I was privileged to write a children's book on the life of C. S. Lewis, the great Ulster writer. I was moved to find how difficult it was for him in the world of academia as a Christian. I learned how he was passed over for academic positions because of his constant preaching, teaching and writing of the Christian Gospel. I was caused to reflect on the fruit of his life's work for Christ. The number of people who have come to faith in Christ because of his witness is absolutely staggering. At the moment three dozen of his titles are still available with over 40 million in print making him the best-selling Christian author of all time. In the United States, for example, he is arguably the most quoted Christian author in the nation. The most fascinating lives continue to be deeply influenced by what he said. He being dead yet speaks: the fruit of light from his being light in Christ is still shining! And his critics? Well, did you ever see a statue raised to a critic in your life?

June *twenty-fourth*

"But rather expose them"
(Ephesians 5:11)

It may be that someone reads today's verse and wonders how they could ever expose the unfruitful works of darkness. The power of Satan seems too strong. The tides of evil seem overwhelming. All around are people who would rather gain the whole world and risk losing their own souls. You feel outnumbered and powerless.

Have you ever read the story of William Wilberforce (1759-1883)? Here was a Member of Parliament who felt that a person of faith could not possibly stay as a colleague amongst such an ungodly crowd of men. Persuaded otherwise by the converted slave-trader, Rev. John Newton, Wilberforce decided to take up the cause of slaves. For forty-five years he and his friends campaigned to abolish the evil slave trade and only three days before his death saw the Bill to Abolish Slavery safely through the House of Commons and the British Government promise to pay plantation owners twenty million pounds to free the slaves. One year later eight hundred thousand slaves in the West Indies were set free in one day!

This, though, was not all the evil that Wilberforce exposed. He campaigned against the evil of overworked children in the great spinning mills of Britain. He helped establish Sunday Schools and orphanages for poor children. He helped found "The Society for the Prevention of Cruely to Animals". He opposed the fearful practice of using chimney boys to sweep chimneys of great houses by which many boys were choked to death by soot. He worked with George III to try to reform behaviour in a nation swamped by drunkeness, immorality, bad language, gambling and profanity. The word in Georgian England for behaviour was "manners". Wilberforce said he had set out to reform "manners". He wrote a book published in five languages setting out the essential Christian doctrines by Scriptural text. It took its readers on a journey to discover how Chrisitanity should and could guide politics, habits, views and attitudes of everyone. John Newton called the book "The most valuable and important publication of the present age". At the height of his life Wilberforce was engaged in sixty-nine good causes!

If you visit the birth-place of Wilberforce in Hull you will read a very moving statement on his statute at the front of the house. It reads "The world owes him the abolition of slavery and England owes him the reformation of manners". His life proves that God can use a life dedicated to Him to expose the works of darkness and bring great reformation. How about your life? Go for it!

June *twenty-fifth*

> *"For it is shameful even to speak of those things which are done by them in secret"*
> (Ephesians 5:12-13)

It is very easy, when eager to expose sinful practices, to get into graphic detail as to what those sinful practices are. We would not want to fortify, by our speech, any inner inclination towards such deeds. In the context of the Ephesian letter the sinful practices referred to are sexual. Better not to speak of what are truly unspeakable deeds. Let's cut out salacious language in our conversation. This will not be easy for such language seeps through a huge section of society.

I know of no greater example in all Scripture the principle in today's text is expounding than that of Nathan, the prophet. David had fallen into gross sin. He had committed adultery with Bathsheba, Uriah the Hittite's wife. She conceived and sent David a message: "I am with child". Then, to cover up his sin, David brought Uriah back from military duty and allowed him to go home, sending a gift of food after him. He was trying to get Uriah to sleep with Bathsheba and thus, he felt, his sin would be covered. But "Uriah slept at the door of the king's house", arguing that "The Ark and Israel and Judah are dwelling in tents and my lord Joab and the servants of my lord are encamped in the open field. Shall I then go to my lord and eat and drink and to lie with my wife?"

David then brought Uriah back to his palace and made him drunk but again Uriah refused to go home to his wife. David then wrote a private letter to Joab, his military commander, arranging for Uriah to be put in the most vulnerable position in the next battle "that he may be struck down and die". So Uriah died and David married Bathsheba.

When, two years later, God sent Nathan to expose David's unspeakably sinful behaviour it is fascinating how he did it without mentioning the word adultery. He did it by telling the story of a rich man and a poor man. The rich man had many flocks and herds and the poor man had nothing but one little ewe lamb. When a traveller came to the rich man, he refused to take from his own flock to give a meal to the travellers but took the poor man's lamb. David erupted and demanded the rich man's death and four-fold restitution to the poor man for the lamb taken. Then powerfully and quietly Nathan looked at David and said, "You are the man!"

The pointed and powerful exposure of David by Nathan was done so by the greatest skill and wisdom but nowhere is salacious language used. Let's keep Nathan in mind next time we are called upon to expose sin.

June *twenty-sixth*

"All things that are exposed are made manifest by the light"
(Ephesians 5:13)

The weight of this very helpful passage of Scripture on exposing sin seems to be that the exposing is more through a Christ-like life than through condemnatory words. Notice carefully that our text tells us that everything exposed is exposed "by the light".

Just watch the sunlight stream into a room and even dust particles you never thought were there are exposed.

Our Lord Jesus is "The Light of the World" and was His power to expose sin never more incredibly exercised than on the infamous day they brought the woman taken in adultery before Him? Knowing very well the wicked hearts of those who brought the woman the Light of the World shone on them to expose them. "He who is without sin among you let him throw a stone at her first", he said. "Then those who heard it, being convicted by their conscience went out one by one, beginning with the oldest even to the last". Notice that the Lord Jesus did not list their sins. He did not say "I know that you stole that money when you were twelve" or "I know that you lied to your mother when you were twenty" or "I know that you blasphemed last Wednesday". It was pure light shining into darkness and there sin lay in all its wickedness. No condemnatory word was used in this instance.

I am not arguing that condemnatory words are not ever to be used in exposing sin. Jesus frequently condemned hypocrisy with scathing language and called money changers in the temple "thieves". All I am arguing is that here in Ephesians Paul is arguing that it is when the powerful light of holiness comes in contact with that which is unholy it doesn't need words to do its work of exposing sin. In and of itself it exposes it. The power of a holy life in an office, village, city, nation, street, in any community anywhere is lethal on sin. Live one!

June *twenty-seventh*

> *"For whatever makes manifest is light"*
> (Ephesians 5:13)

It is wonderful that the exposure of sin by light is not an end in itself. The very light that exposes us is the very light that saves us! "For", writes Paul in 2 Corinthians 4: 6, "it is the God who commanded light to shine out of darkness who has shone in our hearts to give the light of the knowledge of the glory of God in the face of Jesus Christ". The exposing of our sin leads to a revelation of the good news of the Gospel and this leads to transformation on believing it.

Now that we are enlightened we take on the quality of light. "You are light in the Lord", Paul has already told us. "Walk as children of light". And the result? Others who walk in the dark will, through your witness, become light in the Lord, too.

Am I writing today for someone who needs to be encouraged to shine on? You think your witness is insignificant, you think it will never bring any significant penetration or transformation of sinners. I love to tell the story of an immoral, drunken young university student in Germany. No-one could tame him. One evening he happened upon a few Christians who were studying the Scriptures in a drawing room. He influenced them deeply and their influence led to his conversion to Christ. He went to England and one morning shared his breakfast with a few orphan children who were hungry. Soon the few became many and he extended his kindness to giving them not just breakfast but all their meals, every day. A house purchased to accommodate the children soon became two houses, then six, then eight. It all ultimately became an institution housing two thousand children, known as the George Muller Home for Orphans. Millions of pounds came Muller's way, sent by God in answer to his faith.

A record of God's dealings with Muller was published and a copy came into the hands of a Christian in Ireland, a County Antrim man. He was so deeply influenced by Muller's faith that he began to ask "If God could do this for Muller, could he not do it for us?" He began with a few of his friends to pray for revival in Ireland and in 1859 it came: upwards of a hundred thousand souls were converted to Christ in one year. Two of them were my great grandparents. Their influence passed down through our family and I am writing to you today because a few Christians in Germany met and studied the Word and George Muller became a Christian! Get my drift? Shine on!

June *twenty-eighth*

> *"Therefore He says, 'Awake, you who sleep, arise from the dead and Christ will give you light"*
> (Ephesians 5:14)

This, I am told, is a tristich, a primitive baptismal hymn. The congregation would greet the new convert coming out of the waters of baptism with the words of today's text. Their baptism had signified a movement from the sleep of spiritual death into the light of life in response to believing the Gospel. These words mirror all that had happened spiritually to the convert.

The words, taken from Isaiah, also mirror the whole argument Paul has been making about light and darkness. It speaks of the power of Christ's light to shine into spiritual darkness to convict, illuminate and transform. It really is very hard to grasp that we who once knew spiritual darkness are now light in the Lord. When those twelve disciples set out to serve Christ they seemed so weak in comparison to the Aristotles and Platos, the Emperors and Senators, all the people of power in those ancient days. How could a humble tax collector like Matthew or a humble fisherman like Peter blaze spiritual light across an Empire? They did. They turned it upside down.

On down the centuries that light has burned, now low, now more intensely but it has never gone out. You, Christian, are now that light in the Lord in your generation. It's your turn now. If you are even tempted to forget it, remember your baptism and what is declared and what it implied. The early Christians had the wonderful words of today's text ringing in their hearts after their baptism. The clear message was that a Christian is to be light wherever they go. Wouldn't you rather spend your life being a light rather than cursing the darkness? Christ will give you that light in abundant measure. Please, remember what Jesus said: "You are the light of the world. A city on a hill cannot be hidden. Neither do people light a lamp and put it under a bowl. Instead they put it on a stand and it gives light to everyone in the house. In the same way, let your light shine before men, that they may see your good deeds and praise your Father in Heaven". Be an agent of light. What better occupation?

June *twenty-ninth*

> *"See that you walk circumspectly, not as fools, but as wise, redeeming the time"*
> (Ephesians 5:15-16)

Recently, on the Isle of Man, I was taken by some of my friends to visit one of the world's greatest watchmakers. I am informed he only makes one watch a year and each one is worth a hundred thousand pounds. His name is George Daniels.

I asked Mr. Daniels about his work and he told me it has interested him since he was five! Chronology is his passion and his watches are something else. "What is the most important thing you have learned from your studies of time?", I asked.

He replied that human beings measure time because they will die one day. "God knows nothing about time", he said, "He lives in an eternal now". The Gospel, of course, shows that God, who does live in an eternal now, actually stepped into time in the person of Jesus Christ. He in fact knows a lot about it. Mr. Daniels, though, is right about human beings. We measure time because we know it is limited. I have stood by the old clock in Chester Cathedral and read those famous words:

"When as a child I laughed and wept,
Time crept,
When as a youth I grew more bold,
Time strolled,
When I became a full grown man,
Time ran,
Soon I shall find as I journey on,
Time gone".

The thrust of Paul's teaching on time is that we treat it as something to be eagerly bought. The Greek verb which he uses means "an intensive buying" and was used as commerical language in Greek. We are to buy up the time, making the most of every passing opportunity.

June *thirtieth*

"Because the days are evil" (Ephesians 5:16)

The motivation for redeeming the time is that the days are evil. Some think that this is emphasising that we are in the last of the last days. While this is undoubtedly true the wider application of today's text is that Christians have always lived in the midst of spiritual darkness and are called upon to live out their lives for the Lord in a climate which is predominantly evil. The greater the darkness the brighter the light shines! The fact is that because the days are evil that is all the more reason for buying up opportunities to be good.

Is there filthy talk around you? Obscene language is destructive so use your tongue to speak kind and encouraging words. Are people greedy in your community? Then you be selfless. Are parents latch-key parents? Then be there for your children. Are individuals violent around you? Then you be gentle. Are your colleagues dependent on drugs for their alleviation of stress? Then you and I must show by our lives that God has put a beautiful world around us to enjoy.

I return again to the life of Joseph to show you that no matter how evil your environment you can be good. His father was a deceiver. His uncle Esau was weak and chose the immediate and sold his future for a paltry thing. His father was duped into marrying the wrong woman. His beautiful mother Rebecca was a selfish and manipulative person. The events surrounding Joseph's twelve brothers are about as shameful and as sordid as those surrounding his father and mother. They were anything but a good example to their younger brother Joseph.

Incredibly with such parents and brothers, amidst a family dominated by lying, deceit, immorality and manipulation, there emerges one of the most beautiful lives every lived. Here was ability without instability. Here was attractiveness without vanity. Here was cheerfulness without foolishness. Here was gift without lording. Here was courage without rough handling. Here was godliness that was as real to the man as breathing. Here was someone who did not wait for some great occasion but who made every occasion great. And he did it all in evil days! Selah.

JULY

To live together in harmony is described by the psalmist as being like the dew on Mount Hermon. Dew stood for unity in the Jewish poet's mind. No wonder, then, that Gideon sought to see if he could control the dew through his prayers. That wet and dry fleece said a lot to the needy leader of God's army. Why? Because at that time the Israelites had been so scared of the enemy that they had prepared shelters for themselves in mountain clefts, caves and strongholds. They were on high ground all right but for the wrong reasons! They were leaderless and afraid and very divided.

Sometimes marriages and parent-children relationships can be like a battlefield. To have unity in a marriage and a home is one of the most wonderful experiences on earth. Paul addresses this question in the section of Ephesians we will look at in detail this month. In order to have this unity he explains how we can be controlled by the mighty Spirit of God.

Paul also addresses the complex question of masters and their slaves who numbered 60 million in the days of the Roman Empire. The relevance of his teaching is very pertinent to employer-employee relationships in our day.

July *first*

> *"Do not be drunk with wine"*
> (Ephesians 5:18)

Drunkenness is marked down by Paul as a characteristic of darkness. When you have a moment read 1 Thessalonians 5: 5-8 and Romans 13: 12-14. (Other helpful references include Matthew 24: 19; Luke 12: 45; 1 Corinthians 5: 11; 6:10; 1 Timothy 3: 8; Titus 2: 3 and 1 Peter 4: 3). The Scriptures are very clear that drunkenness is a destructive and unacceptable lifestyle. To get drunk is, in the sight of God, the very height of folly. The way of the fool and the way of the wise is being contrasted by Paul and drunkenness is unquestionably the way of the fool.

There has been much argument about whether or not a Christian should drink alcohol but there is one salient point which is often forgotten in the discussion: the effect of alcohol in the body is always depressive and inhibitory, i.e. negative. Paradoxically the effect of small doses appears to bring relaxation, to reduce a sense of stress, to give feelings of pleasure or wellbeing, but alcohol does that by actually depressing the normal inhibitory systems in the higher centres of the brain.

For example, pre-prandial "drinks" at a lunch or party are supposed to lower people's inhibitions and allow them to mix more freely, to give them a feeling of excitement or pleasure and to reduce the normal stresses of meeting strangers. The plain fact is that these drinks do this by "cheating" and exerting a depressant action on protective natural inhibitions rather than giving an added exciting action. In any event this effect is short lived and often it takes more and more to produce the same effect, as many tens of thousands of people can testify regarding the dangers, for example, of "night-cap" drinking. Even in small doses alcohol produces a loss of efficiency, reduces one's critical abilities, slows one's reflexes and allows one's more basic instincts to emerge.

In one year in the United Kingdom, for example, eight to fourteen million working days are lost through alcohol abuse and eight hundred million pounds are lost to industry. Seventy per cent of problem drinkers are at work. In around eighty per cent of all serious road accidents alcohol is implicated because it causes dis-inhibition, impairs judgment, and the process of thinking and leads to impulsiveness. The sad fact is that in ninety per cent of suicide attempts, alcohol is involved. It causes depression to worsen, it leads to impaired thinking processes and produces impetuous actions. Public drunkenness takes up eighty thousand hours of police time and the cost to the criminal justice system is between six to seven million pounds.

However the tee-totalling Christian may be regarded, it must be acknowledged they have wisdom on their side.

July *second*

"In which is
dissipation"
(Ephesians 5:18)

Dissipation? What does it mean? It is obviously a very important word because it is the condition into which a person is led if that person gets drunk. It is the very same word as is used by the Prodigal Son when we are told that he spent his time in riotous living, i.e. wasteful, wild, unrestrained, unbound, dissolute living. It is the opposite of saving and conserving. It is to squander and throw away and to lose control.

Watch a person who is drunk and you will see that all discipline is gone. They squander their time and their energy and sadly they often also throw away their charity and purity and morality. In today's text we are told that drunkenness will lead to sexual excess and debauchery. It is a chilling warning.

I have often wondered how Laban tricked Jacob into "marrying" Leah. The Scriptures tell us that "Laban gathered together all the men of the place and made a feast. Now it came to pass in the evening he took Leah, his daughter, and brought her to Jacob; and he went in to her. And so it came to pass in the morning that behold it was Leah. And he said to Laban, 'What is this you have done to me? Was it not for Rachel that I served you? Why then have you deceived me?'" How could Jacob not have known the difference between Leah and Rachel? It could well have been that he was drunk on that infamous night.

Although Scripture is silent on the reason for Jacob's behaviour it is not silent on what happened to Noah. "And Noah ... planted a vineyard. Then he drank of the wine and was drunk, and became uncovered in his tent." We are told how his sons Shem and Japheth covered him with a garment and "their faces were turned away". On that occasion the great and godly Noah had become a naked fool through drink. The righteous Lot was duped into incest by wine and was so drunk the Scripture comments that "he did not know when she lay down or when she arose" (Genesis 20; 31-38). Why are such things told in such graphic detail in Scripture? Because they are written for our learning.

July *third*

"But be filled with the Spirit"
(Ephesians 5:18)

If alcohol is a depressant then the Holy Spirit is a stimulant! To be controlled by alcohol leads to depression, dissipation and disaster. To be controlled by the Holy Spirit leads to exhilaration and happiness. Show me a person controlled by the Holy Spirit and I will show you a person stimulated to all kinds of positive things underlined with the sheer joy of the Lord in their lives, which is their strength.

Does that mean that the Spirit-filled believer won't have sorrow? Of course not. Peter, though, puts it this way: "In this you greatly rejoice, though now for a little while, you have been grieved by various trials". He says we can "rejoice with joy unspeakable and full of glory" (1 Peter 1: 6-8). Mark carefully the beautiful words of Psalm 4: "There are many who say, 'Who will show us any good?' Lord, lift the light of your countenance upon us. You have put gladness in my heart, more than in the season that their grain and wine increased. I will both lie down in peace, and sleep; for you alone, O Lord, makes me dwell in safety". Beautiful, isn't it?

See the harvesters with their harvest gathered in! The barns are full. It is party time! The hard work is over and winter is a little way off. The wine begins to flow, the effect is immediate conviviality and merriment. Laughter is everywhere. The evening, though, wears on. The music fades and the party-goers move homeward. And the next morning? Hangovers are the order of the day. Party-goers are now bad tempered and out of sorts and curse the fact that they have to go back to work.

See, though, a group of Spirit-filled Christians meet. See them share their faith, see them speak to one another of Christ and of the Scriptures, of salvation, of God's promises. And the next day? The Christ they worship is even more wonderful to them than He was the day before. The things they discussed are even sweeter to their taste as time moves on; better, deeper, grander, higher! That's what being filled with the Spirit does for them.

Note, though, the exhortation is to "be filled with the Spirit". This is a command. It isn't a suggestion. It is a state, a condition. It is possible to be filled with other things and such Christians coming together would be "not for the better but for the worse" (See 1 Corinthians 11: 17). There is no greater need in these days than the need to let the Holy Spirit control our lives. The results will be astonishing.

July *fourth*

> *"Speaking to one
> another in psalms
> and hymns and
> spiritual songs"*
> (Ephesians 5:18)

Fascinating, isn't it, that the focus in today's text is not on the praise of God? The verse clearly states, first, that we are to speak "to one another" in psalms, hymns and spiritual songs. There are two audiences. This obviously isn't a ban on Spirit-filled Christians speaking to each other and an order for them to sing to one another instead! This is all about Christian fellowship in the context of public worship.

Professor Bruce states, "The meetings of those early Christians must have been musical occasions, as they not only sang and made melody to the Lord, in their hearts as well as with their tongues, but addressed one another for mutual help and blessing in compositions already known to the community or in songs improvised under immediate inspiration" (Bruce, pp. 380-381). It is also worth looking at Colossians 3: 16.

The distinction between the words used in the text is not easy to define. Psalms probably refers mainly to the Old Testament Psalter. Hymns mainly refer to songs of praise to God and Christ. We have already seen that Ephesians 5: 14 is such a hymn. Spiritual songs could well refer to sacred themes other than direct praise to God and Christ. All these of course overlap.

In the New Testament the word "Psalms" certainly refers to Old Testament psalms (See Luke 20: 42; 24:44; Acts 1: 20; 13: 33). "Hymn" occurs only in today's text though the cognate verb and is found in Mark 14: 26; Mark 26: 30; Acts 16: 25; Hebrews 2: 12. The word "song" is employed for songs of heavenly worship in Revelation 5: 9; 14: 3; 15: 3. Christians build each other up, instruct each other and exhort each other through all three mediums.

July *fifth*

> *"Singing and
> making melody in
> your hearts to the
> Lord"*
> (Ephesians 5:19)

The emphasis in today's text is that the singing is directed to the Lord, the other audience in our singing. This singing is for His ears. Don't you think we often forget the Lord draws tremendous pleasure from the praises of His people? We enjoy it all but I wonder if we truly have any idea of what He gets from it.

Why does Paul say that we should make melody in our hearts to the Lord? What does "the heart" imply? The heart, in Scripture, refers to the controlling centre of one's being. Paul is asking us to sing with our whole being. Our emotions and our wills and our understanding is involved. We sing in the Spirit but we also sing with our understanding. Our singing, of course, must be intelligible to others (See 1 Corinthians 14: 15). Yet, above all, to sing from the heart implies absolute sincerity. It is not merely a "will-you-please-join-in" mode of singing. It is Spirit-filled singing, welling up from a heart overflowing with worship and praise.

I sometimes think of the very serious situation facing the people of God. Their King "appointed singers to the Lord .... that should praise the beauty of holiness as they went out before the army". A miracle occurred and their enemies were defeated through the power of praise (See 2 Chronicles 20: 14-25). Who can tell the effect of Spirit-filled singing?

July *sixth*

> *"Giving thanks always for all things to God the Father in the Name of our Lord Jesus Christ"*
> (Ephesians 5:20)

There was a coffee shop in which I used to dine regularly called "The Red Fox" in the delightful village of Hillsborough, County Down. Its pleasant soups, its friendly staff cheered many a day, especially the days when my hours were filled with deep, intensive study.

One day a waitress went to a nearby table to take an order. Coming by my table she referred to the lady she had just served, raising her eyes to the heavens, "That woman! She just ordered a baked potato and she says I must give her a round one. What does she think I'll give her? A square one?"

Grumblers, what would you do with them?

"As a rule, man's a fool,
When it's hot, he wants it cool,
When it's cool, he wants it hot,
Always wanting what it's not"

Some people are born pessimists. They always see the dark side of things rather than the bright. An optimist may be wrong as often as a pessimist but he or she is far happier!

Surely the single most significant decision I can make on a day-to-day basis is my choice of attitude. Life is ten per cent what happens to me and ninety per cent how I respond to it. A glance through the story of Israel going through the wilderness is a story of grumbling. After the marvellous parting of the Red Sea and their incredible deliverance, the Israelites sang. To look at them that day you would have thought that they would never have grumbled again. They did, of course, again and again, raising the Lord's anger against them. At the heart of it all was downright ingratitude.

The text is not asking us, of course, to thank God for literally everything. That would be bizarre. It would, for example, be impossible to thank God for evil. The qualifying phrase is that we give thanks always for all things "to God the Father in the Name of the Lord Jesus Christ". It does mean, though, that we must always develop a thankful spirit; our troubles are vastly out-numbered by our blessings. We can always find something for which to be thankful.

July *seventh*

"Submitting to one another"
(Ephesians 5:21)

To be filled with the Spirit of God has certain inevitable consequences. One of them is the joy in public worship when Christians meet as they sing psalms, hymns and spiritual songs. Another is a spirit of thankfulness and gratitude to the Lord for all His goodness. A third is an attitude among Christians of submission to one another.

This is not an easy attitude to define but it is a beautiful attitude, nonetheless. Dr. Martyn Lloyd-Jones in his exposition on Ephesians ('Life in the Spirit' p. 68) sums it up very succinctly: "You who agree about the truth, do so in the right way: do not be opinionated: listen patiently to the other side: do not lose your temper: know how to be indulgent in argument: let the others speak, let them put forward their ideas: do not be censorious, do not condemn a man for a word: be prepared to listen: be charitable: go as far as you can: but when it comes to vital truth, stand, but always do so in the right way, in the Spirit. Do it with humility, do it with charity, do it with understanding, do it with hopefulness. Do not be offensive and bad-mannered".

The person who is controlled by alcohol is self-assertive. He boasts. He has a high view of himself. He is not a good listener, he constantly interrupts.

He also condemns all around him, there is no balance in his thinking, he takes extreme positions in argument. He does not think before he speaks. He doesn't look before he leaps. There is no consideration. Not so the Spirit-filled Christian. Spirit-filled Christians are part of the body of Christ and they think of the good of the body rather than just their own. So, just as parts of the human body submit to each other for the co-ordination of the whole body, so Christians should submit to each other for the good of the co-ordination of the whole body of Christ.

July *eighth*

*"In reverence to
Christ"*
(Ephesians 5:21)

Some translations put today's text as "submitting to one another in the fear of God". But, I understand, the better translation is, "In reverence to Christ". Here we have the motivation for submitting ourselves to one another. Here is the great controlling principle for Christians' behaviour toward one another.

I once met a former Governor of a certain island which had Queen Elizabeth II as its Sovereign. The Governor was an absolute "stickler" for time. If a person arrived late for an appointment he did not take kindly to their behaviour. They were told in no uncertain terms that to be late for his appointment was to be late for Her Majesty, as he was her representative. People tended to turn up on time thereafter.

It is because of who Christ is that we hold Him in awe and reverence. He is the Chief Corner Stone, the Sun of Righteousness, the Living Bread, the Hidden Treasure, the Sure Foundation, the Great Physician, the Rock of Ages, the Righteous Judge, the True Witness, the Pearl of Great Price, the Giver of Rest, the Lamb of God, the King of Kings, the Living God, the Saviour, the Redeemer and Lord. "In reverence to Christ" is the motive for Christian action not only in the relationships of believers to each other but, as we shall see in the next few days, other relationships too. No higher motivation can be found. Is it yours? It certainly marks all Spirit-filled believers.

July *ninth*

"Wives, submit to your own husbands, as to the Lord, for the husband is head of the wife, as also Christ is Head of the Church; and He is the Saviour of the body. Therefore, just as the Church is subject to Christ, so let the wives be to their own husbands in everything"
(Ephesians 5:22-24)

The emphasis in today's text has a particular force. Christian wives are to submit to their husbands "as to the Lord". Does a Christian woman find the headship of Christ in His church impressive and harsh? Does she find the church's Saviour a tyrant? Is the head of the body not the one from whom the body gains its health and growth into maturity? The Redeemer and Saviour of the body is its Head. Christ would not countenance divorcing His church, harming His church or abandoning His church. He cared for it, even to death on a cross.

Our text tells us clearly that "the husband is head of the wife as also Christ is Head of the church". If a husband behaved towards his wife as Christ behaved towards the church would any Christian wife have a problem with this text? Whatever else this text is teaching it is not teaching the mindless obedience of a Christian wife to her husband's every whim.

Submission is not a synonym for "subordination". It is a question of distinction between the sexes and of purpose. In creation man is the one who leads, who has headship, but in our text his headship in the Christian family is defined in terms of the Headship of Christ and His church. It is a deeply important definition. If a husband is not behaving towards his wife as Christ to the church she is not called upon to submit to un-Christlike demands. To be subject to their own husbands in everything certainly does not mean in everything without exception. If he demanded of her to do evil then it would be a sin to submit to him. If however, he does fulfil his role the result will be an enriching and an enhancing of her womanhood and femininity and she will have no problem submitting.

July *tenth*

"Husbands, love your wives, just as Christ also loved the Church and gave Himself for it"
(Ephesians 5:21)

It is my privilege from time to time to speak at the Great Keswick Convention in England's beautiful Lake District. At the time of writing I have just returned from teaching God's Word once more at Keswick and burning in my heart is a beautiful story told one evening by Agith Fernando, a very precious Christian leader from Sri Lanka.

He spoke about a fascinating evangelist of a bygone day called Gipsy Smith who served Christ through many decades and died on a ship on his way to America for yet another evangelistic tour. He was buried at sea. "Someone asked Gipsy Smith what kept him going for his many years of service", said Agith, "and his reply was, 'I have never lost the wonder'". It was quite obvious from looking into Agith's face that he hadn't lost "the wonder" either as he served God across the world. Turning to his large audience the Sri Lankan Christian said, "I am so glad that Jesus loves me, Jesus loves me, Jesus loves me. I am so glad that Jesus loves me. Jesus loves even me!"

Christ's love for us was not self-assertive, it was self-sacrificial. "Show yourself to the world", said His brothers, "no-one does anything in secret while he himself seeks to be known openly". Jesus, though, did not move to their agenda. His love for His bride, the Church, was such that He moved inexorably in absolute self-sacrifice to the cross and gave Himself for His church. Nothing, no nothing, side-tracked Him.

Husbands are called on to love their wives just like that. The wonder of Christ's self-sacrifice should find its counterpart in the daily self-sacrificial love of Christian husbands for their wives. Exhortations to husbands to love their wives outside of the New Testament are few and far between. In the New Testament they could not be more important. So, husbands, go love your wife today not with self-assertion, but with self-sacrifice.

July *eleventh*

> *"Just as Christ also loved the Church and gave Himself for it, that He might sanctify and cleanse it with the washing of water by the Word"*
> (Ephesians 5:25-26)

The goal of Christ's love for His church is now explained. The first goal is that His church might be sanctified. When the Lord Jesus died on Calvary He opened the way back to God for all who trust in Him as Saviour. Such people become a sanctified people, that is a people who are set apart for Him and called to lead holy lives. Christ's death brings forgiveness of sins and peace with God and makes it possible for His people to be holy. Notice how Paul constantly refers to this aspect in the Christian's life by referring to their identify in this letter as the "called-out" ones, the ones who are "set apart" (See Ephesians 1: 4; 4:15, 18: 2: 19; 3: 18; 4:12; 5:3).

How is this sanctification effected? It takes place by cleansing, "by washing of the water by the Word". Notice it is Christ who does the cleansing and, it would appear, this is a reference to Christ as the baptiser (See also 1 Corinthians 6: 11 and Titus 3:5). When Ananias called on Paul to "rise and be baptised and wash away your sins, calling on His name", he was certainly not saying that Paul would have his sins washed away by being baptised in water. If such were true why did the Lord Jesus have to die for our sins? Paul was implying that the outward washing expressed what had happened inwardly. The convert was, of course, baptised "calling on His name". This, as Professor Bruce points out, "Throws light on the phrase 'With the Word' or 'With a word' as in our present text: the "word" or "utterance" is the convert's confession of the Name of Christ as baptism is administered" (Bruce, pp. 388-9).

Millions of women gladly wear an engagement ring to signify publicly a decision they have already taken in their heart. So Christian baptism is a public declaration of an inward decision of the heart. It is the public "answer" or "pledge" of the conscience already cleansed by Christ. (See 1 Peter 3: 21). Have you given that public answer, yet? Baptism is a beautiful symbol and from experience I have found it speaks an incredibly powerful message to those without Christ who witness it.

July *twelfth*

> *"That He might present it to Himself a glorious church"*
> (Ephesians 5:27)

When Napoleon Boneparte was crowned Emperor of the French be brought the Pope from Rome to crown him. It was a glittering ceremony held in the Cathedral of Notre Dame in Paris on December 2nd, 1804. Napoleon was at the very peak of his ambitions. When it came to the moment of crowning, though, he could not resist taking the crown and crowning himself! He then crowned his wife Josephine as Empress. I have always felt a deep aversion to his stupendous pride. He was not worthy of such an action, was he? There is something monstrously arrogant about what he did.

When I come to today's text, though, I have no aversion. In the year of writing, I shall come, D.V. to that fascinating moment in life when I shall present my eldest daughter to her bridegroom at a public wedding ceremony. I shall, of course, do it with deep affection and it will be an honour. Here, though, in our text, the bride is the universal church of Jesus Christ; Christ is the Bridegroom and He does not need anyone else to present His bride. He Himself presents His bride to Himself. It would appear that this will occur at His second coming when He will present His church, all glorious, to Himself.

Why does our Heavenly Bridegroom present His bride to Himself? Because nobody is adequate to do it. He died for her in the first place. He has sought her down through the past two millennia in every corner of earth, day by day adding to her number. From every climate, in every culture, all speaking different tongues and coming from all walks of life, He has called His church. He saved and sanctified her. He is to her wisdom and redemption, He clothed her with His righteousness. All of her salvation is all of Him. He alone is adequate to present her to Himself. What a moment!

(For an interesting study in the context of Christ and His bride see Ezekiel 16: 1-14)

July *thirteenth*

> *"Not having spot"*
> (Ephesians 5:27)

Does the church have spots? Plenty of them. Just ask the unconverted in your district and they will not be long in telling you about them! There is not a Christian on earth either, with any experience of the church, who would not tell you that the church has plenty of spots. When, however, the great day comes we shall "all be changed" (See 1 Corinthians 15: 51). Corruption will put on incorruption and the mortal shall put on immortality. The church will be presented absolutely spotless. Nothing will mar her beauty.

In July 1999 off the Massachusetts coast the tragic death occurred of John F. Kennedy Junior and his sister-in-law Lauren Bessette and his wife Carolyn Bessette. Voted by her High School "the ultimate beautiful person" Carolyn worked for the designer Calvin Klein when John started to court her. They were married on Cumberland Island off the Georgia coast in a tiny wood-framed chapel, lit only by candles and kerosene lamps. It was all hauntingly romantic. Quick-witted, stylish and intrinsically self-possessed, Carolyn understood "the mystical femininity", a friend said. America wept at her death and that of her husband and sister. And no wonder.

Yet, I am sure even Carolyn Kennedy would have been the first to say she was not perfect. Nobody has ever yet been born who was. Talk to people and you will find that they wish they had different colour of eyes or shape of nose or whatever. But this Bride, the Bride of Christ will be seen in that day, flawless, complete, entire, wanting nothing. Spotless. Picture the most beautiful bride, ever. That is what the church is going to be like. He who began a good work in His church will complete it to perfection. Nothing, anywhere will stop that mighty work.

July *fourteenth*

"So husbands ought to love their wives, as their own bodies"
(Ephesians 5:28)

Let us lay the emphasis of today's verse on the word "ought". It is quite obvious that all husbands do not love their wives as their own bodies. Look at many of them: they take exercise to keep their bodies fit, they buy designer clothes to make their bodies attractive, they holiday to give their bodies refreshment, and they choose healthy food to give their bodies nourishment. They also have checkups with the dentist, the doctor, the optometrist, and the osteopath and lots and lots of others to see that all is well with their teeth, their blood pressure, their eyes, their mobility, and so on.

When it comes to their minds they store them with information as they "surf the net", drawing down endless fascinating material. They read books on all kinds of subjects. They watch documentaries on featured material that interest their minds. If their bodies hurts everybody knows it! If they need something vital for their bodies' good they go to endless trouble to ensure that they get it. Anything that harms their bodies is abhorred and anything that helps it is embraced. The money spent on housing, clothing, entertaining, occupying, feeding and enhancing our bodies is astronomical.

In the same way husbands ought to love their wives, "as their own bodies". See how a man grabs his finger when it hurts! See how he warms himself when his body is cold! See how he gets on the suntan oil if his body is being over-exposed to the sun. His body? There is nothing dearer to him, nothing more precious. Draw near to harm it and you will know his wrath. Give him money to aid it and he will spend it. It is a wonderful metaphor that Paul uses for how a man ought to behave towards his wife.

I knew a man, once, who was, because of absolute dedication to his profession, rather absent-minded. When he got married his sister-in-law said that he would be good to her sister, "if he remembered"!! May your wife never have to say of you that "he 'ought' to have loved me 'as his own body'." May she report that "he did!"

July *fifteenth*

> *"He who loves his wife loves himself"*
> (Ephesians 5:28)

"Love your neighbour as yourself", says the Scriptures. "Do to others as you would have them do to you", it exhorts. "He who loves his wife loves himself", says today's text. It this narcissism? Is this setting myself as the standard? What does it mean? Surely it is all about the importance of self-worth. Yes, I am a sinner. Yes, I have broken God's law. Yes, I am helpless to save myself and deserve God's wrath. Yes, salvation is all of grace. But, despite my sin I was created in the image of God and am of eternal value. I am the object of God's love and God sent the Lord Jesus to die for me. I am of such worth to God that divine life became human life in order that I might have everlasting life.

I am not called upon to curse the day of my birth and apologise to everyone for breathing. God's thoughts about me are more than the sand on the seashore and to move through life feeling I have no worth would be a sin. "He loves himself", people say in derision of someone who is proud. I am not writing about pride, I am writing about self-worth. Pride is detestable but a proper understanding of self-worth brings balance and blessing into my life.

If, then, I love my wife, Paul says, I love myself. It means I have a healthy, balanced attitude to self-worth. To neglect, deride, abandon, abuse, ridicule and despise my wife is to do the same to myself, for we are both one. "He has no respect for himself", we say of some poor wretch making a fool of himself somewhere. That is the very point today's text is making. Love your wife and you will do yourself untold good.

July *sixteenth*

> *"For no-one ever hated his own flesh but norishes and cherishes it"*
> (Ephesians 5:29)

Have you noticed the incredible explosion of interest in food in western culture? Cooks of all kinds are turning up on television to cook the most tempting dishes with fresh, organically grown produce. They are growing their own vegetables from broad beans to artichokes, from parsnips to new potatoes, from spinach to lettuce. Restaurants are bringing food to tables of high quality and less bulk. Healthier eating is a very rewarding trend and not before time. People are demanding it. Good food nourishes in all kinds of ways.

Paul draws a very powerful lesson for husbands from the way good food nourishes our bodies. As a person carefully chooses how to nourish their body by giving it the proper food, so a husband should be thinking about what will strengthen, nourish and help his wife. He should know her needs and respond to them. He should make sure she has a safe and spiritual church base which feeds her soul and lifts her spirit. He should delight her with that which gives her encouragement, refreshment, inspiration, and pleasure.

Don't we do that with food? Paul Rankin, Northern Ireland's most famous chef, TV cook and restaurateur once told me how food was very closely related to art. How food looks as it is presented on a plate is as important as what it contains. Paul has shown huge flair in this area and has had a deep effect upon cooking in our Province and further afield. Come on, then, husbands, nourish and cherish that wife of yours. And do it with flair.

July *seventeenth*

> *"Just as the Lord does His Church"*
> (Ephesians 5:29)

Does the Lord nourish His church? Always. He loved her when she was unlovable. He found her in deep need and bled and died for her. He saved her, sanctified her, cleansed her, and filled her with the Spirit. That mighty Comforter comes alongside and empowers His church against innumerable foes. He gave apostles, prophets, evangelists, pastors and teachers for her edification and growth. And He gave us His Word, the sacred Scriptures to nourish us.

How does it do that? When you have time read Psalm 119 and check out how the Word of God nourishes your life and changes it. Notice the way the psalmist puts it. He points out twenty-two reasons why it is worthwhile to invest in nourishing your soul in the Word of God. Let me give them to you. Spending time in the Word of God establishes my way (v. 5), purifies my life (v. 9, 10, 11), gives me counsel (v. 24), removes everything false in me (v. 29), produces reverence for God (v. 38), increases my courage (v. 46), comforts me in affliction (v. 50), guards me from panic (v. 61-62), teaches me discernment and knowledge (v. 66), makes me resourceful (v. 79-80), cultivates patience (v. 87), keeps me spiritually recharged (v. 93), accelerates my understanding (v. 98-100), creates a joyful heart (v. 111), sustains me when I feel helpless (v. 116), enables me to honour right and hate wrong (v. 128), causes me to walk in the truth (v. 133), surrounds me with delight in spite of difficulty (v. 143), develops the discipline of prayer (v. 147), rescues me when I am defenceless (v. 153-154), fills me with praise without and peace within (v. 164-165), and draws me back when I stray (v. 176).

July *eighteenth*

> *"For we are members of His body, of His flesh and of His bones"*
> (Ephesians 5:30)

Just as Eve was formed out of Adam by God's mighty power, so the church has been formed out of Christ. Adam is called the First Man, so Christ is called in the New Testament the "Second Man". Eve was formed as Adam slept. The church was formed on the basis of the Saviour's death. We are members of His body, of His flesh and of His bones.

When Adam saw Eve he said, "This is now bone of my bone and flesh of my flesh: she shall be called Woman because she was taken out of Man". When you and I look at the church in every corner of the earth we say, "We are members of His body, of His flesh and of His bones". We owe Him our very life, and, for all eternity, we are part of Him.

My mother used to say to me that once you are Christ's "you are spoiled for the world". I didn't know as a young person the full truth of what she was speaking but I do now. Once you become a member of His body, of His flesh and of His bones, no matter what the world can offer, you are not truly part of it. Christians who grow cold at heart and slip back to former ways and try to taste its pleasures are "spoiled". They have tasted of Christ, have known Christ, have been nourished by Him and the world's songs, standards, maxims, joys, thrills, and glories are tainted. What the world feeds on is transient but the Church of Christ feeds on Him and at His right hand are pleasures for evermore.

Does some wandering eye, once lit by the radiant commands of the Lord (see Psalm 19: 8) read these words I am writing? Does some wandering heart, once enraptured by the Saviour, now try to look for satisfaction once more from the world and the flesh? I plead with you not to wander anymore. Repent and return to the Lord and He will abundantly pardon you. Christian, you are bone of His bone and flesh of His flesh; you are not rooted in the world and the flesh now. Don't go to it for nurture: it simply will not satisfy. Don't waste your time with it any more.

July *nineteenth*

"For this reason a man shall leave his father and mother and be joined to his wife"
(Ephesians 5:31)

Here is one of the most important ingredients of a good marriage. If a man brings strong emotional, financial and psychological links to his parents into his marriage he will have deep problems. The same applies to his wife. The blueprint of Genesis 2 quoted here by Paul is vital in all marriage relationships. The principles of "leaving and cleaving" are still as relevant today as ever.

In practical terms if a husband is constantly telephoning his father and mother to find out what they think he should do next, what kind of leadership is that to give to his wife? A wife needs her husband's leadership. He needs to seek responsibility and to take responsibility for his actions. Headship, in the context of Ephesians, is leadership and a leadership of love. It is not a general commanding his army, a computer analyst pushing the right buttons or a master in charge of a slave. It is a loving relationship that makes sound and timely decisions, that keeps channels of communication open and clear, that is based on knowing his wife's gifts, talents, strengths, weaknesses and needs. No man would dream of starting a new job without first having a knowledge of the requirements, would he? The categorical requirement of a man in his marriage is to leave his father and mother and be united to his wife. It doesn't mean he should neglect his parents or despise them. It does mean, though, that he is now united to his wife and is called to be the head of his family and to make responsible decisions without harping back to his parents and their views and opinions.

July *twentieth*

"Amd the two shall become one flesh"
(Ephesians 5:31)

This verse is speaking of the mysterious and indescribable depths of sexual union. Sexual pleasure is a gift of God. The pleasure is God's invention, not the devil's. We must not, as they did in the ancient world, make a god out of sex. A Christian is not a hedonist. Nor must we give into Sigmund Freud's maxim that man is a creature whose every action is controlled by the pursuit of pleasure and the avoidance of pain. When we devote ourselves to pursuing pleasure it ceases to be a pleasure.

Sexual pleasure was designed by God to be enjoyed within marriage. The purpose of sex is the ending of isolation and loneliness; reproduction is its secondary and not primary purpose. Sex outside of marriage, of course, is a very lonely thing. There is no promise attached to such behaviour. No commitment binds it. If such has been your behaviour, repent of it and you will find forgiveness. Yet, let us remember that you might promise a life-long commitment in your marriage vows but that merely makes the relationship possible. It does not guarantee it, does it? We must put that commitment into practice.

There is no union to compare with the union of two hearts, minds and bodies in a happy marriage. But remember, a happy marriage is like building a house. While it is new it looks terrific but as time passes, windows stick, paint peels, the roof leaks, taps drip, and those drains clog. Warm passionate fire can die down and the honeymoon is well and truly over. A while back a sign appeared in a jeweller's window. It read, "We rent wedding rings!" Follow the true architect's blueprint and the building of your marriage will be secure and strong and in a state of good repair.

July *twenty-first*

> *"This is a great mystery but I speak concerning Christ and the Church"*
> (Ephesians 5:32)

Paul now draws the symbolism of Christian marriage to an even deeper level. If the true union of a man and woman in marriage is a wonderful, indescribable mystery, what shall we say of the mystical union of Christ and His church? Let there be no argument about it. The analogy Paul is writing about is powerfully applicable to the church? How?

Let's go right back to Genesis Chapter 2. The clear teaching is that Adam was incomplete without Eve. For Adam no suitable helper was found. There was something missing in his life. It was not good that he should be alone, so God created Eve. Eve brought about the "fullness" of Adam, she made up what was missing.

The Lord Jesus is in no way deficient. He is complete and perfect. He has no strong points simply because He does not have any weak ones. The absolute fullness of the Godhead is in Him. "But", as Dr. Martyn Lloyd-Jones has stated ('Life in the Spirit' p. 193), "as the Mediator, Christ is not full without the Church. Now this is the mystery, the most glorious mystery of all. Jesus Christ as the Mediator will not be full and complete and entire until every soul has been gathered in for whom He died - 'The fullness of the Gentiles' and 'all Israel'. It is only then that He will be full, only then will the fullness be complete".

He could, of course, have chosen not to be our Mediator and to let us perish. He could have chosen to be alone without us but He loved His bride and will not be happy until she is with Him forever. It's a mystery but praise Him, it's true!

July *twenty-second*

> *"This is a great mystery"*
> (Ephesians 5:32)

There is an amazing result springing from this great union of Christ and His church. It is that we are raised above angels. These are amazing creatures who obey God's exact commands. Christ said He could have called thousands of them to do His bidding at the time of his crucifixion and there is no doubt that they would have done whatever He asked. They must have watched in utter amazement as He allowed human beings to beat Him beyond recognition and crucify Him in order to effect redemption. The Scriptures tell us that angels desire to look into such mystery.

Did they ever imagine that one day humans whose sins led to the slaying of the Lord of Glory would one day be raised to a position where they would judge them?

In 1 Corinthians 6 we read that Paul is urging Christians not to take one another to court. He is asking them to sort out their problems between themselves. And his reason? "Do you not know", he writes, "That we shall judge angels? How much more things that pertain to this life ..... is it so that there is not a wise man among you, not even one, who would be able to judge between his brethren?"

If I read this Scripture right then difficulties in my life are training for reigning! One day we shall reign with Christ and part of that reigning will be to judge angels. Working out which videos our children should watch or not watch under our roofs or making decisions about fair and just treatment of employees or making moral judgments about abortion, etc. are all part of getting us ready for high office in the coming new earth.

Christian, you have been raised above angels in the union to which you now belong, the union of Christ and His church. Make good decisions today in the light of mightier decisions you will make in the future.

July *twenty-third*

"Nevertheless let each one of you in particular so love his own wife as himself and let the wife see that she respects her husband"
(Ephesians 5:33)

The symbolism of Christian marriage has taught us a lot about the relationship between Christ and His church. Now Paul moves from the great mystery of it all back to his main theme. The mystical union of Christ and His church is a theme which will occupy our minds for eternity. Marriage, though, needs to face the practicalities of everyday life. The way Christ loves His church obliges husbands to similarly love their wives every day of their lives. Paul repeats unquestionably that a husband must love his wife "as himself". He really drives this truth to the fore, doesn't he? Why, then, do we not hear more of such teaching in the modern day church? Let's restore the teaching to its proper place. It would solve a lot of problems. Note the emphasis to husbands in its final repetition: "Each one of you in particular". No husband is allowed to escape his responsibilities.

"And", adds Paul, "Let the wife see that she respects her husband". Respect? The word literally means "fear" and certainly does not mean terror, though sadly, many an abused wife has been terrified of her husband. Such a situation is disgraceful and will bring the judgment of God on such unrepentant men. "There is no fear in love", the Bible says. The word used for "fear" is used of citizens toward the state (Romans 13: 3, 4, 7), children towards parents, slaves towards masters (Ephesians 6: 5; 1 Peter 2: 18) and Christians towards Christ (Ephesians 5: 21).

If a state, parents and masters earn respect and co-operation, they deserve it. If a Christian husband earns it, Paul commands that he gets it.

July *twenty-fourth*

"Children, obey your parents in the Lord for this is right"
(Ephesians 6:1)

It is interesting that nowhere in Sciptue are wives commanded to obey their husbands. Submission, yes, but obedience, no. The submission is love's response to love, not a response to a whim or to a command. When Paul now turns to deal with the relationship of children with their parents they are called upon to obey. This applies to children of both Christian and non-Christian parents.

Paul argues that the obedience of children belongs to the natural law, it is part of the "nature of things". Down through the centuries people have recognised that children's obedience is fitting and proper within a family, it is righteous. We feel that when we see a child in rank disobedience to their parents there is something desperately wrong about it all. In Paul's day, the appeal of what is held to be naturally right or just was common. It was, for example, part of Stoic teaching and this kind of appeal can be found in the New Testament in Luke 12: 57; Philippians 4: 8 and Colossians 4: 1.

There is a major problem which arises in this command, though. How far are we to take this obedience? "Children obey your parents in all things for this is well pleasing to the Lord", says Colossians 3: 20. Does "in all things" mean that children must obey their parents in absolutely everything they ask them to do? If a child's parents, for example, were to prohibit the worship of God are they expected to comply? If parents were encouraging their children to sin, are they allowed to refuse?

The balance of this teaching is brought out very clearly in today's text. The command is for children to obey their parents "in the Lord". The Lord Jesus is the one to whom they must be primarily loyal. Anything that is incompatible with that priority is out. No child is asked in the Scriptures to obey their parents in everything without exception. Loyalty to the Lord Jesus is the exception. Allegiance to Him is bound to affect every other allegiance. Conflict does come and Jesus said His teaching would bring division between father and son and mother and daughter.

Outside of allegiance and loyalty to Christ parents are to be obeyed. Children should be always doing their very best to obey their parents. Why? For it is right. Huge problems in our society would be solved if they did.

July *twenty-fifth*

> *"'Honour your father and mother', which is the first commandment with promise: 'that it may be well with you and you may live long on the earth'"*
> (Ephesians 6:2-3)

Paul has been dealing with the motivation behind children's obedience. The first was their Christian commitment "in the Lord" and the second, which applies to both Christian and non-Christian children, namely, that it is the right thing to do. Now he underlines his teaching with the third motivation which is that it is the very first Scriptural commandment with a promise.

This poses an interesting problem for all who commentate on the Scriptures. Why? Because the second commandment, it is argued, carries a promise before the fifth commandment! The second commandment is against idolatory and says God will show "mercy to thousands of those who love Me and keep My commandments". Professor Bruce has commented very succinctly on this problem. He says that the last words of the second commandment "are a declaration of God's character rather than a promise" (Bruce, p. 121). Others argue that it is the first commandment in rank, not order, to carry a promise. The scribe, for example, asked Jesus, "Which is the first commandment of all?" (See Mark 12:28). I go for Professor Bruce's argument!

What relevance has this promise for us today? The call to honour our parents is clear enough though in the original form of the commandment the promise of long life was to be enjoyed "in the land which the Lord your God is giving you" (See Exodus 20:12; Deuteronomy 5:16). Paul, of course, is generalising the promise and saying it applies to obedient children everywhere. He is also perhaps particularly emphasising that a society where aged parents are respected and cared for by their children is a healthy and stable one.

The promise, then, is not confined today to one land or to one people. The question, though, is often asked, "Are obedient children guaranteed a long life?" The answer is that as a general rule this is true. Let's let Charles Hodge, Professor of Biblical Literature and Theology at Princeton for over 50 years, have a word on our text. He writes (Hodge, p. 203): "That some obedient children are unfortunate and live short lives is no more inconsistent with this promise than that some diligent people are poor is inconsistent with the declaration 'the Lord of the diligent makes rich'. Diligence, as a general rule, does secure riches; and obedient children, as a general rule, are prosperous and happy. The general promise if fulfilled to individuals just so far 'as it will serve for God's glory and their own good'."

July *twenty-sixth*

*"And you, fathers,
do not provoke your
children to wrath"*
(Ephesians 6:4)

I have seen it, haven't you? I have seen fathers goading their children to resentment, provoking them to anger. They are too severe in their discipline, they make unreasonable demands, they abuse their authority, they are patently unfair in their judgments, they are sarcastic and cutting in their remarks, they do not shrink from humilitating their children, they are insensitive to their needs. They are, in fact, arrogant bullies.

In Roman times we are told by one Dionysius of Halicarnassus that "the law-giver of the Romans gave virtually full power to the father over the son, where he thought proper to imprison him, to scourge him, to put him in chains, and keep him at work in the fields, or to put him to death: and this even though the son were already engaged in public affairs, though he were numbered among the highest magistrates and though he were celebrated for his zeal for the Commonwealth". We are informed that a father had authority to decide on the life and death of his newborn children: weak and deformed children could be killed, usually by drowning and unwanted daughters were often exposed or sold. All children were reckoned to be under a father's control. A father had legal control over all of his children living with him and also legal control over the children of his sons. A mother had no legal power. The father was also legally liable for the actions of members of his household. All this was peculiar to Roman citizens and was found in no other nation.

Paul has taught that the husband is the head of his household and that pre-supposes he is to have authority over his children but Paul sets a very clear boundary to that authority. Every child has its own personality and gifts. These are to be lovingly nurtured and nothing should be said or done to discourage or exasperate a child and cause it to become resentful.

Does God as our Heavenly Father, provoke us to wrath? Does He not discipline us in ways that are for our good but always in a spirit of love? So, fathers let's be like our Heavenly Father.

July *twenty-seventh*

"Servants, be obedient to those who are your masters according to the flesh, with fear and trembling in sincerity of heart, as to Christ"
(Ephesians 6:5-6)

There were 60 million slaves in the Roman Empire. The whole social and economic structure of Roman life depended on slavery. Nowhere does the New Testament condone the practice of one human being owning another and Paul knew very well that the Gospel he preached would be the seed that would split the rock. The Gospel was already undermining slavery by transforming the relationship between slave and slave owners who knew the Saviour (see the letter to Philemon).

The application of this teaching on the relationship between slaves and masters is powerfully relevant to all work relationships. The highest priority and responsibility on any Christian is to serve the Lord Jesus. In any work relationship we must remember we are willing slaves of Jesus Christ. He is to have absolute sway in every act of our lives. He is our motivation, we act out of love to Him; and let's not assume we do, let's make sure.

The slave is called to be obedient to his master. "With fear and trembling" does not imply literal quaking but refers to the deference of the slave to his master in the work relationship (see 1 Peter 2:18). They are do everything "as to Christ": so must we in all our work. We must treat our employer with deference as we would treat Christ. We must do it with sincerity, or singleness of heart. Our work for him or her is to be seen as an opportunity to serve Christ and we must do our work as if we were doing it for the Lord. So, go to your work with such a motivation and see how it transforms the most mundane task.

July *twenty-eighth*

"Not with eye-service, as men pleasers, but as servants of Christ, doing the will of God from the heart"
(Ephesians 6:6)

Eye-service. It is a miserable business, isn't it? Here is an employee who works hard, behaves pleasantly and speaks carefully when his or her employer is watching. When the employer's back is turned then shady behaviour and all sorts of "corner - cutting" takes place. It is a hypocritical lifestyle underlined with fawning.

Men - pleasing. It is also a miserable business. Why? Men are hard to please. Trying to curry favour with them is the hardest taskmaster you will know because men are fickle and what pleases them today may not please them tomorrow. No two men are the same, are they?

Paul now gives us the beautiful contrast as to how sincere servants of Christ behave. They seek to please the Lord. Their principle of obedience is not an external but an internal thing. They serve the Lord from their very hearts and for them the will of God has not only to do with being adopted (1:5), experiencing salvation present and future (1:7-12), but has to do with the very chores of everyday life, in house, in home, and in all duties of public employment. The balance of the teaching of Ephesians is that it soars to the very highest of doctrinal teaching but it also gets into the nitty-gritty of life. "Put Christ at the centre of your life and the circumference will take care of itself", goes the saying. That circumference includes the whole gamut of our lives.

Living for Christ is not a passive existence, it is active existence: we "do" the will of God from our hearts. It is the eye of God that matters most. It is His pleasure that is a priority. When Joseph was tempted by Potiphar's wife to sin, far from the eye of the public, he refused, but notice the thinking behind his refusal. "Look", he said, "my master does not know what is in the house, and he has committed all that he has to my hand. There is none greater in this house than I, nor has he kept anything from me but you, because you were his wife. How then can I do this great wickedness and sin against God?" Joseph in his action perfectly epitomises Paul's teaching regarding a slave-master work relationship. He is a starlight of encouragement to all who would seek to serve God in their employment.

July *twenty-ninth*

> *"With goodwill doing service as to the Lord, and not to men"*
> (Ephesians 6:8)

This text is urging us to serve in our employment with good will, that is with enthusiasm. It is a very attractive quality! So much service is done with only a sense of duty and is done grudgingly out of sheer necessity.

Our Lord talked of going "the extra mile". As I understand it, a Roman soldier was allowed to command a civilian to carry his military baggage for one mile. After that the civilian was not under any obligation to carry it further. Jesus was saying that people should go beyond the call of duty and carry it another mile ! "Going the extra mile" involves all kinds of extra touches to our service.

I was in a little place called "Pine Mountain" in Georgia, the other day. The day had involved a lot of preaching and we headed for a little restaurant called "Maguire's" and arrived to find it shut. The proprietor, though, who was closing up told us of another restaurant he though might be open and, what do you know, he phoned up to check it out for us! No wonder we had our breakfast at "Maguire's", Pine Mountain, the next morning! He went the extra mile.

I like soup but when I get it with parsley on top it tastes even better! When the man selling me my newspaper passes a cheery comment he is more than just a newspaper seller. When a steward or hostess on a airline serves me with enthusiasm it is a memorable flight. When a teacher finds that Jimmy has tried hard but written a lousy essay and the teacher picks out one good line and enthuses about it, what happens? Jimmy writes a better essay next time!

Let us do our work with enthusiasm. Treat no one as unimportant. Treat all as you would treat Christ. Whether you meet a cab driver or a President, a rich banker or a poor man, a little child or an older person, touch their life with enthusiasm. Your life is not a rehearsal. It is the real thing. Whatever service you are about be enthusiastic about it!

July *thirtieth*

**"As to the Lord and
not to men"**
(Ephesians 6:7)

"It was the best prayer ever delivered to an American audience", the man said. He might have been right but prayer is not meant to be to an earthly audience, is it? "Many people spend their lives seeking respect and admiration from a poorly defined audience", writes Klyne Snodgrass (Snodgrass p. 333) "but as interests become focused, the audience becomes more defined. We choose the sector we want to impress".

Think it through. You can dress to suit a certain audience. You can prepare material to target a certain audience. You watch what you say with a certain group of people. If they are not around, you don't put in the same effort. "This is why", writes Snodgrass "we demean some people but go overboard to impress others. With the first we do not care about the audience: with the second we do".

We are reminded, again, by Paul in this text that Christians have only one audience and that is God. He knows our down sitting and up rising and there is not a word on our tongue but he knows it, altogether. The very hairs on our head are numbered. There is nowhere we can go to get away from His presence. If there was He would cease to be God, wouldn't He? He is omniscient. I don't know where you will go today, who you will meet, what circumstances will cross your path, in private or in public. Wherever you go and whatever you do try to remember that you have an audience. The Lord is watching every move and derives huge pleasure if you do all as to Him. Sure, if you please Him what does it matter who else you please or don't please?

July *thirty-first*

**"Knowing that
whatever good
anyone does, he will
receive the same from
the Lord, whether
he is either slave
or free"**
(Ephesians 6:8)

Good deeds done on earth can go unrecognised. Some of the greatest acts of bravery or kindness can go unrewarded. People can be very selfish or simply forgetful. They can also be very fickle. God, though, is not fickle. He never forgets whatever good anyone does. No social distinction on earth makes any difference with God regarding reward. This truth applies to both "slave or free", Paul says.

There is documentary evidence that in certain households in Roman times some discussions of household management record that slaves could be motivated by more food, more praise, better clothing and even shoes. Our prime motivation is to bring glory to God in all that we do but there is a very definite promise of reward from our Lord for service given. Moses, we are told, had respect for the recompense of the reward. We also need to have the same respect.

In the story of the parable of the men who went to work in the vineyard the workers who worked for one hour were paid as much as those who worked for twelve hours. The twelve hour workers grumbled. They had borne the burden and heat of the day. Yet, why did the owner of the vineyard pay the one hour workers as much as the twelve hour workers? Because he wanted to point out that the twelve hour workers had a contract and all the rest of the workers he hired that day, didn't. The twelve hour workers had agreed to be paid a denarius a day. To the rest of the workers the owner had said "You will also go into the vineyard and whatever is right I will give you".

We must not try to make contracts or bargains with God. He will give us "what is right" and it will be exceedingly, abundantly, above all that we could ever ask or think. Not only will it be right but, today's text reminds us, it will be good. Trust Him for it. No one who did was ever disappointed.

AUGUST

How lovely on the mountains are the feet of the one who brings good news! All who are in Christ have for the resource of having their feet fitted with readiness that comes from the gospel of peace. And, of course, there is much more. There is the belt of truth and the breastplate of righteousness. In addition to this there is the shield of faith with which to put out all the flaming arrows of the wicked one. The helmet of salvation is augmented with the sword of the Spirit.

There is no question that the Christian life is a battle and opposition is certain. This month our Readings are concentrated on Paul's teaching about the armour of God available for all Christian warfare: it is awesome in its scope and practicality. His great letter to the Ephesians ends with a benediction that reminds us that God provides all a believer needs through our Lord Jesus Christ. What a resource! What a Saviour!

August *first*

> *"And you, masters, do the same things to them giving up threats, knowing that your own Master also is in heaven and there is no partiality with Him"*
> (Ephesians 6:9)

The emphasis of today's text is on the impartiality of our Lord Jesus. He is our Master in heaven and a person's social status on earth does not give that person any edge over anyone else in His sight. There is no favouritism with the Lord.

Seneca, in his day, reminded masters that they were under the same power, Chance, as their slaves. He taught that they were in fact both slaves. Paul certainly did not believe or teach that Christian slaves or their masters were under the power of Chance. But in today's text he is implying that both were under the Lordship of Christ and were both His slaves. In this teaching were the seeds of true emancipation.

Look around society today and you will see a very clear hierarchy and people are given value within that hierarchy. Some are treated as being of virtually no value. In the Christian community, in the sight of God, there is seniority but there is no superiority. All are of equal value.

I heard of a young student who put his head into a local Church building to inquire of a man who was "sweeping up" as to whether or not Professor so-and- so belonged to that Church. The "sweeper" turned out to be Professor so-and-so! Let us not show deference to the intelligent or the rich or the powerful and little attention or respect to the poor and powerless. Let us, if we are in a position of influence and power never use any threats to bring service from those we employ. Threatening is a "big stick" which is used a lot by people in the society where I happen to live. It hasn't helped heal that society, I can tell you. For which, in the light of today's text, would you rather be remembered? Someone who is a threatener or someone who goes about doing good?

August *second*

"Finally, my brethren, be strong in the Lord and in the power of His might"
(Ephesians 6:10)

We are, as Christians, in a conflict. We have a relentless foe called the devil who is a liar, who is very strong, who fights dirty and seeks to oppress the Christian by constantly dogging his or her footsteps. He will use anything or anyone is his desire to divert a Christian from closely following the Lord. We should take Satan very seriously because he has immense power. Yet we should not take him too seriously because he has been defeated and the Scriptures tell us he will ultimately perish. Let's keep the balance right.

Before Paul depicts the battle we are in he indicates the unsurpassable resources which are available to Christians in the fight. They begin from a position of strength. They are "in the Lord". We have learned that this is a favourite expression of Paul's. Because the believer is in Christ then that believer has direct access to Christ's power. That power should be constantly drawn upon in the battle. As we are to pray for strengthening through the Spirit in the inner person (3:16) so we are to draw from Christ's power. Here is a call to act on what we know. To rush into battle without acknowledging Christ and without putting our trust in Him would leave us confused and defeated. We begin, then, from a place of unparalleled strength.

"In the power of His might", speaks of "the vigour derived from His strength". Christ is our food and drink, the New Testament teaches. That food is found in the Scriptures. When the temperamental and even frightened Timothy was facing the battle Paul reminded him that "all Scripture is given by inspiration of God, and is profitable for doctrine, for reproof, for correction, for instruction in righteousness, that the man of God might be complete" (1 Timothy 3:16-17). As we feed on the Scriptures we draw from Christ's strength. And prayer, too, is another way of drawing sustenance for the battle. As we turn to the Lord in prayer we have fellowship with God and, as Revelation 3:20 puts it, our Lord "dines" with us and we with Him.

Partaking of the Lord's Supper is also reinvigorating for the battle, it feeds us. I do not believe in transubstantiation but I do believe that partaking of the Lord's Supper is of a huge spiritual blessing to us. As we partake of the emblems they remind us of Christ's death and resurrection and imminent return. Meditating on such themes strengthens us for the battle. So, to be strong in the Lord and in the power of His might is not a passive experience, is it? We need to feed on Christ and then His strength will become ours.

August *third*

"Put on the whole armour of God"
(Ephesians 6:11)

If we are not to be passive in gaining strength and vigour for Christian warfare neither are we to be passive in defending ourselves against the attacks of the enemy. We are not, as Paul puts it in 2 Cor 2:11 "to be ignorant of his devices". We must not be shocked and amazed that Satan's attacks come from hugely unsuspected corners. He is wily, subtle, highly skilled and superbly organised and it is absolutely necessary to defend ourselves against him.

Think in Scripture of the string of characters upon whom Satan has inflicted serious injury, from King David to Peter, from Noah to Samson, from Lot to Demas. We need protection at all times and in all circumstances and God has provided armour for us, specially and intricately designed to protect us in everything we face in the battle. The armour, of course, is spiritual and consists of knowing, understanding and applying the truths of the Gospel in our journey through life.

The word "whole" in our text is not in the original but is necessary in order to translate the word Paul uses which is "panoply". This word meant the complete equipment of a fully armed Roman soldier. The Christian, then, is to "put on" the whole "panoply of God".

What use is a soldier's armour is he doesn't put it on? From the armour of ancient knights to modern day flat jackets, protective equipment must be put on in a battle. Don't just only study the Gospel and its truths but make sure you also "put them on", applying them in the battle against Satan. You will find that your enemy will be defeated again and again. You have, in the armour of God, one glorious secret for the whole emergency you face.

August *fourth*

"That you might be able to stand"
(Ephesians 6:11)

Stand! What a word! Here is no wimp. Here is no deserter. Here is no feeling-sorry-for-himself individual. Here is no unstable, weakly, "blown about in the wind" uncertain or half-hearted person. Here is no dull and constantly melancholic individual, either. This person is not frightened nor foolhardy; fully realising the power of the enemy, this person is not overwhelmed.

Here we have the successful Christian soldier who is able to "stand". It is important to realise what to "stand" means because it is the key word of this section of Ephesians. It means to "remain firm in the face of assault". Huge pressure may bear upon you but you are not running from it, you are facing it: you brace yourself, there is to be no provision for or even thought of retreat. The armour that God gives you is sufficient protection from everything that the enemy will throw at you. In this armour you can stand because in it you are able to withstand.

Does today's reading catch the eye of someone who is tempted to flee the battle? Are you tempted to do what Paul's fellow-soldier Demas did? He left the field of battle for an easier place."Demas has forsaken me", writes Paul in his very last letter to Timothy "having loved this present world". The battle was hot, threatening Demas' very life and he deserted. He did not stand, he fled. Yes, I believe that his soul was saved, but he lost the joy of victory in battle for his Lord. Thereafter he had a saved soul but a wasted life. To save your life, said Jesus, is to lose it and to lose your life for His sake and the Gospel's is to find it. Come on, discouraged one, look who your Captain is! I know only too well that the battle is sore because I too am in it but victory through Christ is sweet, is it not?

Sunsets for Demas at Thessalonica, I am sure, were a lot easier than house arrest with Paul in Rome but which man was used by God to help change the world?

August *fifth*

"*Against the wiles of the devil*"
(Ephesians 6:11)

"Wiles" literally mean "methods" or "stratagems". The devil's methods and stratagems are what the believer is up against. There is a personal centre at the heart of evil. Our text implies that the devil does not always attack in an obvious way, he employs cunning and is very wily. He means to catch the believer unawares. The devil never signs his name to anything.

The Bible tells us that the devil is comparable to a roaring lion. That's true but he doesn't always act as a roaring lion. He can slink in like a wolf. He can also masquerade as an angel of light. He does not always appear ugly and harsh and cruel. Sometimes he is most pleasant and very affable. One day he is attacking Scripture, the next he is quoting it. One day he is telling you that you are not good enough to be a Christian and next he is telling you that you are! Henry Law wrote this challenging piece about Satan. Let's heed it. "He never slumbers, he is never weary, never relents, never abandons hope. He deals blows at childhood's weakness, youth's inexperience, manhood's strength and the tottering of age. He watches to ensnare the morning thought. He departs not with the shades of night. He enters the palace, the hut, the fortress, the camp, the fleet. He visits every room of every dwelling, every pew of every sanctuary. He is busy with the busy. He hurries about with the active. He sits by each bed of sickness, and whispers in each dying ear. As the spirit quits the tenement of clay, he still draws his bow with unrelenting rage. What I say unto you, I say unto you all - watch!"

August *sixth*

"For we do not wrestle against flesh and blood, but against principalities, against powers, against the rulers of the darkness of this age, against spiritual hosts of wickedness in the heavenly places"
(Ephesians 6:12)

When you realise the nature of your enemy then you realise your great need for the armour of God. Paul tells us specially that we are not in conflict with mere human beings but rather that we are in a battle against evil spirit powers. Flesh and blood can be much more easily overcome than evil spirit powers.

What, then, is the nature of our enemy? First we struggle against "principalities and powers", that is, personal demonic intelligences. They can exploit human, social, political, judicial and economic structures. We read of the city of Pergamum in Revelation 2:13. The Lord says that Pergamum is the place "where Satan's throne is". That means that "the principalities and powers" can shift their attack from one place to another and from one "corridor of earthly power" to another. The Lord, of course, can invade that centre of power with His Gospel and it can become a centre of good.

Secondly, we wrestle against "the rulers of the darkness of this age". This probably refers to the highest in rank amongst demons. "The darkness of this age" is the present order of things in the earth where there is alienation from God. In such a situation Satan and his demons rule over the spiritual darkness. The god of this age has "blinded the minds of those who do not believe, lest the light of the Gospel of the glory of Christ, who is the image of God, should shine on them" (2 Cor 4:4).

Thirdly, we wrestle against "spiritual hosts of wickedness in the heavenly places". These spirits are wicked by nature and always have wicked intent. They dwell "in the heavenly realms". Professor Bruce states that "the heavenly realm may be envisaged as comprising a succession of levels, with the throne of God on the highest of these and the hostile forces occupying the lowest" (Bruce, p. 406). These levels are unseen but real.

All of these forces are spiritual forces and must be resisted with spiritual resources. As we have been reviewing our resources in Christ in this book we shall in the next few days review the resources available for Christian warfare. The armour of God is perfectly adequate for all that we face. Knowing the nature of our enemy we will need that armour. Never, ever underestimate his power and reach.

August *seventh*

"Therefore take up the whole armour of God that you may be able to withstand in the evil day"
(Ephesians 6:14)

What is the meaning of "the evil day"? Some say that it is the time of special tribulation just before the end of the earth as we know it: a last attack by Satan. Some say that it is a special time of crisis or temptation in one's life. Others say that it is the reference to the whole of this present age in which we live. The answer lies, Andrew Lincoln has pointed out, in a combination of the first and third interpretations (Lincoln, p. 445-446). How?

The Bible speaks of a final evil day that is to come (see Amos 5:18-20, Daniel 12:1, 1 Cor 7:26, 1 Thessalonians 7:26, 1 Thessalonians 5:2-4, 2 Thessalonians 2:3-12). Paul's Ephesian letter has already spoken of the fact that we are in evil days at present (5:16). Just as we have already experienced redemption (1:7) and will yet experience a final day of redemption (4:30), so we live in evil times and there will yet be a final evil day. The point of today's text is that God's armour will enable a Christian to gain victory both now and in the future, whatever that may hold.

You may feel that the Christian church is being overwhelmed in the midst of the present evil day but do not be discouraged, it will spring back. There is no power on earth can finally keep it down, or you, either, Christian. "At least five times", noted G.K. Chesterton, "the Faith has to all appearances gone to the dogs. In each of these five cases, it was the dog that died!" 'The Everlasting Man' (Garden City, Image Books, 1995, p. 260-261). No, we are not whistling in the dark, God has given us our armour and has promised that it will see us through.

August *eighth*

> *"And having done all, to stand"*
> (Ephesians 6:13)

I have, before writing today's entry, just spent a few hours with a Christian leader who has been through some tremendous battles recently in his Christian service. The onslaught against him was awesomely frightening and here he was, at the end of his experiences, still standing firm. I was inspired.

Are you in a similar place? Despite all that has happened to you, you are determined to stand firm. Why? Because of the one you are serving. It is an honour to stand firm for Him. A. B. Cave once said "the system of human meditation falls away in the advent to our souls of the living Christ. Who wants the stars, or even the moon, when the sun is up". The dignity of the service of Christ brings dignity to those who serve Him. Augustine said "God is not greater if you reverence him but you are greater if you serve Him". The battles you fight, are not your own personal ones for "the battle belongs to the Lord". We are in the army of the living God and it is an honour to serve Him in it.

"You are living on the planet Zob", the media moderator commented after I had tried to present Christian truth on his radio discussion panel: "You are an angel on a pinhead", he added for good measure! I reeled under his tongue, but then, who cares what you are called if you drawing fire for Christ?

I once met an Ethiopian Christian who had been in prison for Christ and he told me that he was sorry the day he left prison. Why? Because of the joy he experienced while being in prison for the Lord's sake! I believed him.

As Nehemiah and his people stood firm at Jerusalem against the enemy they were ridiculed for rebuilding the city wall. As they held both "the sword and the trowel" the enemy mocked by saying that if "Even a fox goes up on it, he will break down their stone wall". But they stood firm, finished their work and, as Nehemiah put it, the joy of the Lord was their strength.

So, having done, all, Christian, stand firm. Remember for whom you stand.

August *ninth*

"Stand therefore, having girded your waist with truth"
(Ephesians 6:14)

Paul calls us, once more, to take up our position in the battle, resisting and prevailing against the enemy. As we do so the first necessary action in the battle is to fasten on the belt of truth around our waist. The idea of "girding" in the ancient world was to gather up long and loose garments and to bind them together with a belt. Then a person was ready to move freely. It has the idea of readiness, of being totally unimpeded. Such a stance was vital preparation for any vigorous activity. In the context of the Roman army the Roman soldier's belt or girdle was a leather apron worn under the armour like breeches: it supported and braced the soldier for action. It gathered his tunic together and also held his sword.

Paul tells us that the Christian's belt is truth. Much discussion has gone into a definition of what he means. Is it the truth as revealed in Scripture or does it mean integrity? William Gunall in his famous book "The Christian in complete armour" thinks it is both. He states: "Some by truth mean a truth of doctrine; others will have a truth of heart, sincerity; I think best that comprise both. One will not do without the other."

Can you imagine what it would be like to be found in battle with a soldier who is not reliable and someone who is without integrity? The enemy would soon come in like a flood. Soldiers who have integrity and knowledge of warfare are a formidable force. So, those who know the truth of Christian doctrine and who live with integrity need not fear the enemy. As Philip Brooks put it "Truth is always strong, no matter how weak it looks and falsehood is always weak, no matter how strong it looks". So, belt up with truth!

August *tenth*

> *"Having put on the breastplate of righteousness"*
> (Ephesians 6:14)

Let us stay for four days reading with this vital piece of armour. On the Roman soldier the breastplate generally extended from the base of the neck to the upper part of the thighs, so it covered what we would now call the thorax and abdomen. It covered, then, some very vital organs: the kidneys, the bowels, the heart and the lungs. In ancient times people believed that these various organs were the seat of the "affections". When they had various feelings they believed that the cause of the trouble was in a particular organ. We still speak in our language of people "venting their spleen" or being "liverish" or being "heartbroken" etc.

It is vital that we have a protection for our feelings, affections, desires and will because we are engaged in a conflict with the world, the flesh and the devil. That protection is our standing in Christ. Christ is the believer's righteousness, a righteousness which is imputed and there is, now, no condemnation for those who are in Christ Jesus (see Romans 8:1-2). "For", writes Paul, in 2 Corinthians 5:21, "He made him who knew no sin to be sin for us, that we might become the righteousness of God in Him".

It may be that some Christian who reads these lines is being assailed by Satan as to their salvation. You might be wondering if you are a Christian at all. You have begun to be introspective and are all too well aware of sins and failures in your life. Satan is saying to you "What right have you to pray? What right have you to witness? What right have you to participate of the Lord's Supper? What right have you to teach others?" As he assails you depression begins to seep into your life like fog from the sea. You are weakened in the battle and soon become ineffective in your service.

Come, then, Christian, remember that you have a breastplate of righteousness to "take up" and "put on". Your sins were all future to the cross and were dealt with there by Christ. He is your righteousness, no matter what Satan says. Let your feelings and moods be controlled by the fact that Christ's righteousness covers you and will cover you forever against any accusation and any accuser. Christ is your confidence and assurance. Enjoy!

> "When Satan tempts me to despair
> Telling me of evil yet within
> Upward I look and see Him there
> Who made an end of all my sin."

August *eleventh*

"Having put on the breastplate of righteousness"
(Ephesians 6:14)

The company was most interesting and the food was excellent. When coffee time came we went "through", as they say in Scotland, to the sitting room. Lifting a Bible from the coffee table my good friend, Donald MacCuish handed it to me."Do you know whose Bible that is?" he asked. On the flyleaf I read the words "Mr McCheyne's Bible". I was thrilled to be handling the Bible of the Rev. Murray McCheyne, one of the greatest Christian ministers Scotland has ever known who sadly died in his twenty-ninth year.

The company that day in Inverness included Lord and Lady MacKay of Clashfern. Lord MacKay is a former Lord Chancellor of the United Kingdom and is a devout Christian. Donald then told us all the fascinating story of the Bible he had handed to me.

When Mr McCheyne was dying he was in a delirium and said to Jessie Stewart, his housekeeper, "Jessie, 'be ye steadfast, unmovable, always abounding in the work of the Lord for as much as ye know that your labour is not in vain in the Lord'." The verse he quoted came from 1 Corinthians 15:58. When Mr McCheyne died they gave his Bible to Jessie who wrote in the margin against the verse in 1 Corinthians "Last text given to me by my Pastor and Master, Mr McCheyne, before he slept in Jesus". She took the Bible to South Africa and gave it to a friend who in turn gave it to a minister. The minister eventually returned to Holland where the Bible entered the Dutch Royal Family for many years.

One day in The Hague in Holland a man was contracted to clear the house of a minister who had died. He found lots of books in the house and before throwing them away the thought crossed his mind that a Christian gentleman that he knew in the district might like some of them. The Christian eventually came round to find a Bible with the words "Mr McCheyne's Bible" on the flyleaf. It so happened he had come to faith in Jesus Christ through reading one of Mr McCheyne's sermons! He took the Bible home and said in his heart "this Bible belongs in Scotland. The first Scot to come through my door who appreciates the ministry of Robert Murray McCheyne will have it".

One day, my friend Donald MacCuish arrived at The Hague for a wedding and stayed in the home of a Christian gentleman. When asked about Mr McCheyne he waxed eloquent and was given the Bible!

So it was that Lord MacKay and I sat that Sunday afternoon in Inverness and shared some of the texts Mr McCheyne had underlined in his Bible. As he left the home Lord MacKay signed the MacCuish's visitors book and in the comments box he wrote "1 Corinthians 15:58"!

Amazing, isn't it, that the dying words of a Scottish Minister travelled through history to inspire the heart of the first Scottish Lord Chancellor in history, 154 years later?!

In the Old Testament we read of Jehovah Tsidkenu (Jeremiah 23:6) meaning "The Lord our Righteousness". During his short lifetime Robert Murray McCheyne wrote a beautiful hymn and one of the verses states:

"When treading the valley the shadow of death
This watchword shall rally my faltering breath,
And when from life's fever my God sets me free,
Jehovah Tsidkenu my death song shall be"

And Jehovah Tsidkendu actually was Mr. McCheyne's death song, wasn't He? The godly Donald MacCuish uncovered that fact for us all.

August *twelfth*

"Putting on the breastplate of righteousness"
(Ephesians 6:14)

I wrote, yesterday, the story of Robert Murray McCheyne as he approached death. Few Christians studying Ephesians in-depth in a modern day do not turn to the works of Martyn Lloyd Jones. His longest series of expositions at Westminster Chapel in London,on Sunday mornings, from 1955 to 1968 ,was on this great letter. I want to think today about the dying moments of Dr. Lloyd-Jones because I think you will find them inspiring.

I was invited by my friend, Dr Alan Gillespie, when he was the President of the Cambridge University Christian Union to come and stay at the University halls and hear Dr Lloyd-Jones speak. I had my life turned around by what I heard that weekend. I shall always remember having tea with the Doctor in a little tea room in Cambridge and finding a passion continuing to rise in my heart to truly give myself to the teaching of the Scriptures. That weekend was a defining time in my life.

On today's verse the Doctor stated "It is a part of putting on the breast-plate of righteousness that I remind myself daily of where I am and where I am going ... you say to yourself 'I do not belong here, I am passing through this country ... I am making for Heaven, for light, for glory'" ("The Christian Soldier", page 263-4). He speaks of the fact that the Christian is a traveller: "It means therefore he does not settle down in this world, and feel anxious to do so, and regret the fact that he has to go out of it".

As Mr McCheyne epitomised what he had written by his death, so Dr. Lloyd Jones did the same. I am told that as he neared death, his daughter, Lady Elizabeth Catherwood was praying by his bedside and audibly asked the Lord to spare her father to be a further blessing to His people. The weak and dying Doctor reached for a piece of paper and wrote the following note; "Don't hinder me from the glory!" The man had his breastplate on even as death approached him. He didn't regret that he had to go because he was anticipating the glory that would follow. Live a good life for Jesus Christ but die, if the Lord has not come, a good death for him too!

August *thirteenth*

> *"Having put on the breastplate of righteousness"*
> (Ephesians 6:14)

I don't think we can leave our meditations on the truth of the breastplate of righteousness without looking at another side of the teaching. In Isaiah 59:17 we read that Jehovah put on "righteousness as a breastplate". This surely refers to a moral quality of God which we, as his people, are called upon to reflect in our actions. It is an ethical quality which is most attractive. Surely we must guard our lives and hearts by living righteous lives, consistent with our calling. "The completeness of pardon for past offence and the integrity of character that belong to the justified life, are woven together into an impenetrable mail" (G.G.Findlay, p.415).That's the kind of "chain mail" we should always have on!

"When the enemy comes in like a flood, the Spirit of the Lord will lift up a standard against him", the Scriptures teach (Isaiah 59:19). The saving life of Christ lived out in your life is that standard for the Lord which will be lived out in your office, on your farm, or factory, or home, or business, or classroom, or community or whatever. As the poet said:

Not merely in the words you say,
Not only in your deeds confessed,
But in the most unconscious way,
Is Christ expressed.

Is it a beautific smile?
A holy light upon your brow?
Oh, no, I felt His Presence
When you laughed just now.

For me,'twas not the truth you told,
To you so clear, to me so dim,
But when you came to me, you brought,
A glimpse of Him.

And from your eyes He beckons me,
And from your lips His love is shed,
Til I lose sight of you, and see
The Christ instead.

August *fourteenth*

"And having your feet shod with the preparation of the Gospel of peace"
(Ephesians 6:15)

There is a huge paradox in today's text. The context of the verse is the Christians conflict with the world, the flesh and the devil and yet here is talk of the Gospel of peace. What is this paradox of peace and war?

The answer lies in the emphasis in the text on the word "preparation". It means readiness, preparedness. In the context it is not readiness to proclaim the Gospel but a readiness for battle and a firmness of foot in the battle that the Gospel of peace gives. The paradox is that when we appropriate the Gospel of peace it makes us ready for war! Think of the peace that the Gospel had brought these Ephesian Christians. It had brought them peace with God, peace in their hearts and lives and peace between Jews and Gentiles who were once at emnity. One day in the fullness of time, God will gather "together in one all things in Christ, which are in Heaven and which are in earth - in Him" (1:10). One day the "manifold wisdom of God" will be made known "by the church to the principalities and powers in the heavenly places" (3:10). Do you think the devil likes the situation? He opposes it entirely and brings intense opposition to it. So the peace the Christian knows gives that Christian a firm standing against the enemy of that peace and makes him or her ready for combat.

Who knows what opposition will arise against you, today? Who knows what the devil will throw at you this week? You need not fear because you will have a firm standing in the Gospel and all the truths it teaches. The Roman soldier had his "caliga" or half-boot. It was a sandal which consisted of a leather sole with straps that held it firmly to the foot. It had a heavy studded sole that prevented his foot from sliding. So it is that the Gospel of peace will prevent us from sliding. One of the best translations of our text puts it this way : "having shod your feet with the equipment of the Gospel of peace". No better equipment than the Gospel to help you stand firm when the onslaught comes, no matter how unexpected. Keep your boots on, tight!

August *fifteenth*

> *"Having shod your feet with the preparation of the Gospel of peace"*
> (Ephesians 6:15)

All great military commanders in history have been those who are masters of mobility. They see an opportunity and grasp it, even in the midst of a battle: insistence on the mobility of troop movement has been a vital strategy in many a famous victory. Sadly at Singapore the British had their guns pointed out at sea and the Japanese came "on bicycles" from behind and defeated them. They won on mobility.

You and I must be mobile in the service of God. Sluggishness, lethargic attitudes, slowness to react, thoughtless, unintelligent living will make no impact on the enemy. The gates of Hell are not offensive weapons, they are defensive weapons, they can be driven back. They will not be driven back, though, by sluggish Christians. There is a battle raging all around us and we need to be prepared and ready to take advantage of any opportunity that arises to advance the kingdom of God. We have to be ready to move at the Lord's bidding. To do that we must be unencumbered and certainly not heavy - footed. We are to have our feet shod with the preparation of the Gospel of peace.

Are you ready to respond to the Lord's every call to you? Are you so lethargic and "stuck-in-the-mud" that you are even unwilling to move out of your present situation for the greater advancement of the kingdom? Have you any idea of what you are missing? If Moses had stayed in the Egyptian Palace he would never have seen the Red Sea open or manna fall from Heaven. If Gideon had stayed down on the farm he would have never seen a 32,000 manned army reduced to 300. He would then never have witnessed an enemy, like locusts for number, flee as those 300 were used by God to rout them! If Ruth had stayed in Moab she would never have met Boaz in Bethlehem and eventually had her name put in the genealogy of Christ.

So, move it, Christian, move it!

August *sixteenth*

"Having your feet shod with the preparation of the Gospel of peace"
(Ephesians 6:15)

Goliath was a formidable enemy. He was over 9ft tall. He had a bronze helmet on his head and wore a coat of scale armour of bronze weighing around 57 kilograms. He had a bronze javelin strung on his back and his spear was like a weaver's beam and its iron point weighed about 7 kilograms. For 40 days he had presented himself to the army of Israel every morning and evening mocking the living God and crying "I defy the armies of Israel this day: give me a man that we might fight together".

And who stood up against him? The young David. He said to King Saul, "The Lord who delivered me from the paw of the lion and the paw of the bear, he will deliver me from the hand of this Philistine". And what did Saul do? He "Put a bronze helmet on his head: he also clothed him with a coat of mail. And David fastened his sword to his armour and he tried to walk, for he had not tested them. And David said to Saul 'I cannot walk with these, for I have not tested them'". Taking his staff in his hand and five smooth stones from the brook and putting them in a shepherd's bag he took up a sling in his hand and went up the valley of Elah and slew the giant.

What is the moral principle in David's story? It is that he used his own method of fighting, not Saul's. He knew his own limitations; he knew what he was capable of in God's hands within those limitations. Saul's armour was beyond him.

How does this apply to today's text? It is that you must be ready to repel the attack of the evil one with that which you have proved. The Gospel of peace has reached you and you are in Christ but you have certain gifts given to you by God and it is best to stick to them in the battle. The modern army has all kinds of soldiers with all kinds of skills. So does God's. The tank commander is not in the infantry. The rear guard is not the front line but all are in the battle and one cannot do without the other. Fight with what you have proved and when God wants you to move to new ground, he will show you when and where. Make sure you obey Him when he does.

August *seventeenth*

"Above all, taking the shield of faith"
(Ephesians 6:16)

In addition to fastening on the belt of truth and the breastplate of righteousness and shodding your feet with the preparation of the Gospel of peace, further armour is indispensable. Paul calls us to take up the shield of faith. The term Paul uses is "sartum" which was the large shield used by the Roman soldier, 4ft in length and 2ft wide which protected the whole body. It was generally made of wood with a thick coating of leather.

The first three pieces of armour Paul mentions have to be fastened on but the shield of faith has to be taken up. You grab your shield when you have to engage with the enemy but you don't use it when resting.

The teaching here is that the Christian has his or her faith to deal with everything with which the enemy attacks. Faith is a mighty shield in the time of battle. What is faith? Faith is based on three things. Someone must first make a promise. There must be a very good reason for believing in the integrity of the person making the promise. There then follows an assurance that what has been promised will be delivered.

Who has made the promise? God. As we study the Scriptures we come across hundreds of God's promises. We are as sure of what God has promised as we would be if it were in front of our very eyes. If you want greater faith then you will find that the promises of God are faith's native food. Faith will lift your life from mediocrity. "Faith," wrote F.B.Meyer, "does not under rate the power of man but magnifies omniscience. Faith is not callous of present pain but weighs it against future joy. Against ill-gotton gains she puts eternal treasures: against human hate, the recompense of reward: against the tears of winter sowing the shoutings of Autumn sheaves: against the inconvenience of the tent, the permanent city". So, get into those promises, Christian, and soon you will be wielding the shield of faith with skill.

August *eighteenth*

> *"Above all, taking the shield of faith"*
> (Ephesians 6:16)

Let us try to grasp the reach of faith. "By faith we understand", says Hebrews 11, "that the worlds were framed by the Word of God so that the things which are seen were not made of things which are visible". God, in fact, spoke to nothing and it became something. Faith believes in creation! "By faith", we are further told, "Abel offered to God a more excellent sacrifice than Cain." Faith believes in redemption!"By faith", adds the writer to the Hebrews, "Enoch was taken so that he did not see death, 'and was not found because God had taken him'" Faith believes in glorification!

Look, in the Bible, at what faith did for people. It inspired Noah to build an ark. It helped Abraham to quit the sophistication of Ur and head out for the city whose builder and maker is God. It helped Joseph to believe that Israel would pull out of Egypt for the promised land, so much so, that he gave instructions that his bones go with them when they pulled out! It inspired the parents of Moses to put their baby in an ark of bullrushes and so he was saved from certain death. Faith brought Daniel through the den of lions and his three friends through the fiery furnace. Faith fired the New Testament Christians despite the incredible persecutions they endured to the point where it was actually said of some of them that they had "turned the world upside down"(see Acts 17:6). Need I go on?

No matter what position you are in, faith can overcome in insuperable difficulties. It is the best shield you can have. If you walk by sight you will be overwhelmed. If, though, you walk by faith you will have "the evidence of things not seen".

Let me give you some quotations on the subject of faith. I trust it will inspire you to use the shield of faith in whatever you face, today.

"A weak faith may receive a strong Christ" (Thomas Watson). "Simple faith honours God and God honours simple faith" (Mary Winslow). The poor man's hand is Christ's bank" (John Trapp). "So many Christians badly need a faith lift!" (Anon). "Faith has no back door" (Paul Madsen). "Faith is dead to doubt, dumb to discouragement, blind to impossibilities" (Anon). "Faith is the daring of the soul to go further than it can see" (W.S.Clarke). (These quotations are taken from "Gathered Gold," compiled by John Blanchard, Evangelical Press 1984).

August *nineteenth*

> *"Above all, taking the shield of faith with which you will be able to quench all the fiery darts of the wicked one"*
> (Ephesians 6:16)

I remember talking, once, to a very godly Christian leader. He told me that some of the filthiest thoughts he had ever had came to him as he was partaking of the Lord's Supper. So it is that as we are going along in our Christian lives, right out of the blue, in the most unexpected places, our minds are invaded by unsought blasphemous thoughts, filthy words, lust, fear and horrible suggestions. We panic and spiritual depression sets in because we begin to feel we are not Christians at all. How, we surmise, could we ever be Christians if such thinking is present in our lives?

Today's verse shows the way out of such depression. What we are actually experiencing is the flaming, fiery darts of the wicked one. He has hurled such thoughts into our imaginations and his deception is to make us think that such thoughts are ours, not his. "The point that we must grasp is that they obviously come from outside ourselves. They are not generated by us; they come to us" (Lloyd-Jones, "The Christian Soldier", p.301).

I am quite certain that no Christian reading today's meditation has not experienced doubt invading their thoughts. Sometimes after a huge victory in your Christian life doubt about the very validity of the Christian faith or even the very existence of God can seek to overwhelm you. You love the Saviour, you love the Scriptures, you love God's people, you love the Gospel, yes? You were led by the mighty Holy Spirit and have discovered the Father- heart of God, yes? But those fiery darts come in on you and threaten to burn you alive.

Just as the Roman soldier had a shield which was made of wood and had a fireproof metal lining placed on it, so you have the shield of faith which is able to "quench" all the fiery darts of the wicked one. It is not faith in faith but faith in the object of all faith ,which is the living God, that will see off all fiery darts.

August *twentieth*

"And take the helmet of salvation"
(Ephesians 6:17)

The importance of the mind cannot be over-estimated. Our life and the co-ordination of all that it entails is deeply influenced by the state of our minds. Healthy positive attitudes to the challenges of any day comes from what we are thinking. Let a negative, unhealthy thought get the hold of our mind and we can be paralysed in our actions and withdraw into ourselves and be useless in any given situation.

Paul tells us that in Christian warfare we are to take the helmet of salvation. This means that we are to receive the helmet of salvation. It is offered to us by God as a gift. In chapter 2 verses 5 and 8 Paul has reminded us that we are saved by grace and that such salvation is the gift of God. When this truth conquers your mind it gives you huge confidence in the battle. If you are "in Christ" you are "in Christ" forever. Your sins are forgiven and Hell you will never see because of Christ's atoning work accomplished at Calvary. What a helmet to protect your mind!

Notice the order. The Roman soldier would first take the shield in his left hand and then, before taking the sword in right hand, he would put on his helmet. You have been saved by grace through faith and now you can apply the sword of the Spirit.

Of course, salvation also involves salvation in a present - continuous sense. You "are being" saved, every day. The work that Christ has begun in you continues. When you and I fail and the tempter assails us we remind him that we are not perfect yet but the Lord is at work in us ("How do you get a horse out of that?", someone asked the sculptor. "Everything that isn't horse has to come away", he answered!)

This truth brings us to the final stage of salvation when we shall be perfected for we shall be like Him one day. "For now our salvation is nearer than when we first believed", says Roman 13:11. "Being confident of this very thing", writes Paul in Philippians 1:7, "that He who has begun a good work in you will complete it until the day of Jesus Christ". Nothing will stop that work. You "have been" saved from the penalty of sin, you "are being" saved from the power of sin and you will "yet be" saved from the very presence of sin, one day. There is no better helmet in all the world than the helmet of salvation.

August *twenty-first*

> *"And the sword of the Spirit which is the Word of God"*
> (Ephesians 6:17)

The sword Paul has in mind is the Roman short sword as opposed to the long sword. It was absolutely vital in close combat. It is the only weapon mentioned in the Christian's armoury which can be used for attack as well as defence.

Paul tells us that the Christian sword is the sword of Spirit and defines it as the Word of God. In what sense does he mean this? He means that our greatest defensive weapon in our fight against Satan is the Bible which was first given and inspired by the Holy Spirit. Only men of God down through the centuries spoke "as they were moved by the Spirit", Peter tells us. "All Scripture is given by inspiration of God", Paul wrote to Timothy. The Scriptures are not a series of books which contain mans ideas or philosophies, the Holy Spirit is the author.

The Holy Spirit also helps you to understand and interpret Scripture for "the natural man does not receive the things of the Spirit of God, for they are foolishness to him; nor can he know them, because they are spiritually discerned" (1 Corinthians 2:14). The Holy Spirit will also help you when you are called upon to defend the Gospel. Jesus told his followers "you will be brought before governors and kings for my sake, as a testimony to them and to the Gentiles. But when they deliver you up, do not worry about how or what your should speak. For it will be given to you in the hour what you should speak; for it is not you who speak, but the Spirit of your Father who speaks in you" (Matthew 10:18-20).

The Holy Spirit awesomely uses the Scriptures to speak to people. Do not be afraid to sensitively quote them when you are evangelising because "the Word of God is living and powerful and sharper than any two edged sword, piercing even to the division of soul and spirit, and of joints and marrow, and is a discerner of the thoughts and intents of the heart" (Hebrews 4:12).

There is absolutely no telling what the Holy Spirit will do with the Word of God through you today. Let absolutely nothing shake your confidence in its power. Uninspired Scripture would be as a broken sword in your hand. What you have is no broken sword.

August *twenty-second*

> *"The sword of the Spirit, which is the Word of God"*
> (Ephesians 6:17)

The story is told of President Richard Nixon one evening in Washington. The next day a huge demonstration against his policies in Vietnam was to be mounted by young people in particular. Thousands were gathering and the President could not sleep. Restlessly he phoned friends all over the nation to talk to them. He played some music but that did not calm him either.

Eventually the President went out in the wee hours of the morning and much to his Secret Servicemen's consternation he got out of his car at the Abraham Lincoln memorial and started to talk to some of the protestors already gathered there, awaiting the demonstration the next day. He then took his valet, a man called Sanchez up to Capitol Hill and told him that he wanted to show him around. The curator of the building simply could not believe his eyes that the President wanted into the place at such an hour.

As the President was showing his valet his first seat as a Congressman and other highlights of the place a black cleaning lady espied the President. She was cleaning brass at the time. She approached him and reaching into her pocket drew out a Bible and asked him to sign it. He instantly agreed and as he signed his name bemoaned the fact "we" don't read the Bible enough, these days. "I read it all the time, Mr President!", the lady replied. He then began to tenderly reminisce about his godly mother.

Interesting, isn't it, that in all the United States on that momentous evening the one who could calm the President down in the dark night of his soul was a precious Bible loving cleaning lady on Capitol Hill! The Word of God is truly mighty to bring down strongholds and even to arrest the attention of a distraught President. Selah.

August *twenty-third*

> *"Praying always with all prayer and supplication in the Spirit"*
> (Ephesians 6:18)

This is a call to pray in the Spirit on all occasions with all kinds of prayers and requests. Prayer is not, please note, an additional piece of armour. It is something that is to pervade all our Christian warfare. A very important question to ask when considering prayer is "Why pray?" We pray, for a start, because the Lord Jesus prayed. He began his ministry with prayer (Luke 3:21). He prayed early in the morning (Mark 1:35). He prayed at the end of the day (Mark 6:46). He prayed when in great demand (Luke 5:15-16). He prayed before making important decisions (Luke 6:12). He prayed before accomplishing great miracles (Matthew 15:36; Matthew 14:22-23; Mark 9:14-29). His ministry ended in prayer (Luke 23:46). He is still praying for us today (Hebrews 7:25).

In his book on prayer ("Between heaven and earth" Harper Collins,1997) the author Ken Gire gives some very helpful answers to the question, "Why do we pray?" In part four of his book (pp.79-152) he puts it this way: "Why pray? Because we are grateful. This kind of prayer is called thanksgiving. Why pray? Because we are sinners and need forgiveness. This kind of prayer is called confession. Why pray? Because Jesus Christ is Lord. This kind of prayer is consecration. Why pray? Because we need help. This kind of prayer is called petition." In today's text Paul highlights our petition prayers.He tells us that we ought to keep alert and persevere in our prayers. He particularly calls for prayer for fellow Christians.

It is very easy to get so absorbed in the busy world around us that we forget to "watch and pray" for the needs of others in the body of Christ. They need our prayers just as we need theirs. Anyone who has experienced trauma and suffering will know that the prayers of other Christians are of huge comfort at such a time. Let's remember that a battle is going on against believers at all times and the need for prayer support is always present. Notice the word "all" in our text. "Praying always" (i.e. "at all times"), with "all prayers", with "all perseverance" for "all saints". It is not occasional prayer that we are called to but constant prayer. The days are evil, the Lord is coming, the time is short, the battle is raging, so let us wake up in our prayer life. Here we will renew our strength, here we will have communion with God, here we will become mighty overcomers. So pray, Christian pray!

August *twenty-fourth*

"And for me"
(Ephesians 6:19)

Paul asks for prayer for himself. Does personal prayer work? Imagine a small, poverty stricken house in London. In that house lived a very hard working woman, her back was bent because of years at the wash tub. Taking in washing was her only source of income. Despite the pressures of her life she prayed constantly for her son who was press-ganged into Navy service and ended up a slave of the wife of a slave owner in Africa. Elizabeth Newton prayed that her son would find the Saviour. She died before her prayers were answered.

Answered? Were they what! Her son John was eventually converted in the middle of a horrendous storm in the middle of the Atlantic ocean on board a slave ship. He was used to lead thousands of people to Christ and his famous hymn "Amazing Grace" is still sung around the world. John Newton was used to bring a learned but sceptical man called Thomas Scott to the Lord Jesus. Later Thomas Scott's writings led a man called William Cowper to Christ and Cowper became one of the most powerful Christian poets in his day ("God moves in mysterious way his wonders to perform" etc.). Newton was, of course, used by God to help the great William Wilberforce to faith. He also encouraged him to stay in the House of Commons where he became one of the greatest statesmen of history. Wilberforce was then used by God to abolish the slave trade.

Just a few weeks ago I was preaching at some services in Normandale in Minneapolis, Minnesota. There one evening a blind Afro-American Christian sang some beautiful solos. He gave me the loan of a very, very, old book to peruse and I discovered it was published in 1810! It turned out to be the works of John Newton and it contained poems I have never come across before. As I leafed through those old yellowed pages I marvelled that such, a wicked, blasphemous, cruel, godless man ever found Christ. Millions of people still go on being touched by his witness. The inspiring thing is that we can trace all that blessing to the prayers of a woman bent over a wash tub in a poverty stricken house in London all those years ago. No wonder Paul asked the Christians to pray for him. No wonder.

"More things are wrought by prayer,
Than this world dreams of. Wherefore, let thy voice
Rise like a fountain for me night and day".

Alfred Lord Tennyson
(Idylls of the King)

August *twenty-fifth*

*"That I may open
my mouth boldly to
make known the
mystery of the
Gospel"*
(Ephesians 6:19)

Have you ever wondered why great spiritual awakenings come? Have you ever considered why great exponents of the Gospel have come on the scene with incredible courage to the blessing of multitudes? There are three answers. (1) Prayer! (2) Prayer! (3) Prayer! Take the 16th and 17th Century. The church was staggering along, crippled by dead orthodoxy. Christian leaders in America decided to develop "prayer societies" which were small cells of Christians meeting in homes. They also organised similar cells in Schools, Colleges and Churches.

Meanwhile in Europe Count Zinzendorf gathered Christians from across Europe. Prayer made the Christians of one mind. The whole history of the church changed. The great awakening of 1725-1740 came out of that united effort in prayer touching America, England and parts of Europe. Millions became Christians and up-front were people like Wesley, Whitfield and Jonathan Edwards.

As a result of the awakening another prayer movement called "The Concert of prayer" gathered Christians to pray for an outpouring of God's Spirit. At one of those gatherings William Carey was called to India and the second great awakening in America came in the 1800.

I have preached in Korea in modern times and witnessed the extraordinary effect of concentrated prayer. What shall we say of the church in Africa which, according to statistics originally produced by the Interdenominational Foreign Mission Association in co-operation with the U.S. Centre for World Mission and reprinted in " A.D. 2000 and Beyond" November/December 1990, is increasing by 20,000 people per day on average? According to the same source the church in China is growing by an average of 28,000 people per day and conservative estimates indicate that there are in China between 40 and 50 million Christians. We are also told that 3,500 new churches are opening every week world-wide .The vast majority of evangelical churches in the world are now found, by far, in the Third World. We need another great movement of prayer in the West again. Will it start with you?

August *twenty-sixth*

"That I may open my mouth boldly"
(Ephesians 6:19)

What have we not missed in our Christians lives by not speaking up when it was necessary? We know that God will powerfully use what we say in witness for Him, but we hold back. Are you like that? Would you allow me to give you some advice I learned long ago about witnessing? I learned it through a study by Paul Little in a little book called "How to give away your faith" published by Inter Varsity Press. It was a little section on the story of the woman of Samaria that really helped me.

Here was a woman who was contemptible to Jews because of her faith. Researching the backgrounds of the Samaritans' religion I have found that it was based on the Pentateuch (the first five books of the bible) alone. At one Passover during the Governship of Coponius (A.D.6-9) some Samaritans invaded and polluted the holy place by scattering human bones in the porches. Samaritans were, after that, excluded from the services. They were cursed in the temple and their food was considered unclean. Of course apart from her despised faith, the woman had had five husbands and the one she now had was not her husband.

This woman now comes to a well by which the tired and thirsty Saviour is sitting. How could he ever begin to witness to her? Watch his approach. First he makes contact socially. He spoke to her. He identified with the woman despite the fact that the religious differences between them were great. Next he found something he had in common with the woman and that became his bridge of communication. Notice that he did not get right to the point immediately and boldly. What would Christ the Saviour of the world and the woman of Samaria have in common? They were both thirsty. He began with water and asked her for a drink. That simple request led him, eventually, to her very soul.

He then aroused interest by speaking of living water. Notice that he did not at first explain what it was all about. He did not go too far. He did not condemn either; as she answered him about her husband, her own sin itself condemned her. He hadn't come to condemn her; he had come to save her. Let us learn not to condemn. He also stuck to the main issues. When she tried to talk about where the Samaritans worshipped and where the Jews worshipped he told her that God the Father was looking for people to worship Him in spirit and in truth. Then he boldly confronted her with his Messianic claim and she was faced with a decision to be either for him or against him. Do you see the process? Then try to follow it. The Apostle Paul did and he was asking for prayer that he might do it boldly. Got it?

August *twenty-seventh*

*"To make known
the mystery of the
Gospel"*
(Ephesians 6:19)

Let's pause and think deeply about the context of Paul's prayer request in today's text. He asks that he may be given "clarity" and "courage" in his making known the mystery of the Gospel.

John Stott points out (Stott, p. 287) that Paul uses the word "parresia" twice, first as a noun and then as a verb in the expressions "that I may open my mouth boldly" (verse 19) and "that I may speak boldly" (verse 20). The first reference seems to refer to the need for clarity in his communication and the second for courage.

These are vital words to understand in the communication of the Gospel. You can have communicators who are very bold in their Christian witness but are muddled and mixed up in the way they present it. It is absolutely vital to be clear with our courage.

Others in their communication are extremely lucid but they are terrified! Fear of what others think of them and what might happen to them as a result of their witness makes them ineffective witnesses. We need courage to face the enemy but the Lord will give us that courage no matter how formidable our foe. Ask God, then, for clarity and courage in your witness. Paul certainly got his prayers answered, didn't he? So will we. All around us people will benefit as a result.

August *twenty-eighth*

*"For which I am an
ambassador in
chains"*
(Ephesians 6:20)

The other evening I happened to dine in company with the ambassador of a certain country. At my table was one of his Scotland Yard detectives who was a most interesting individual. He told me he once earned "Royal Slipper" money. "Royal Slipper" money? That was pay for a policeman wearing slippers while he passed the Royal apartments in Buckingham Palace at night! The ambassador obviously had enemies and needed to be guarded day and night.

If you are an ambassador you must, I think, have an extremely difficult job. Fine if everything goes well between the country you are in and the country you represent. But if anything goes wrong who is called onto " the carpet"? You are! You also must have great balance in your approach to your work for if you get too close to the country you are in you will not represent your own country too well. You must also watch and balance every word and action in your life because people judge your country by what you do and say.

Paul was an ambassador for Christ. He was an ambassador, though, in chains. Normally an ambassador would be granted diplomatic immunity and could not be imprisoned by those to whom he was sent, but not this one. In chains though he was, see how this great Christian sees himself. He sees himself as a representative of Christ and one through whom Christ speaks. He sees no embarrassment by his imprisonment. In ancient times on festive occasions ambassadors wore ornamental chains as a mark of the prestige of the country they represented. Paul saw his chains as a fitting symbol of his link to his crucified but now risen and exalted Lord.

Now, then, Christian are you in a tough spot because of your commitment to Christ and his Gospel? Remember who you are because you too are an ambassador for Christ. May you, like Paul, speak in your difficult circumstances "as you ought to speak"? The right word in the right place and even emperors' households can be reached by the Gospel (see Philippians 4:22). Paul writes in Philippians that "it has become evident to the whole palace guard and to all the rest that my chains are in Christ" (Philippians 1:13). If God can use Paul's chains for the furtherance of His kingdom in difficult times at the heart of the Roman Empire, He can certainly use your difficult circumstances for the same purpose in your day and generation.

August *twenty-ninth*

> *"But that you also may know my affairs and how I am doing, Tychicus, a beloved brother and faithful minister in the Lord, will make all things known to you; whom I have sent to you for this very purpose, that you may know our affairs, and that he may comfort your hearts"*
> (Ephesians 6:21)

Paul had a genius for friendship. No person in the New Testament had fiercer enemies but few had better friends. One of them was Tychicus, the letter carrier. In our day of e-mail and fast postage the role of the letter carrier is obscured. In Paul's day things were very different. Private letters were carried by private messengers or were sent along by people who were known to be travelling to the desired destination. If the letter carrier was a close friend of the sender then the letter carrier would be expected to give all the news or further detail of the contents of the letter.

Tychicus, when he carried the Ephesian letter was carrying a document which, in God's hands, was going to carry many a believer to highest ground. As he walked the dusty roads, over hills and mountain passes he carried price-less truth. Paul entrusted him with it and he did his job well and untold millions have benefited.

Tychicus couldn't write a letter like Paul could he? No, but he could deliver it. One couldn't do without the other. The letter carried great theology, sublime doctrine and exquisite exposition, but, for all its God breathed contents, the Christians in Ephesus needed a human face to encourage them as well. Tychicus was that human face and he had a ministry of encouragement and comfort. The letter writer and letter carrier have both gone to their reward but their works follow them. Beloved Tychicus is an inspiration to all who serve the Lord in doing the mundane tasks of the kingdom. He shows us that Christian truth is all very well and good but carried by a loving heart and a friendly face it is even better.

August *thirtieth*

> *"Peace to the brethren and love with faith, from God the Father and the Lord Jesus Christ"*
> (Ephesians 6:23)

Ancient correspondents ended their letters with a wish for their readers. So does Paul for his. He wishes them peace and love and faith from God our Father and the Lord Jesus Christ. If only the world knew and understood where these wonderful things are sourced.

I will always remember listening at a Convention one evening to Elvis Presley's stepbrother speak. He told how the world famous singer was approached by one of his entourage."This girl keeps ringing me", he said, "and says that it is high time I was living for Jesus. What do you think, Elvis?" "It is", replied Elvis, "high time we were all living for Jesus". Three days later Elvis was dead. He had lived the latter years of his life in a horrendously zany way showing deep restlessness. He knew, though, where true peace and love could be found. They could be found by faith in Jesus Christ. Sadly he lived for other things which could not deliver on the things he needed most.

Looking back over the 20th Century as I write in its last few dying days I would have to say that peace is not a word that springs to mind to describe its history. In the First World War, (1914-18), the total dead from all nations was 10 million. In the Second World War (1939-45), 55 million people died. I think also of the purges of Stalin and the purges of Mao Tse Tung and the slaughter in Vietnam. I think of the killing fields of Cambodia and the unbelievable slaughter of Rwanda. I think more recently of Kosovo and East Timor. Even as this Millennium peters out peace between nations and peace between people is as elusive as it was in Paul's day. Love is what people desperately seek but where in the world can they find it? Faith, even at this hour is still one of the most divisive of words.

When "The Times" asked a number of writers to contribute an essay on the topic "What it wrong with the world?" they received one reply which was somewhat brief.

Dear Sirs,
I am
Sincerely Yours,
G.K.Chesterson.

The plain fact is that world wide peace and love and faith will not be known until the Lord returns. Peter in his great sermon at Jerusalem put it this way: "But those things, which God foretold by the mouth of his prophets, that Christ would suffer, he has thus fulfilled. Repent therefore and be converted, that your sins may be blotted out, so that times of refreshing may come from the presence of the Lord, and that he may send Jesus Christ, who was preached to you before, whom Heaven must receive until the times of restoration of all things, of which God has spoken by the mouth of all his holy prophets since the world began" (Acts 3:18-21).

As we await the return of our Lord and the great restoration that He will bring, the message of Ephesians is clear. It is that any individual who seeks and finds God in Christ whether in the Ephesus of Paul's day or in the atomic and jet age in which we live, they will find a peace, faith and love which the world simply cannot deliver. It is a peace, faith and love which, once found, will not be taken away.

August *thirty-first*

"Grace be with all those who love our Lord Jesus Christ in sincerity. Amen"
(Ephesians 6:24)

It has been a challenging climb with you, my reader, up the slopes of Ephesians, the Switzerland of the Bible. As we have surveyed our resources we have found them to be truly magnificent. We have spiritual blessings beyond fathoming, we have a salvation and a redemption which is matchless, we have a power available to us which is enough to overcome the grave itself. On top of all this we have a unity which is unbreakable, riches which are unsearchable, and a love whose width, length, depth and height which passes knowledge. We have an armour which can protect us from everything the enemy can throw at us. We are part of a new creation which can impact our home and public life and touch a dark world with a message of hope.

As I have surveyed these things with you I have sensed a deep conviction in my heart, soul and life. In the midst of all the problems we face locally, nationally and internationally, there is a Saviour who is Lord. All of these incredible things are mine because, I am, as Ephesians teaches, "In Christ" along with all those millions who have trusted Him. It has nothing to do with sects, denominations; and lists of rules, philosophies of men or women, or schools of thought. It has nothing to do with money, or education, or social position or status. It has nothing to do with the lack of things, either. All I have spiritually is because I belong, by God's grace, alone, to the Lord Jesus. I have found that the bottom line of everything is whether a person is "in" or "out" of Christ.

So Paul closes his letter by wishing God's grace on all those who love our Lord Jesus with undying love and unpolluted sincerity. In grace it all began, with grace it all continues, and through grace it will never, ever, end.

SEPTEMBER

Moses was about to climb the high ground of Mount Nebo in Moab. He would be able to view the Promised Land. His death, though, was imminent and after his death on Mount Nebo he would have the great honour of being buried by God.

First, though, Moses made a great speech to his people. The last words of great men are fascinating as were those of Moses. Speaking of God's blessings on Israel, Moses said, "As an eagle stirs up its nest, hovers over its young, spreading out its wings, taking them up, so the Lord alone led him and made him ride the heights of the earth."

So, this September, let's soar with the eagle. Mr. Bill Gothard of the Institute in Basic Youth Conflicts in Oak Brook, Illinois has published an intriguing book called, "The Eagle Story". I am assured that I can take some of Mr. Gothard's material and apply it to my own situation. I pray you and I will soon soar as the eagle to the highest ground.

September *first*

> *"Bless the Lord,*
> *O my soul .. Who*
> *satisfies your mouth*
> *with good things so*
> *that your youth is*
> *renewed like the*
> *eagle's"*
> (Psalm 103:1,5)

Eagles have been seen soaring almost motionless in near hurricane force winds; moving only the tips of their feathers to adjust for the varying wind speeds. It seems almost as if the eagle is nailed to the sky in a storm. It is not nailed. An eagle's amazing ability to manoeuvre has to do with those all important feathers. One eagle was found to have 7,182 feathers!

Each year the eagle is renewed, replacing every single feather in its entire body over a period of several months. The eagle, unlike other birds, is not severely handicapped because no two adjacent wing feathers fall out or moult at the same time. This enables the eagle to continue flying throughout the entire renewal process!

So it is that God's people are constantly renewed while serving Him. I preached for a week once, with my friend Dr. Alan Redpath who was then 75 years of age. I shall never forget praying with him in that Co. Wicklow town. One evening before we went out to preach: 'Lord,' he said, 'we want to serve you to our very last ounce of strength and to our very last drop of blood.' Amen, to that!

September *second*

> *"As an eagle*
> *stirs up its nest ... so*
> *the Lord"*
> (Deuteronomy 32:11)

Eagles mate for life and return to the same nest every year, making necessary repairs and additions. One pair of eagles was observed for 25 years in the same location. Their nest grew to be 20 feet deep and over 9 ft across! Support trees often give way under the ever increasing weight of such nests!

But staying in such a nest for all of its life will not get the young eaglet into the sky. The care of the parent is phenomenal, even to replacing its body shade with a layer of sticks and debris to shade the young from the sun's heat while it goes hunting. But the time must come for progress from the nest so the parents begin to stir the nest. It is time to move on.

We usually don't like it when the Lord stirs our nest. We are often very stubborn about it. But it is a call to a great adventure. You may think it cruel that you must lose your job, or change your job, or move house or that you do not get what you desire. Don't resist God's stirrings. He wants you to soar.

September *third*

> *"As an eagle ... hovers over its young"*
> (Deuteronomy 32:11)

In the brood of an eagle there is keen competition between eaglets. The first eaglet to hatch is usually the largest and demands the most food. The nestlings are fed by the mother eagle. The father does the hunting and the meal comes to be broken into bite-size portions for the eaglet. That breaking up of the food for the eaglets is vital to their survival.

A preacher once arrived to find only one man in his congregation to listen to his preaching: 'I will give him what I would have given a packed congregation.' he thought. When the service was over he asked his patient listener what he thought. 'I am a farmer,' said the man, 'if I went out with a full load of hay to feed my cattle and only one lonely critter showed up, I tell you one thing, I sure wouldn't dump the whole load on him!' Wise words.

Let's break the bread of God's word carefully to meet the needs of those we are feeding. He is a fool who gives a steak to a little baby and he is equally a fool who only feeds a grown person on milk.

September *fourth*

> *"I bore you on eagles' wings"*
> (Exodus 19:4)

After spending two or three months in the security of the nest the young eaglet is ready to learn to fly: the 'stirring up' process is over. The first flight is usually from the nest to a rock but on subsequent flights the adult eagle may actually accompany the eaglet using its primary feathers to create an air current which lifts the eaglet.

I was always of the impression that eagles actually carry their young on their wings, dropping them into the abyss and then diving to catch them, taking them higher each time. I always thought that by the principle of 'must do' being a good master eaglets learned to fly! Research with those who know of these things tell me that is aerodynamically impossible; the eaglets by the time they are ready to fly are too heavy for their parents to physically carry them on their wings. Rather, the eaglet flies itself and the parent creates the conditions for flight.

The primary meaning of the Hebrew word 'bare' in today's text means 'to lift'. When God puts someone out to serve Him or sends a Christian on an errand for Him He 'bares' them, He creates the 'air currents' to lift them to the task. No matter how difficult the day, God will bare His own on eagles' wings.

September *fifth*

"As the eagle ..."
(Deuteronomy 28:49)

The eagle's vision is exceptionally sharp: each eye has two areas of acute vision as compared with the human eye which has only one. The eyes are placed forward on the eagle's head giving him acute depth perception and this is very important as the eagle must know precisely when to pull out of a dive. The forward placement of its eyes also enables the eagle to see to each side, peripheral vision. The eagle's area of vision covers almost 270 degrees which is much more than a man's and this enables it to spot an object as small as a rabbit from a distance of almost two miles.

Another fascinating fact is that an eagle can see with its eyes shut. In addition to its normal pair of eyelids the eagle has a set of clear eyelids called 'nicitating membranes'. These eyelids can be closed for protection from the wind, hungry eaglets or the violence of the kill without affecting the eagle's vision.

Double vision is a great asset to the eagle but it is also of great asset to the Christian. Human eyes are wonderful but it is much better to have spiritual eyes as well. The young man with Elisha saw a huge army of Syrians but Elisha saw the mountains around him filled with chariots of fire as well. Use your double vision, Christian, as you live out your life today.

September *sixth*

> *"Riches ... fly away like an eagle towards heaven"*
> (Proverbs 23:5)

In the ancient world nothing was safe: moths went for clothes, rats went for poison, worms went for buried treasure, thieves broke into homes. Now, of course, modern man would argue all is changed, treasures can be protected, we have insecticides, rat poison, mouse traps, rust proof paints, burglar alarms, insurance, and lasers. Let us not be fooled because with all of man's devices his riches can still fly away as swiftly as an eagle toward heaven.

An eagle flies in storms when other birds seek shelter. So it is with riches when the storm of an economic slump comes, or inflation, or devaluation: man's riches fly away in a storm like an eagle toward heaven.

One great irreversible fact is that treasure in heaven can never fly away. It is incorruptible. What is it? It is the development of Christlike character. It is active endeavour to introduce others to Christ. It is investing money in causes whose dividends are everlasting. It is the only gilt edged security whose gilt will never tarnish. Let's set our heart on it.

September *seventh*

> *"The forth living creature was like a flying eagle"*
> (Revelation 4:7)

From Napoleon to the Romans, from Charlemagne to the United States the eagle has been the official symbol of nations and armies. There is something about the bird, its grace in flight, its royal pose, its size, its spread, its awesome power. An eagle gives people a feeling of fear and wonder at the same time. If the head of an eagle is studied carefully, just above each eye is a bone protrusion which extends over the eye much like a furrowed eyebrow. These protrusions lend to the eagle's face the human expression of decisiveness. If it were not there the eyes would look much like a chicken's, and with all due respect to the chicken, no nation or army on earth has a chicken as its symbol!

It is good to be decisive in life. We must not 'chicken out' of making important decisions and sticking by the consequences. How often the church seems to take no position on any issue and therefore loses its effectiveness.

Got a decision to make today? Then be decisive. And again, don't forget that old motto: 'Always gently refuse that which you intend to ultimately deny.'

September *eighth*

> *"Too wonderful for me ... The way of an eagle in the air"*
> (Proverbs 30:18-19)

Tack. It is a little word with great importance, especially in relation to wind direction. It applies to the eagle in the air just as much as a yacht at sea. God has built into the eagle's wings aerodynamic possibilities that give it the ability to change its tack when the wind changes direction. The eagle's wings are characterised by primary feathers which are separated at the tips like the fingers of a hand. The separations play a major role in the power and stability of the eagle in flight. Whirlpools of air are formed by each primary feather. These collide and cancel the drag effect on the wing, allowing the eagle to fly almost effortlessly.

Tack is so vital in the Christian life. The winds of change can come hurtling down from one direction this week and come hurtling up from another next week. God has made the Christian's body the temple of the Holy Spirit and because of the Spirit's power He can give the Christian the exact 'tack' needed to meet oncoming winds.

It was the same Spirit who guided Philip into the desert as guided Philip into Samaria. The Spirit said to Philip, "Go near and join thyself to this chariot." Philip ran and got up into the chariot the Ethiopian was riding in to discover he was reading a verse about Jesus! If Philip had not run he would have arrived at the wrong verse! The tack used was perfect. The Spirit behind such tack makes no mistakes.

September *ninth*

> *"As the eagle ...*
> *so with the Lord."*
> (Deuteronomy 28:49)

A soaring eagle, gliding effortlessly at altitudes of over 2,000 feet, can give the illusion that an eagle moves almost at a snail's pace. To the casual observer 'the monarch of the sky' appears sluggish. He is a fool who is so deceived by his eyes. When an eagle spots its prey it will turn sharply, fold its wings into a tight, aerodynamic formation and dive at speeds of up to 200 m.p.h. That's faster than a Porsche in the fast lane!

'As with the eagle .. so with the Lord', says our text: it was the last address to the children of Israel ever given by Moses and he knew what he was talking about. God's ways to the casual observer appear slow. People demand instant action from God and then say He is not there when He does not give it. When God does act the speed of light appears sluggish in comparison. Do not be deceived, God is not passive at any time. God demands all men, everywhere, to repent and trust the Saviour. If they do not, He will act. The judgement of God when it falls is swift and he who hardens his neck will suddenly, says the Scripture, be destroyed and that without remedy. Again and again the swiftness of the eagle is emphasised in the Bible, and Moses in today's text knew God's judgement at first hand and so he compared its swiftness to the eagle's. Let's keep it in mind: whether in judgement on the unbeliever or in the chastisement on the believer, God can move very swiftly.

September *tenth*

> *"Believe not every*
> *spirit, but try the*
> *spirits whether they*
> *are of God"*
> (1 John 4:1)

An eagle is a majestic bird but it can be brought down. A trapper can lay out some fish on a daily basis to lure an eagle in. Once the daily habit of eating the fish is established a trap can be sprung. The most deadly traps are hidden but if an eagle follows its instincts it will be able to see visible evidences of their presence. Why would fish be lying in grass day after day? It is not their natural habitat.

The devil's incognito is one of his cleverest tricks and he can appear to us as an Angel of Light. So we must test every sermon we hear, every book we read, all the teaching we come across with the Word of God. Things that are unfamiliar should be very suspect and very weighed up before being accepted. The wiles of the devil are set to stop us soaring and to trap us and cage us for the rest of our lives. It is a sad thing to have a saved soul and a wasted life. Let's just remember: hidden dangers have visible evidences. Make sure you look for them.

September *eleventh*

"For we wrestle not against flesh and blood, but against principalities, against powers, against the rulers of the darkness of this world, against spiritual wickedness in high places"
(Ephesians 6:12)

We want to continue on yesterday's theme today: the most dangerous enemies are unseen. The eagle who ignores this can be trapped and so can the Christian. There are unseen principalities and powers operating in the sphere of invisible reality against the church of Jesus Christ. They have no moral principles, no code of honour, no higher feelings. They are utterly unscrupulous, ruthless and cunning. Darkness is their habitat, the darkness of falsehood and sin.

Unfortunately, today, the fact of the existence of these hierarchies of evil is being forgotten by the church. Everything is being attributed to the psychological. Was the attack of Satan on the lovely children of Bethlehem, through Herod's selfish ambition, psychological? Were the fiendish insinuations of the devil on the Saviour in the wilderness just mere imagination? Why did that bloodlike sweat pour down that sacred face in Gethsemane? Satan was sorely tempting the sinless Saviour. Why did the Lord Jesus say to Peter 'Get behind me Satan', when Peter had protested against the Lord's determination to go to Calvary? Satan can attack you through your very best friends. Let's never forget that Satan is a master at covering his tracks.

September *twelfth*

> *"And when the woman saw the tree was good for food ... she took its fruit and ate"*
> (Genesis 3:6)

Deadly traps always appeal to basic needs. What works in trapping an eagle also worked in trapping Eve. Satan attacked Eve along the line of her appetite. He did the very same when he tempted the hungry Lord Jesus in the wilderness; "If you are the Son of God, command that these stones become bread." When Demas left the path of serving God, Paul, his colleague, said "Demas has forsaken me having loved this present world!" Satan had tempted Demas with present comforts as Demas wrestled with the persecution, loneliness and imprisonment afforded to a keen servant of God in the early days of the Roman Empire. Demas left the track for the comforts of by-path meadow.

Let's watch for the attack of Satan through our basic needs. From Eve to David, from Adam to Peter, we can be trapped and led to deny the life of faith and to deny the Lord His rightful place in our hearts and lives.

September *thirteenth*

> *"Obey those who rule over you, and be submissive, for they watch out for your souls"*
> (Hebrews 13:17)

A trapper, once he has lured an eagle in by fish, then sets up a net over the fish. It is a strong hoop net with a long handle dug into the ground. Fish are set under the net. The eagle swoops down for his fish and is, at first, very suspicious of the net. He flies around it, eyes it carefully and approaches with caution. With beak and claw he pulls the fish from under the net and hops quickly back. The eagle has senses to detect danger but ignores them to get food. The next day he goes under the net without apprehension.

Again and again God uses not only the Holy Spirit to warn us but wise parents, godly friends, spiritual pastors, wise elders. Often Satan tempts us to throw aside their cautions and to go our own way. We ignore their advice, if it is Bible based, at our peril. I remember a warning coming from a preacher in a pulpit, once, and unknown to him, it was so relevant to the person sitting beside me that the person gripped my arm with fear. Don't ignore such messages. They are warnings of hidden danger.

September *fourteenth*

*"Do not be deceived;
God is not mocked:
for whatever a man
sows, that he will
also reap."*
(Galatians 6:7)

We all love something for nothing but everything has its price. An eagle soon discovers that free fish leads to the trapper's net and often the Zoo's cage. I stood one summer's day and gazed at a golden eagle in Edinburgh Zoo and I must admit his misery caused me long, long thoughts. The caged eagle looks the saddest of birds.

In life adultery appears to be as soft as down but, in the end, it is a screaming vulture. Compromise seems to be an easy option but in the end undermines the very principles of living and brings collapse. Laziness in the form of a little folding of the hands and a little more sleep seems the thing but poverty is soon knocking on the door. Everything has its price. The wages of sin seems easy money at the time but the actual wages of sin is death. Watch free provisions for they have hidden costs. Whatever a man sows, that he will also reap.

September *fifteenth*

*"For he who sows
to his flesh, will of
the flesh reap
corruption, but
he who sows to the
Spirit will of
the Spirit reap
everlasting life."*
(Galatians 6:8)

There are two root causes behind the circumstances which affect our lives: God or Satan. These things that come are not mere coincidences or accidents. We must discern the source. I often feel today's text perfectly sums up success or failure in the Christian life.

In the Christian life there are definitely two powers struggling, the one against the other. The law of the Spirit of life in Christ is greater than the law of sin and death because Satan was defeated at the cross. Christ faced Satan where he exercised power and broke that power. The Lord made a public example of Satan and overcame him and if we submit to the Lord Jesus we will overcome Satan too.

An eagle is also subject to a law which would drag it down. If an eagle in flight folded its wings it would plummet by the law of gravity. Despite the power of gravity, the eagle overcomes it. We cannot overcome the law of sin and death, but in the Christ who bears us on eagle's wings we can overcome.

September *sixteenth*

> *"I will say to my
> soul ... take your
> ease"*
> (Luke 12:19)

Our aim should never be to work for a life of ease. Easy fish costs the eagle freedom. The rich man of the Bible thought he had a long time to enjoy ease. He forgot about his soul and the reality of death and God called him a fool. He died that night.

Soberly I write it, my reader: what if this were your last day on earth? It could be. How do you plan to spend it? Are you dreaming of ease and rest and merriment? Don't let such dreams dull your alertness to impending danger. The Bible says that it is better to go to the house of mourning than the house of feasting. It makes us wise up. We get our priorities right. Easy meat and a life of ease does not prepare us for eternity. Just as there is no Utopia of easy fish for an eagle on this earth so there is no Utopia of rest and ease on this earth. Anyway, what would it profit anyone if they were to gain the whole world and lose their soul?

September *seventeenth*

> *"Sir, we wish to see
> Jesus."*
> (John 12:21)

Some Greeks expressed the desire to see Jesus. Through Philip and Andrew they sought an introduction. At the very moment those Greeks came Israel had decisively turned against the Lord Jesus. What a sore temptation it must have been to welcome this approach from out beyond Israel in the wider world He had come to win. But he immediately said 'Unless an ear of wheat falls into the ground and dies, it remains alone; but if it dies, it produces much fruit ... now my soul is troubled.'

Why was His soul troubled? The answer is that He was being tempted to by-pass the cross and turn to the Gentiles. It was only if he were 'lifted up from the earth' He would draw all men to Him. Satan was using a lovely request to halt Calvary. Deadly traps look harmless until they are sprung. The eagle accepts the presence of the trap when he comes to eat the trapper's fish. It becomes part of his world. The Lord Jesus knew the deadly destruction of Satan's harmless looking traps and avoided them. So by His grace, must we.

September *eighteenth*

> *"Can a man take fire to his bosom and his clothes not be burned?"*
> (Proverbs 6:27)

The trapper now moves to catch the eagle. At the dead of night he ties a strong cord to the rim of the hoop. Then he runs the cord down to the ground, under a shallow root and into a nearby thicket. He pulls the cord. The net bends down until it covers the rock. When he releases the cord the net rebounds to its former position. He loosens the dirt at the base of the handle and after satisfying himself that all is in readiness, he baits the trap and creeps into the thicket to await the growing dawn.

Mighty wings are soon heard above him. This time there is no hesitation, the bird has been lured into accepting the structure as part of the established order. He starts to eat the fish. Suddenly there is a movement and, despite a last moment attempt by the eagle to spring free into the safety of the air, the trap is sprung and closes too swiftly for escape.

"Can a man take fire to his bosom and his clothes not be burned?", asks Scripture. No. Only pride and false confidence tell us we can enjoy the pleasures of sin and not get caught in sin's consequences. No more powerful figure than Samson strode across Israel. But he took fire to his bosom and his testimony for God was burnt alive. The eagle is no match for a trap once sprung and neither are we.

September *nineteenth*

> *"Do you not know that to whom you present yourselves as slaves to obey, you are slaves of the one whom you obey, whether of sin to death, or of obedience to righteousness?"*
> (Romans 6:16)

Two possibilities face a trapped eagle: captivity or death. No matter how furiously he beats his wings, tears with his beak, clutches with his talons, he will find any effort to free himself only results in greater destruction and bondage. Unless the victim is freed the azure blue will know him no more.

So it is when Satan's trap of sin is sprung in our lives. Unless someone gets us out we've had it. Praise God there is a way out. It has to do with yielding to the Lord Jesus and this brings incredible freedom from the bondage Satan brings. For the next few days we shall study how the Saviour faced Satan's attacks and how he overcame them. Meanwhile watch to whom you yield for:

"He breaks the power of cancelled sin,
He sets the prisoner free,
His blood can make the foulest clean,
His blood avails for me".

September *twentieth*

"No temptation has overtaken you except such as is common to man; but God is faithful, who will not allow you to be tempted beyond what you are able, but with the temptation will also make the way of escape, that you may be able to bear it."
(I Corinthians 10:13)

Recently I was suddenly tempted to do wrong. The temptation was strong but the Lord gave the victory and the temptation passed. Suddenly I felt guilty, unclean. I shouldn't have. There is no sin in being tempted, the sin is yielding to temptation. It is important to remember that sin does not necessitate sinning. With every temptation God will provide a way of escape.

When the Lord was tempted in the wilderness He was alone. Solitude does not prevent temptation, in fact it often greatly increases it. But for Him, as for us, there was a way of escape. Learn this principle and learn it well for even to the very brink of Jordan you will find Satan nibbling at your heels. When tempted pray "Lord Jesus come close to me now and shew me the way of escape." He always will, if you ask Him.

September *twenty-first*

"Then Jesus was led up by the Spirit into the wilderness to be tempted by the devil. And when He had fasted forty days and forty nights, afterwards He was hungry. Now when the tempter came to Him he said, 'If you are the Son of God, command that these stones become bread.'"

(Matthew 4: 3)

Notice the setting of this great onslaught of Satan against the Lord Jesus. It was in the wilderness. It was a shimmering, solitary, burning wilderness. The Bible has a lot to say about the wilderness because the nation of Israel had failed there so miserably. Now Satan attacks in the wilderness again. The timing of his attack was also very significant. The Lord Jesus had just been baptised and the voice from the heavens had said, "This is my beloved Son in whom I am well pleased." Satan's favourite time for attack is following a time when God has been honoured. Elijah after Carmel, David after Goliath, even Paul after his great writing is struck with "a thorn in the flesh, the messenger of Satan to buffet me." After blessing comes buffeting.

Notice that he does not give a point blank denial, he just casts a doubt, 'If thou be the Son of God.' The Lord had proved for 30 years that He was just that but the devil casts doubt over it. And he will do the same with you. Recently, maybe, you enjoyed a special time of blessing from God. You would never doubt again, you said. But the devil has come and cast doubt by saying "It was just excitement, there was nothing in it!" Remember those times at the Lord's table when the Lord drew near? The devil calls it "just imagination". Don't let Satan rob you of past blessings or past experiences of God.

Notice that the Lord Jesus often used His power to meet human need: Cana of Galilee and the 5,000 on the mountainside knew that. But Jesus was not going to be pushed into making stones bread at the devil's instigation. The lesson is clear, trounce, by God's power, Satan's "If's" and don't be pushed into the good to miss the better.

September *twenty-second*

> *"But he answered and said, 'It is written, 'Man shall not live by bread alone, but by every word that proceeds from the mouth of God'"*
> (Matthew 4:4)

If the Lord needed to have recourse to the Scriptures as "The sword of the spirit which is the Word of God" it is certain that we do. The Lord could have used angelic force against Satan, or, He could have unveiled His glory, or, He could have used devastating logic and reason, but He used the best weapon, and, so must we. His adversary shifted his point of attack constantly, because error can have many forms, but the Lord continually used His one defence: the Word of God.

The Lord also displayed a most marvellous trust in His Heavenly Father. He was willing to do without food if necessary in order to do His Father's will. Where Eve fell, He overcame. Two more lessons for every Christian are clear from our text: use God's Word as a defence against every attack of the evil one and trust in God even if it means going without to do so.

September *twenty-third*

> *"Then the devil took Him up into the holy city, set Him on the pinnacle of the temple, and said to Him, 'If you are the Son of God, throw yourself down. For it is written, 'He shall give his angels charge concerning you,' and 'in their hands they shall bear you up, lest you dash your foot against a stone'"*
> (Matthew 4:4)

Satan is an excellent theologian: he is good at quoting Scripture. So, the Lord Jesus trusts in His father, does he? Right: there is a promise in a marvellous Psalm of safety for those who do that, is there not? Satan quotes it while tempting the Saviour to do the very opposite. He was wanting Him to either get killed or make a public exhibition of Himself. He would have been "a King for a day" had it come off. But those who would have marvelled would have remained firmly in Satan's camp at the same time.

It was in a high and Holy place the Saviour was tempted. High and Holy places are a favourite hunting ground for Satan. If your cup is full of spiritual blessing, watch out. Satan would just love to spill it all out. It will take a steady hand to carry it. Walk humbly and carefully and do not tempt the Lord your God by trying to force His hand to do anything. No jumps for fame, please. Trust Him and all will be well.

September *twenty-fourth*

"Again, the devil took Him up on an exceedingly high mountain, and showed Him all the kingdoms of the world and their glory. And he said to Him, 'All these things I will give you, if you will fall down and worship me'"

Matthew 4:8-9

Ambition is a very powerful force in a person's life. Obviously the Lord's main ambition was to do His Father's will but Satan, the grasper, assaults the Lord Jesus with the offer of the kingdoms of this world if He will worship him. Here is the very heart of the tempter. Satan wants world dominion by disobedience: the Lord Jesus was going to have world dominion by obedience by taking on Himself the form of a servant. Satan just could not break down the Saviour's single-mindedness: no compromise or inducement could make Him turn back.

How did the Lord harrow Satan on this temptation? He had no discussion on the matter, He harrowed him by not asking him to go but by telling him to go. Does it work? I was staying with a family recently and after the evening service was over I sat down to an excellent meal with my friends. My hostess had had a difficult day. "Do you know what I did?", she smiled, "I was so tired of Satan's attacks all day, I simply opened the door and told him to get out!" I was glad Satan had got that treatment and not me! My hostess was right in line with Scripture: "Away with you, Satan!" said Jesus.

September *twenty-fifth*

"There is therefore now no condemnation to those who are in Christ Jesus."

Romans 8:1

Calvary has inflicted on Satan a fatal blow. At Calvary the Lord Jesus stooped to conquer. Satan means "accuser", and, as a result of Calvary every man, woman and child who hides in His completed work cannot be condemned. The occult and all other cults, indeed the whole world of demonic activity have been ultimately robbed of their power by Calvary.

Death and sin, disobedience and rebellion were overcome at Calvary and such was the size of the victory that whenever Christ's name is named in faith, Satan is bound to flee. Where the first man failed the second man from Heaven won. Lift up your heart today and thank God for Jesus. As September nears its end let this word ring in your heart in your afternoon walk amidst falling leaves. No condemnation! No condemnation! Calvary is the greatest barrier to Hell and the very door to Heaven.

September *twenty-sixth*

"That I may know Him and the power of His resurrection, and the fellowship of His sufferings"
Philippians 3:10

We have, in a spiritual sense, seen the eagle released over the last few days. What now? The answer is that turbulent winds will batter us constantly until our "soaring" days are over. We must expect it. As September days draw to a close let's think of what benefits turbulent winds will bring.

The happy truth is that turbulent winds cause the eagle to fly higher! There is tremendous lifting power in the thermal updrafts of turbulent winds. These updrafts cause the eagle to reach great heights as it soars with them. The turbulent winds of persecution that came against the early church only caused the church to grow as they soared spiritually with the situation, going everywhere preaching the Word. Make sure you use every turbulence that comes your way today to soar for God. Rejoice when the turbulence comes. The power of Christ's resurrection will carry you far, the fellowship of His sufferings will bring you joy unspeakable.

September *twenty-seventh*

"You are the salt of the earth."
Matthew 5:13

Turbulent winds give the eagle a larger view. Remember an eagle, from a height of half a mile, can survey an area some four and a half square miles! As the winds of life cause you to wait on the Lord and you soar as a result you will be able to see things that no one else can see. Is it true that Peter and Andrew knew more than Aristotle and Plato did? Is it true that those disciples of Christ described by some onlookers as 'without grammar and idiots' had knowledge the philosophies of men could not match? Jesus said so: "You are the salt of the earth," he said, "You are the light of the world." A fisherman, the light of the world? Why? Because he knew the Lord.

So it is, in your office, or school, or factory, or shop, if you know the Lord you can shed more light than Einstein on the real issues behind this universe. God says He has hidden things from the wise and the prudent and revealed them to babes. So shine, Christian, shine.

September *twenty-eighth*

> *"But the Lord ...*
> *strengthened me"*
> 2 Timothy 4:17

Turbulent winds lift the eagle above harass-ment. At lower elevations the eagle is often harassed by suspicious crows, disgruntled hawks and other smaller birds. As the eagle soars higher it leaves all these distractions behind.

So it is when we live by the law of life in Christ. Listen to Paul writing to Timothy: "All those in Asia have turned away from me ... Demas has forsaken me ... Alexander the coppersmith did me much harm ... at my first answer no man stood with me, but all men forsook me." From this writing we learn that the winds of loneliness and desertion were fiercely against him. Suddenly, in the midst of it all, up comes this mighty sentence: "But the Lord stood with me and strengthened me, so that the message might be preached fully through me, and that all the Gentiles might hear. And I was delivered out of the mouth of the lion. And the Lord will deliver me from every evil work and preserve me for his heavenly kingdom. To him be glory forever and ever. Amen." Some soaring, isn't it!

September *twenty-ninth*

> *"... and not be weary"*
> Isaiah 40:31

Turbulent winds allow the eagle to use less effort. The wings of the eagle are designed for gliding in the winds. The feathers' structure prevents stalling, reduces the turbulence, and produces a relatively smooth ride with minimum effort, even in rough winds. The rougher it gets the smoother the ride.

How many an unbeliever has gazed in disbelief at the strength a believer gets in the face of great odds? A lady once told me that the first great influence to touch her life regarding the reality of the Gospel was to watch the believers and unbelievers die in a hospital where she worked. The believers' faith had stirred her to faith in Christ. May God give us incorruptible faith: a faith that burns like a fire that cannot be put out. The greater the storm, the more we can lean on what God has provided for us to combat the turbulence. We can do all things through Christ who strengthens us.

September *thirtieth*

> *"But those who wait on the Lord shall renew their strength; they shall mount up with wings like eagles"*
> Nehemiah 8:10

The eagle uses the winds to soar and glide for long periods of time. In the winds the eagle first glides in long shallow circles downward and then spirals upward in a thermal draft. The eagle must feed and care for its young. It must fight off enemies and come down to earth, often. Long soaring, despite the nitty-gritty, is a tremendous part of its life and universal appeal.

With due respect to the parrot, I prefer the lifestyle of the eagle, don't you? The parrot loves to be stroked, to repeat what it hears and, of course, it keeps eating those dry seeds day in and day out. The eagle, though, soars up there in the azure blue.

The world is full of people who are parrot-like. Thy just keep on repeating what they hear others say and the repetitive nature of their lives is incredibly boring. I'm glad the Scripture takes the eagle as a metaphor for what true spirituality is like, aren't you? Wait upon the Lord and you will soar. It's guaranteed.

OCTOBER

W e speak of Zion's hill. Zion, or Jerusalem as we know it, was taken by David and his men. They took it by surprise. "You will not get in here," said the occupants, the Jebusites, "even the blind and the lame can ward you off." They were wrong. It became known as the city of David and his city was to know many incredible events within its boundaries. In David's life, though, few days were to match the day he brought the ark to Jerusalem.

David wrote a psalm about that great zenith of his life. In the psalm he poured honour, praise, glory, power and majesty upon the Lord. Here was the great centre of the resources he had drawn upon in his life. The psalm was delivered into the hand of Asaph, the leader of Israel's praise, the day the ark was "set in the midst of the tabernacle David had erected for it." It is as fresh today as the day it was delivered. Let's spend some time during the month of October enjoying it.

October *first*

> *"And there was war again, and David went out and fought with the Philistines"*
> (I Samuel 19:8)

A new month. This year has, perhaps, been a very troubled one for you. You thought old arguments had been resolved but there is "war" again in your circumstances. You were trying to get your life into some sort of settled routine but crisis after crisis has arrived. Money problems have come. Ill health, maybe, is worrying you. Bereavement in your family has stunned you. Relationships have recently soured with one whom you first loved, deeply. A medical doctor friend of mine puts it down as "A conspiracy of things". The truth is, there always will be "war again", no matter how long we live on this present earth. What is the answer?

I have always found in my life that the main cause of discouragement and disappointment is a temporary loss of perspective. David's life shows us the true perspective for living like few other lives. He was, you will remember, training for reigning. So are you, Christian. This present trouble that you are experiencing will make you stronger, wiser, better. Learn from it. Experience brings patience and patience, hope. That hope is not "hope so". You will reign with Christ and there will be no more war.

October *second*

> *"So David fled and escaped, and went to Samuel at Ramah, and told him all that Saul had done to him. And he and Samuel went and stayed in Naioth"*
> (I Samuel 19:18)

It's good for a David to have a Samuel in his life. What if Samuel had said, "Sorry, David, I'm too busy being a judge to talk to you today". What if Samuel had let the fear of man become a snare to him? The court was anti-David and Samuel took his life into his own hands by identifying with this young man.

Is there a David knocking on your door? Because he is out of favour with the hierarchy, the establishment, the in-set, your association with him will be frowned on. Samuel read the situation clearly. David was putting God first and suffering for it and he must protect him and above all, listen to him. How many a Christian could have been inspired to go on for the Lord if only they had had a Samuel to sit and listen to their fears and hopes? How many a person would have become a Christian if only somebody had stopped to listen to their questions? Be careful in your busy life today; a David may call.

October *third*

"Then David fled from Naioth in Ramah"
(I Samuel 20:1)

There comes a time in all our lives when God begins to remove all the familiar things we lean on to make us lean on Him. Is that happening to you at the moment? It certainly happened to David. Let's trace it.

Take David's job; he had to flee from his work as a trusted officer in Saul's army (19:8-10). Take David's wife; Michal had to persuade David to escape for his life by letting him down through a window and putting a dummy in his bed (19: 11-12). Take David's mentor; Saul discovered where David and Samuel were hiding at Naioth and David had to flee again (20:1).

It is not a pleasant experience to have your props removed but if your props have become a substitute for the Lord you are in trouble. There is, in fact, nothing wrong with leaning if you are leaning on the Lord. Remember, one with God is a majority.

October *fourth* Friday

"Then David ... said to Jonathan, What have I done? What is my iniquity, and what is my sin before your father, that he seeks my life?"
(I Samuel 20:1)

I can recall an occasion in my life when I had to tell a lady some tragic news. The lady looked up at me and said in anguish "What have we done wrong?" She was overwhelmed with a feeling of guilt. She felt she had sinned and God was punishing her with the tragic circumstances in her family circle.

David had exactly the same experience. He was so overwhelmed with the pressure of Saul chasing him that he was sure that he had done something wrong. In fact he was being chased for the precise reason that he had done right! It is my experience that a wife whose husband has walked out on her often feels she is the guilty one, the person who is approached for money by one who has squandered his own is almost made to feel the other person's debt is their personal debt etc. Such feelings are a delusion from the devil. Don't panic, just because you are under pressure does not automatically mean that you have sinned.

October *fifth*

"Truly, as the Lord lives, and as your soul lives, there is but a step between me and death"
(I Samuel 20:3)

Where is the spirit of the David of the valley Elah, now? Where is the lad who defied the godless giant in the name of the Lord of Hosts? He never even thought of dying when he faced the Philistine, did he?; now, he is overwhelmed with the thought of death at the hand of an Israelite king! Had not God promised David that he would reign on Israel's throne? Was he not immortal until his work was done? What had gotten into him?

Discouragement; that was the root of his loss of vision. Just like you, Christian? You can hear the whirr of the hurled spears of your critics and you have joined Elijah under the juniper tree and said "I am no better than my fathers; let me die". Away with discouragement, today, away with it! You too are immortal until your work is done and you must not go around saying, "There is but a step between me and death". You must change it to "For me to live is Christ and to die is gain".

October *sixth*

"Nevertheless, if there is iniquity in me, kill me yourself for why should you bring me to your father"
(I Samuel 20:8)

David had, momentarily, lost his vision, his sense of security and his confidence. Familiar surroundings of home and family, job and position had been removed. He got his attention off the Lord and he begins to look in, rather than up, and makes an extraordinary request of his friend Jonathan; he says, in effect, if you think I am a bad person, kill me yourself.

To walk through David's life is to touch virtually every mood of human experience. Today's mood is what some folk would call "hitting the self-destruction button". David was so discouraged that he thought if Jonathan killed him Jonathan would be justified in doing so. David had no right to treat his precious life so lightly and neither have you, yours. God has a special purpose for you and you must not put your life exclusively at the mercy of anybody's whim. You know that people just don't have to kill you to ruin your life; you just have to let them take you over. Resist their whims and only be mastered by the Master.

October *seventh*

> *"But you shall not cut off your kindness from my house forever ... So, Jonathan made a covenant with the house of David"*
> (I Samuel 20:14-15)

Jonathan had no notion of killing David, he never wavered in his belief that David was Israel's Saviour. Though he knew better than to try to be king himself, he was determined to have a covenant with the one who would be. The covenant he made carried the promise that David would never cut off his kindness to Jonathan's family when he came to power.

The Lord Jesus is certainly in his day of rejection at the moment. Few there are who love Him and honour Him. Millions seek the number one spot for themselves. You, though, are different. Like Jonathan you know who the true Saviour is and have trusted Him as your very own personal Saviour. Be sure of this; he has made a covenant with you. When all his enemies are put down and he rules and reigns, his kindness to you will never be cut off.

October *eighth*

"But if I say thus to the young man, 'Look, the arrows are beyond you' - go your way for the Lord has sent you away"
(I Samuel 20:22)

The message of the arrows was a sad one for David. Jonathan arranged with David to try to find out how his father really stood with David. He then arranged to return to a place where David would be hidden and if he shot three arrows to the side of the stone Ezel and shouted to his servant boy "Go find the arrows, they are on this side of you, get them and come" the message would mean David would have to flee from Saul. When Jonathan talked to his father of David, Saul got so angry he tried to kill Jonathan. The arrows eventually said to the hidden David; "The Lord has sent you away".

Is that the message to you today? Is it time to go? Is it time to move out from the familiar to the unfamiliar? Don't be afraid. If the Lord sends you away, then he will go before you. David longed to stay; God had other plans. Remember, we don't give the orders, we just turn up for duty. If we do the results will be out of this world. It's guaranteed.

October *ninth*

"For as long as the son of Jesse lives on the earth, you shall not be established, nor your kingdom. Now therefore, send and bring him to me, for he shall surely die"
(I Samuel 20:31)

This text is the very heart of King Saul's philosophy. He wanted the kingdom of Israel for himself and for his son, following. No matter that Samuel had distinctly warned him long before that " The Lord has torn the kingdom of Israel from you today and has given it to a neighbour of yours who is better than you". He was now fighting God; he wanted to kill God's anointed.

Saul's argument to Jonathan was that he would never be established as long as David lived. Be careful that such a subtle argument does not creep into your heart. We don't pray "My kingdom come. My will be done", do we? If you want to be truly established in life be established in David's greater Son. "For", says Hebrews 13:9, "it is good that the heart be established by grace". All other kingdoms eventually perish. His is a kingdom that cannot be shaken.

October *tenth*

> "And they wept
> together, but David
> more so"
> (I Samuel 20:41-42)

These last moments together were highly emotional ones for David and Jonathan. David outwept Jonathan because he knew the cost of what Jonathan had done for him. The spear that had been hurled towards him had now been hurled against Jonathan (see 1 Samuel 20:33). It is a costly thing to be associated with God's anointed one.

It still is. Do you not think the Lord knows the price you pay for your association with Him? Your king is touched with the feelings of your infirmities. He knows that people often hate you for His sake. It is called "The fellowship of His sufferings". Yet, remember, He has outwept you. He "Who", says Hebrews 5:7-9, "in the days of His flesh, when He had offered up prayers and supplications, with vehement cries and tears to Him who was able to save Him from death, and was heard because of His godly fear, though He was His son, yet He learned obedience by the things which he suffered. And having been perfected, He became the author of eternal salvation to all who obey Him". Selah

October *eleventh*

> "So David said ...
> 'The king has ordered
> me on some
> business'"
> (I Samuel 21:2)

A lie is always a lie. Sheer panic can make you tell one. David now fled for his life to a place called Nob, a town of the priests in the tribe of Benjamin just north of the city of Jerusalem. The tabernacle stood at Nob and David went there in sheer panic. When asked by Ahimelech the priest why he was alone, David replied he was on a secret errand for the king. It was a lie; it was saying that which was not true with the intention to deceive.

Concealment is not lying. Life would be intolerable if we were required to disclose all the truth we know. Withholding truth is often both necessary and kind but here David told a lie to conceal the truth and that was where he went wrong. Nowhere does the Scripture allow for a lie to be justifiable. It will find us out. So, let's stick to the truth. Let's remember the words of Horatius Bonar: "Truth is not the feeble thing which men often think they can afford to disparage. Truth is power: Let it be treated and trusted as such."

October *twelfth*

> *"So the priest gave him holy bread; for there was no bread there but the showbread "*
> (I Samuel 21:6)

David was the Lord's anointed and it was no sin for him to be fed showbread. Showbread was strictly consecrated to God and to the priests to teach Israel the holiness of the Lord, the sacredness of His service and the sanctity of those whom He chose to minister to Him in the special ministry of the priesthood.

The Scriptures teach that the showbread was for God and then to be eaten by those dedicated to His service. Does God get hungry? He certainly does. He gets hungry for our worship and fellowship. What else do the words of Revelation 3:20 mean?; "Behold, I stand at the door and knock. If any one hears my voice and opens the door, I will come in to him and dine with him, and he with me". When we worship, we feed God and He feeds us. Can you think of a higher occupation for your heart and mind? Whither it be on the top of a bus or sitting on an aeroplane, or quietly in a church service; worship.

October *thirteenth*

> *"So the priest said 'The sword of Goliath the Philistine, whom you killed in the Valley of Elah, there it is ... and David said, 'There is none like it; give it to me"*
> (I Samuel 21:9)

There is something haunting, wistful, even pathetic about this action of David's. The priests of Nob had kept Goliath's sword wrapped in a cloth. Often people must have asked to see it. Can't you hear them?; "What a sword!" "He must have been some giant!" "To think that David's faith in a wonderful God overcame such an enemy!" "He never even got to using his sword on young David, Praise God!" Now, David whose faith never rested in a sword, takes Goliath's sword, of all swords, to defend himself from Saul. "There is none like it", he says. Are there more haunting words in all of David's life story?

Are you depressed, today? Is your spirit choked by somebody who has risen to criticise you? Are the ungodly laughing at the divisions, even in the ranks of Christians, around you? Don't hide behind the defences of the ungodly. The name of the Lord is a strong tower and the righteous run into it and they are safe. Run into that name, today; don't fight the ungodly with their own weapons.

October *fourteenth*

> *"And the servants of Achish said to him, 'Is this not David the king of the land? Did they not sing of him to one another in dances, saying; Saul has slain his thousands, and David his ten thousands?'"*
>
> (I Samuel 21:11)

Even David's enemies recognised that he was the Lord's anointed. Imagine the Gentiles calling him "The King of the land" when his very own people were hunting him to death! Shades of the coming Lord Jesus are very clear in David's life at this time. All analogies break down, and David as an analogy of Christ certainly breaks down at various stages in his life, but the spiritual teaching from the historical setting at this stage is crystal clear.

Even Pilate, Rome's representative governor in Jerusalem wrote "This is the King of the Jews" above Christ's head as He was crucified by His own people. "Surely this is the Son of God", said the Centurion in charge of Christ's crucifixion.

There is coming a day when the Lord Jesus will be received by the nation of Israel. "They shall look on Him whom they pierced", says Scripture. "All Israel will be saved", writes Paul. Meanwhile Christ, like David, is in the hands of the Gentiles because more Gentiles believe in Him in our day than Jews do. But, " The crowning day is coming". Meanwhile;

"King of my life I crown You now,
Yours shall the glory be,
Lest I forget Your thorn crowned brow,
Lead me to Calvary."

October *fifteenth*

> *"So he ... feigned madness ... scratched on the doors of the gate and let the saliva fall down on his beard. Then Achish said to his servants, 'Look, you see the man is insane'"*
> (I Samuel 21:11)

I will never forget quietly sitting in my friend Professor Gooding's home talking of David. "Who", he asked me one morning, "had saliva fall down his beard, apart from David? Who was also called a madman?" "Christ", I answered. The Professor smiled. He had given me a key to the life of David.

The older I grow the more I am convinced that just as every lane and alley in the country in which you live will lead you to the road which will lead you to the metropolis, so every part of Scripture, no matter how seemingly obscure, will lead you to the heart of it all which is Christ Himself. Look for Him in it all and you will surely find Him.

October *sixteenth*

> *"David ... escaped to the cave of Adullam ... and everyone who was in distress, everyone who was in debt, and everyone who was discontented gathered to him"*
> (I Samuel 22:1-2)

How often have I heard certain churches described as "Caves of Adullam"? People who were in debt, discontented and in distress gathered to David at Adullam and so churches that draw such people get dubbed as "Adullams".

Such trite remarks draw away from the beauty of David's character. There was something about him that drew troubled hearts. In our day where do millions of people turn when they are in trouble? They read the Psalms of David! No wonder. Can you find an individual in Scripture or in history whom God used greatly until he first allowed them to be hurt, deeply?

Who flocked to the Saviour; the religious, the comfortable, the established? Certainly not. If the distressed and troubled are heading for your local church it is a great sign.

October *seventeenth*

"Then David ... said to the king of Moab, 'Please let my father and mother come here with you, till I know what God will do for me"
(I Samuel 22:3-5)

We all have times when we don't know what to do next. David did a very wise thing at this time in his life. He cared for his parents and waited on God for guidance. Often we will find days when we are not called upon to do anything more than the every day duties of caring for our family, waiting all the time for the Lord to show us the next step in his plan for our lives. Be certain of this; the guidance that you need will come. Just as God sent a prophet to guide David, he will send his messenger to guide you. It may come in the form of a telephone call, a magazine article, simply bumping into a friend on the street, whatever, but come it will. God's prophets come in rare guises. Meantime? "I can say", said Dr. Barnhouse, "from experience that ninety-five per cent of knowing the will of God consists in being prepared to do it before you know what it is".

October *eighteenth*

"Then Saul said, 'Will the son of Jesse give everyone of you fields and vineyards ...' Then answered Doeg ... 'I saw the son of Jesse going to Nob, to Ahimelech'"
(I Samuel 22:7-9)

Betrayed! The greatest hero in Israel's history was betrayed by a man who loved property and position. Doeg was as Judas; money and what it could buy made him reveal the haunt of God's anointed to his enemy.

I know that a lot has been said about money. I have come across all kinds of views. If you run after money, you are materialistic. If you don't get it you are a loser. If you get it and keep it, you are a miser. If you don't try to get it, you lack ambition. If you get it and spend it you are a spendthrift. If you still have it after a lifetime of work, you are a fool who never got any fun out of life! Yet, beware of the Doegs in life. Money motivates them, prestige inflates them. They would sell your very soul, if it were profitable. The love of money is the root of all kinds of evil.

October *nineteenth*

"Then Saul said to him, 'Why have you conspired against me, you and the son of Jesse ... and have inquired of God for him, that he should rise against me, to lie in wait, as it is this day?'"

(I Samuel 22:13)

The man was paranoid. Jealousy was blinding his reason, his conscience, his view of everything. Saul could see David lying in wait at every corner ready to take his throne from him by force. Ahimelech the priest desperately tried to persuade him that David was in fact one of his most loyal servants but he would not be persuaded.

Watch jealousy, it is a fiercesome thing. It will make you think your friend an enemy, it will make you believe his talents to be a threat. It will turn even his most innocent act into a flame of suspicion in your heart. Many lovely things pass out of life when jealousy comes in. If only Saul had put out the hell spark of jealousy in a sea of prayer. Selah.

October *twentieth*

"And the king said to Doeg, 'You turn and kill the priests!' So Doeg the Edomite turned and struck the priests, and killed that day eighty-five men who wore a linen ephod"

(I Samuel 22:18-19)

Saul's soldiers refused his order to kill the priests of Nob but Doeg was only too ready to do it. Of course, as our verse tells us, he was an Edomite. Edomites were the descendants of Esau who sold his birthright for lentil soup. Lentils are red and Edom means "red", a nickname given to Esau.

Edomites, in the Bible, constantly chose the immediate benefit rather than the long term blessing. Here Doeg, for example, would rather have had the friendship of Saul than wait for the coming reign of God's anointed, David. Herod, the last Edomite mentioned in the Bible, would rather have ruled as king than recognise the little baby of Bethlehem as the King of all Kings. There are a lot of the descendants of Edomites who still choose the immediate pleasures of sin rather than the long term rewards of the righteous. Are you one of them?

October *twenty-first*

"So David said to Abiathar, 'I knew that day, when Doeg the Edomite was there, that he would surely tell Saul. I have caused the death of all the persons of your father's house"
(I Samuel 22:22)

The older you grow, the more you will discover that your life has an influence far beyond your imagination. David fled in panic to Nob, tried to cover his tracks with a lie and before his action was finished it caused the death of eighty-five priests and the sacking of a city, including the deaths of many women and children.

Be careful, today; a word, a hint, an action, even a telephone conversation could, before it is finished set a church on fire, break a marriage, ruin a relationship, bring a tide of heartbreak in its wake. If only David had trusted the Lord instead of taking things into his own hands the community of Nob would have lived. Trust in the Lord with all your heart, and lean not to your own understanding, in all your ways acknowledge Him and He shall direct your paths.

October *twenty-second*

"Then David enquired of the Lord, saying, 'Shall I go and attack these Philistines?' And the Lord said to David, 'Go'"
(I Samuel 23:4)

Have you really made a terrible mess of things and caused hurt to a lot of people, recently? You, like David, panicked and the result has been catastrophic. Find hope in today's text.

What could have been worse for David than the mayhem he caused at Nob? Yet, he learned from it all. He got to prayer and told the Lord that he needed guidance. God did not refuse guidance on the grounds that David had recently disastrously neglected to ask for it. That is what the love of God does. When Peter denied the Lord he was amazed to discover that the Lord loved him, still. Divine love, unlike human love, is not dependent on its object. God's love is not drawn out by our lovableness. Ask him today for guidance, despite the fact that you recently omitted to do so. He will not fail you.

October *twenty-third*

> *"And David stayed in strongholds in the wilderness ... Saul sought him every day, but God did not deliver him into his hand"*
> (I Samuel 23:14)

It is that little phrase, "every day" in our text that evokes the pain and the anguish David went through. There was no let up. Everywhere he went David daily expected death to strike. It's like a situation here in Northern Ireland where a friend of mine is on a terrorist hit list and every time I approach his house and ring his doorbell I know it strikes fear into his heart. He is daily expecting death at his very door.

It may not be fear of a terrorist that haunts you every day but some pain, some anguish, some problem that seems to eternally hound you.

Take it from me that no problem lasts forever. It's a long road which has no turning. Catch hold of the little phrase "but God" in our text. Yes, you are in trouble, "but God". Yes, your problem seems eternal, "but God". Yes, all seems hopeless, "but God". Comforting, isn't it!?

October *twenty-fourth*

> *"Then Jonathan, Saul's son, arose and went to David in the woods and strengthened his hand in God"*
> (I Samuel 23:16)

Notice Jonathan's approach to David, just when he needed him most. He didn't try the old "Tighten your belt and get going" approach. He didn't paint an unrealistic picture of what was happening, either, with a "Come on, it's not as bad as you think" approach. Jonathan simply redirected David's perspective on life by focusing his attention upon his Lord, not his enemy. There was David hunted, frightened, weary, panic stricken, and hiding in a forest and Jonathan got up out of his comfortable seat in the palace, found David and strengthened his hand in God.

One thing is certain, if my friendships do not enable me to strengthen my friends in the Lord then I need to deepen my commitment to Christ. If I can urge a friend to be directly dependent on the Lord I can do that friend no greater service. Get out there into the woods of life today and strengthen someone's hand in God.

October *twenty-fifth*

"Then the Ziphites came up to Saul ... saying, 'Is David not hiding ... and our part shall be to deliver him into the king's hand?'" And Saul said, 'Blessed are you of the Lord'"
(I Samuel 23:19-21)

Beware of attributing to the Lord actions that are not His. It is so easy to say "The Lord sent me" or "The Lord sent you" and later find that circumstances prove that the Lord was not in the thing at all. God often gets blamed for things He has nothing to do with.

I am reminded that the great John Newton who wrote the hymn "Amazing Grace" once read the verse in the Acts of the Apostles where the Lord had encouraged Paul to serve him in Corinth because he had "Many people in this city". Newton felt this verse was God's guidance to him to go to Cheltenham to serve in the Christian ministry. He later wrote, "I very soon discovered that Cheltenham was not Corinth and that I was not Paul". Selah.

October *twenty-sixth*

"So David made haste to go away from Saul, for Saul and his men were encircling David and his men to take them"
(I Samuel 23:26)

Imagine a king of Israel employing an army to stalk and kill one of his most gifted and loyal subjects out of jealousy while he should have been protecting and guarding God's people from an enemy that threatened the whole nation's security.

The Christian church, too, unfortunately, is not backward at in-fighting when it should be concentrating on the big and wider issues. It is very easy to get drawn in amongst a set of Christians who are bent on hounding a fellow Christian, for whatever reason. May the Lord give us grace to focus our fellow Christians' attention on issues that are vital and important and to try to encourage them to fight Satan's kingdom and not each other. You wouldn't want to be party to a crowd who shot their own wounded, would you?

October *twenty-seventh*

> *"Then the men of David said to him, 'This is the day of which the Lord said to you, 'Behold, I will deliver your enemy into your hand'"*
>
> (I Samuel 24:4)

If you had been hiding in a cave, hunted by King Saul and three thousand men and King Saul came, alone into the cave to relieve himself and your men said "Let's kill him", would you have let them? I reckon my human nature would have gone into overdrive!

The temptation open to David to kill Saul was all the stronger because David's soldiers excused their desire to get even with Saul by saying it was God's timing, God's will. We must never rationalise wrong behaviour and sin as being part of God's plan for our lives. Not everyone who says to you "This is the day to act" is necessarily in God's will, no matter how spiritual they may appear and no matter how highly you might regard them.

October *twenty-eighth*

> *"Let the Lord judge between you and me"*
>
> (I Samuel 24:12)

The conversation between David and Saul in the cliffs of En Gedi is full of rich instruction. It really is a very moving example of a young, highly gifted man dealing in a godly way with an older, cantankerous, jealous leader. He did not give Saul a tirade of venom and viciousness but showed him respect and let the Lord judge who was right.

Got a nasty letter, recently? Been badly treated by your boss? Have you been snowed under by false accusations and sheer wickedness on the part of those who do not like you? David reminded Saul that "Wickedness proceeds from the wicked". He decided that joining the ranks of the wicked in order to get even with Saul was a very foolish practice. Why should you stoop to wickedness when you have the Lord to vindicate you?

October *twenty-ninth*

> *"And Saul lifted up his voice and wept. Then he said to David: 'You are more righteous than I'"*
> (I Samuel 24:16-17)

There is nothing more wonderful than to see the love of a woman for her child, the love of a husband for his wife, the love of grandparents for their grandchildren, or the love of a friend for a friend. This kind of love, though, is not the test of our Christian life. If you simply love those who love you and are kind to those that are generous to you then you are doing no more than those who act at the prompting of their own human heart. If that is all Christianity does for you it is no better than the religion of the Pharisees. Our Lord draws us to a higher challenge, by far. "Whoever slaps you on your right cheek, turn the other to him also", he said. He calls us to love those who do not love us. This is the litmus test of our Christian lives. It is not a charter for any unscrupulous tyrant, beggar or thug to abuse us. God sets up government law enforcement agencies to deal with such people. In our personal relationships, though, there is not to be a trace of retaliation. David's dealing with Saul is a shining example of such behaviour.

October *thirtieth*

> *"I remember the days of old; I meditate on all your works; I muse on the work of your hands"*
> (Psalm 143:5)

It is easy when you are depressed, discouraged and downhearted to think that your past days were the best days. Why, when the new temple at Jerusalem was built the young men rejoiced and the old men wept! The younger generation did not feel that the glory of the latter could ever be as great as the glory of the former. They were wrong then and such thinking is wrong now.

Is it wrong to remember good times in the past? Certainly not. We should be glad to remember victories of faith, occasions of joy and God's deliverance in the past but the whole direction of scriptural teaching is to spur us on to the future. The past is full of nostalgia but the future for the believer, no matter what way you look at it, is full of hope. Forgetting those things which are behind we press toward the mark of a high calling of God in Christ.

As David had taken on a few onery bears and lions in the past, it was now time to take on greater tasks. As Moses had seen God open up the courts of Pharaoh he had to now step out and see God open up the Red Sea. Paul had seen God work tremendously in the past in his life but he now set sail for Jerusalem, "Not knowing what will happen to me there". It certainly beat watching full sunsets at Miletus for the rest of his Christian life.

Go on, get out there and prove that God is the God of your future, not just the God of your past.

October *thirty-first*

"Then David went on and became great and the Lord of hosts was with him"
(I Chronicles 11:9)

I commend to you, today, a poem, written by my late friend, Mr. R. J. Wright, Christian Missionary to Japan. It reads:

"Go on. Go on. Go on. Go on.
Go on, Go on. Go on.
Go on. Go on. Go on. Go on.
Go on. Go on. Go on.

Go on. Go on. Go on. Go on.
Go on, Go on. Go on.
Go on. Go on. Go on. Go on.
Go on. Go on. Go on.

Go on. Go on. Go on. Go on.
Go on, Go on. Go on.
Go on. Go on. Go on. Go on.
Go on. Go on. Go on."

NOVEMBER

Life on high ground is not always easy, is it? When David reached the high ground of his youth and was anointed King of Israel, everything seemed set for a time of great victory. The very next day the Philistines attacked and soon poor David was hunted by the jealous Saul and his army "as one hunts a partridge in the mountains".

Driven out into the mountains and hills by an establishment that despised him, the young King-elect faced the raw elements with a loving heart. It is not pleasant to be rejected, particularly when you have not done anything wrong: "What have I done? What is my sin before your father, that he seeks my life?" said David to his friend Jonathan. Yet, though blasted by the winds of criticism and discouragement he refused to get bitter. True, he wavered. True, he wondered what on earth was going on. True, he made mistakes. The loving way, though, in which he refused to harm his persecutor, King Saul is an example which still inspires, even to these November days.

November *first*

> *"Oh give thanks to
> the Lord!"*
> (I Chronicles 16:8)

David's first theme is a good start for this month. Thankfulness. To have a thankful spirit can make a great difference to any day. Do you have a happy spirit of thankfulness in your life? It's like the minister who was always praising the Lord and his congregation wondered one wet, windy, miserable morning what on earth he had to praise the Lord for on such a day. "Thank you, Lord", he said in prayer, "that every day is not like today!"

I'm always moved by the story of the young lieutenant who died while saving the life of one of his soldiers in Vietnam. His parents invited the soldier he had saved to dinner, after he had returned to the United States. He arrived for dinner, drunk. He spent the meal telling filthy stories and using blasphemous language. Mercifully he left. The mother of the dead lieutenant fell into her husband's arms and said "To think that our darling son had to die for that!" It is certain that God the Father will never say that about you. Yet, can there be in all the world a sin more grievous to the heart of the Father, if, after Him giving His Son for us, we in turn show little gratitude?

November *second*

> *"Glory in His holy
> name!"*
> (I Chronicles 16:10)

As I quietly walked around a synagogue in Manchester, which is now a museum, a Jewish gentleman pointed out a stained-glass window in the building which contained the name of God. "We put a picture of that window on a brochure", he said, "to advertise this museum but the orthodox Jews wouldn't let us use it in case the brochure would fall on the ground and the name of God would be desecrated by someone stepping on it".

Such a high view of God's name is not the average view in our western world. The two top swear words in the United Kingdom at this time are, sadly, "God" and "Christ". Let those of us who know the Lord be different. Let's glory in His holy name.

The story is told of a famous leader of an American baseball team who was attending a meeting to negotiate a contract for professional football in

New York. Suddenly he threw down his pencil, pushed back his chair and said "The deal is off". Surprised, the other man asked why there had been such an abrupt break-off when all seemed to be going well on a deal involving big money on both sides. "Because", said the leader, staring at one of the football representatives, "I don't like the way you've been talking about a friend of mine". "But what friend? I haven't been talking about anyone, let alone a friend of yours". "Oh, yes you have", countered the leader, "you mentioned him in almost every sentence". Then he pointed out the man's repeated profane use of the name of Jesus Christ. "I get you", the other man said quietly, "I won't do it again. You can count on it". May the time never come when our ears no longer negatively tingle to hear the Lord's name flippantly juggled in virtually every other sentence by thoughtless people.

November *third*

> *"Talk about all His wondrous works"*
> (1 Chronicles 16:9)

So many people waste words. According to the New York Academy of Sciences, the average man speaks 12,500 words a day and the average woman more than 25,000. How many of those words are positive, helpful and inspiring? How many are negative, sarcastic, hurtful, and a real put-down? Words have igniting power, for good or bad. "Life and death are in the power of the tongue", says the Bible. Some of the most damaging individuals have never fired a gun or incited a riot. They have simply used the power of words to break down and destroy marriages, families, friendships and businesses.

Those who use words to benefit others are such a breath of fresh air. Those who talk of God in a positive and healthy way can bring enormous comfort and hope to those in need. Let the words of William Cowper inspire us to healthy talk;

"Have you no words? Ah! Think again,
Words flow apace when you complain,
And fill your fellow creature's ear,
With a sad tale of all your care.
Were half the breath thus vainly spent,
To Heaven in supplication sent,
Your cheerful song would oftener be;
'Hear what the Lord has done for me!'"

November *fourth*

> **"Seek the Lord and His strength"**
> (1Chronicles 16:11)

My friend John Merson, a worker in the oil industry in the North Sea was called by God to, at that time in his life, service for God in Brazil. I shall never forget his valedictory service in Aberdeen. It was quite a night and I felt somewhat embarrassed in carrying a large box onto the platform with me. I got quite a few "looks". Still, I bore them for I had method in my seeming madness.

What can you give a young fellow about to give his life to Christian service abroad? There are no Oscars or Emmys or Nobel Prizes for such heroes, so, while preaching I opened my box and drew out a pair of scales. "See", I said, "on this pan of the scale is the word 'AS' and on the other the word 'SO'. As your day gets going the pressures mount". I tipped the scale down on the 'AS' side. "Yet", God has said, "as your day so shall your strength be". Down on the 'SO' side comes "God's strength", I rebalanced the scales, dead even. "God's balance is always perfect. As your day, so His strength will match it".

I expressed the wish that maybe one day God might bring to my friend John, a scale-polisher. Months and many letters later, I received a wedding invitation to Copenhagen where John told me a lovely Danish scale-polisher would begin work on a certain date!

(P.S. It is worth noting that Mr. Stephen Cordiner, Senior, and I, hunted shops in Aberdeen that morning for a pair of scales. In the end he and his good wife Carol gave me a pair of scales from their home as a present to John. Mr. Cordiner always noted that when I arrived at his home "His scales fell off!")

November *fifth*

> **"Remember ... the judgements of His mouth"**
> (1Chronicles 16:12)

David wants us to think about the way God judges things. I listened to Lord Tebitt, a former Conservative Party chairman, and Member of Parliament, in the British House of Commons, recently attempt to answer the question "Do you believe in a benevolent God?" He replied that he was an agnostic and explained that if there was a God then if we could explain him or analyse him he would no longer be God.

I was immediately reminded that, in fact, the Bible claims from beginning to end that God has explained Himself, and has actually revealed His thinking and His motivation. He has particularly explained Himself regarding judgement. We all deserve the judgement of God, but, nevertheless, the very wrath of God that should have fallen on us, fell on the very God it came from. Christ died for our sins! That God, incarnate, should bare the punishment of His own wrath and set those free who accept Christ's death as enough to atone for their sins, is the best news on earth. What was God's judgement on Calvary's work?; Christ expressed it perfectly when He cried just before his death "It is finished". Nothing more needs to be done. Rest, then, where God rests.

"The other gods were strong; but Thou wast weak;
They rode, but Thou didst stumble to a throne;
But to our wounds only God's wounds can speak,
And not a god has wounds, but Thou alone."
(Edward Shillito)

November *sixth*

"Remember His covenant always, the word which He commanded, for a thousand generations"
(1 Chronicles 16:15)

"There are", said Vance Havner, "sickly Christians living on crackers and cheese when they have a standing invitation to feast of the grace of God. His promises are cheques to be cashed, not mere mottos to hang on the wall!"

David had proved right through his life that when God makes a promise (a covenant), he delivers. No amount of skullduggery on Saul's part or the Philistines' part, or even on the part of traitors within his own camp, could turn around the promise God had made to make David, king of Israel. In David's lowest moments that promise held.

You cannot starve a person who is feeding on God's promises. Take God's promises, boldly, and say "These are mine". You will never pray better than when you plead the promises of God. You will never behave better than when you are motivated by the promises of God. You will even sleep better when you lay your head down on the promises of God. Your future is as bright as the promises of God.

"His every word of grace is strong,
As that which built the skies;
The voice that rolls the stars along,
Speaks all the promises."
(Isaac Watts)

November *seventh*

> *"And confirmed it
> to Jacob for a
> statute"*
> (1 Chronicles 16:17)

My friend, Dr. R. T. Kendal says that there was a time when he identified most with Joseph but that the older he gets the more he identifies with his father, Jacob. He says the older you get the more you can see the mistakes you have made and the more there is to feel guilty about. Jacob provides a classic study in the problem of guilt.

Too right. Even when Jacob was presented to Pharaoh, all he could say was "Few and evil have been the days of the years of my life". What a frightening summary! Do you, like Jacob, feel overwhelmed with guilt? Take heart, Christian. Where does Jacob end? We read in Hebrews chapter 11 that "Jacob when he was dying, blessed each of the sons of Joseph and worshipped, leaning on the top of his staff". Surely his final reflection was to understand, to quote my friend "R. T." again, "That which once gave him the great sense of guilt now gave him the greatest sense of gratitude. God sanctified to him his deepest distress. All that was wrong in his relationship with Joseph became the very springboard of the good he had seen". God confirmed even to guilty Jacob all his promises.

"Depth of mercy - can there be mercy still reserved for me?
Can my God his wrath forebear? Me the chief of sinners, spare?
There for me the Saviour stands, shows his wounds and spreads his hands,
God is love, I know, I feel,
Jesus lives and loves me still."
(Charles Wesley)

November *eighth*

> *"To you I will give
> the land of Canaan
> as the allotment of
> your inheritance"*
> (1 Chronicles 16:18)

"It is", said an Arab recently on BBC's Radio 4, "difficult to negotiate with the Bible". The Arab was right; the Bible is not filled with phrase, "But, on the other hand!". David knew Gods promises regarding the land of Canaan and today, although millions in the world would want to wipe Israel out, she still has that special protection from God. Just the other day I took a friend to see the house in Belfast where C. S. Lewis lived as a boy. C. S. Lewis wrote of that time when, as a schoolboy of 13, he was "Soon altering 'I believe' to 'one does feel'. And oh the relief of it? From the tyrannous noon of Revelation I passed into the cool evening of Higher Thought, where there was nothing to be obeyed and nothing to be believed except what was either comforting or exciting" ('Surprised by Joy' by C. S. Lewis, Inspirational Press, New York. 1991, p.34).

Are you tempted to live in such a world? Thank God C. S. Lewis came out of it to the blessing of millions. God's word is fixed. It is not negotiable. Whether it is God's promises to Israel or God's promises to you, no one can sell them, re-write them, undermine them, or alter them. As they are, so they stand. From promised land, to promising heaven, there will never be a heavenly voice to say "But, on the other hand!"

November *ninth*

> *"When you were
> but few in number,
> indeed very few, and
> strangers ... He
> permitted no man to
> do them wrong"*
> (1 Chronicles 16:19-
> 21)

David reminds Israel that because they were few in number their numerical position did not affect God's promises to them. David's reminder is a timely reminder for all of us. Don't you think 20th Century Christianity needs to recover from its love affair with bigness? After Christ's ascension the disciples must have looked a sorry bunch as they made their way towards Jerusalem.

There were no computers, no fax machines, no aircraft, no portable phones, no huge stadiums or tents, no media campaigns, no big choirs or recording equipment, no video or audio recordings, no celebrity guests in those days. What was there? A lot of tramping about in ones and twos or threes and fours, conversing and preaching in homes and synagogues and market places and prisons. Why did the Gospel spread so far, so fast? Because average Christians lived out their faith and took it with them as they moved around the empire. The result? They moved an empire for God until the very Roman Emperor himself fell in line.

We are often into big events, big projects, big budgets, big personalities, big institutions. Are we getting big results? Often, the answer is "No". Are you few in number down at your place? Don't get discouraged. Little is much if God is in it.

November *tenth*

> *"When they went from one nation to another, and from one kingdom to another He permitted no man to do them wrong"*
> (1 Chronicles 16:20-21)

You do not need to know key men in order to know true success; you need to know the keeper of the keys. When God opens a door no man can shut it. As Israel were on the move across the nations, he preserved their identity, their ultimate safety as a nation. David reminds Israel of God's preserving care, for few knew it as intimately as he did, whether from a javelin throwing Saul or the warring, threatening nations around him.

You can know it, too, for you are immortal until your work is done. Listen to Paul; "For a great effective door is open to me, and there are many adversaries" or "Furthermore, when I came to Troas to preach Christ's gospel ... a door was opened to me by the Lord". What better word could come to any of us than the word given by the angel of the church in Philadelphia, in Revelation 3:7, "These things says He who is holy, He who is true. He who has the key of David, He who opens and no one shuts, and shuts and no one opens"? The key of David, indeed. The key that opened the door of victory in the valley of Elah, the key that sent Abigail across David's path, the key that brought all Israel to Hebron to make David king, the key that opened the flow of Psalms from David's pen, like the one we are now studying to bring untold help, comfort and inspiration to millions, was the same key!

He who has the key of David is the same one who holds the keys to your life. When He opens, no one shuts, and when He shuts, no one opens. With such a key holder, what are you worried about?

November *eleventh*

*"Yes, He reproved
kings for their sakes"*
(1 Chronicles 16:21)

There is no earthly power structure which is impenetrable to God's power. There is no mistake too great that God cannot, despite it, make all things work together for good. Our text proves it. David is referring to an incident at the beginning of the life of the Hebrew people when Abraham panicked in a time of famine in Canaan and went down to live in Egypt. He knew that there could be a threat to his life because of his beautiful wife Sarah because they might kill him and keep her. So, Abraham persuaded Sarah to say that she was his sister.

Pharaoh was actually attracted to Sarah and had her brought to his house and he treated her "brother" right royally. Suddenly great plagues began to sweep across Pharaoh's life and the life of his family "Because", says the Bible, "of Sarah his wife". When Pharaoh discovered the truth he threw Abraham and Sarah and all that they had out of Egypt.

Think of it! Abraham makes a great mistake and God reproves a king for his sake and pulls Abraham out of the mess he was in. Now if that isn't commitment, I don't know what is. Scripture shows us a string of saints making great and grievous mistakes; Moses murdering the Egyptian, Peter boycotting Gentile believers, Elijah running away from Jezebel. Yet, none became incurably second class. They were, as Abraham was, forgiven and restored. God does not condone wrongdoing and even Abraham smarted for it but wrongdoing on the part of a believer does not change God's commitment to that believer. Comforting, isn't it?

November *twelfth*

*"Do not touch My
anointed ones, and do
My prophets no
harm"*
(1 Chronicles 16:22)

"I made a vow", wrote J. Sidlow Baxter, "over 30 years ago, now, never to criticise another evangelical minister behind his back. That vow has not spared me from being criticised - often wrongfully, cruelly, and with no chance to reply but it has spared me those wretched feelings of self-despising which follow after we have jealously or hurtfully defamed others; and it has saved me from one of those leading faults which becloud or completely fog divine guidance".

David writes our text about God's warning against those who would seek by tongue, pen or sword to wrongfully harm those He has called to serve Him or to deliver His word. David himself was anointed of God to service and few have suffered within a lifetime as much as he did from those who wrongfully opposed that service; they, not he, lived to regret the day they lifted their hand against him.

Voltaire, the French atheist dedicated a lot of energy in trying to destroy the Christian faith. The maid in his house told of him screaming on his deathbed two haunting words; " The Nazarene! The Nazarene! The Nazarene!" She said, "Not for all the wealth in Europe do I ever want to see another infidel die". Be careful that you don't lift your tongue or anything else against God's anointed. Selah.

November *thirteenth*

*"Sing to the Lord,
all the earth"*
(1 Chronicles 16:23)

Do you remember when you fell in love with your husband or wife, first? Your's was an unselfish, ardent, humble love. No low motive lurked. Your love was bright with the promise of hope. First love is the abandonment of all for a love that has abandoned all. You cannot put it into a mathematical formula. It forgets calculation. It is the crowning consciousness of life.

Such was the love of the Ephesian church for Christ. But something had happened. Christ confronted the great church and told them that He missed their first love. They were, it seems, "Faultily faultless, icily regular, splendidly dull".

I like what Dr. G. C. Morgan said about the Ephesian church. He said he reckoned the Lord did not hear from the Christians at Ephesus a song "At the unusual hour". You know what he meant, don't you? It's easy to sing at the usual time of worship, when it is expected, but, what about first love-to-Christ singing? In the car as you travel, about the house as you work, a quiet hum as you walk on a city street? Is there no "unusual hour" singing to the Lord in your life, any more? "Sing to the Lord, all the earth", wrote David. Never were you busier for the Lord, but activity in the King's business will not make up for the neglect of the King. You will even do more harm by your defence of the faith if you have left your first love. Christ told the Ephesian church "I will come to you quickly and remove your lampstand - unless you repent"

(Rev 2:5). Without first love we may retain ceaseless activity, doctrinal purity, severest orthodoxy, and even have a great Christian reputation but there will be no light shining in a dark place and certainly no song at the unusual hour. Without it we are but as sounding brass or a clanging cymbal.

November *fourteenth*

"Proclaim the good news of His salvation from day to day"
(1 Chronicles 16:23)

I was on a plane between San Francisco and Chicago and a young lady, about eighteen years of age sat beside me. She was in no mood for talking and any attempt I made to be friendly was rebuffed, so I gave up.

About halfway through the flight she suddenly turned round to me and asked "What is your job, sir?" I thought if she didn't talk to me when she didn't know what my work was, she would never talk to me once she discovered it! Still, I said, quietly, "I preach the Gospel". "I am a Roman Catholic", she said. "I'm pleased to meet you", I said. "Tell me", she asked, "when you go preaching do you tell people they need to be born again?" "What interests you in such a subject?", I asked. "Well there was this fellow in my class at school. He was the dirtiest tongued, filthiest minded individual in the class. His mind was like a sewer pipe and the girls detested his stories and his language. One day he walked into class and there was no more filthy talk or bad language. I couldn't believe it. I watched and listened to him for three days and then I could stick it no longer. I walked up to him and asked him what on earth had happened to him. He told me that he had been born again. Is that what you preach each, sir?" "I do indeed", I replied. If we would heed David's good advice we will seek to speak of the Good News every day.

November *fifteenth*

"Declare His glory among the nations"
(1 Chronicles 16:24)

In Mineralogy there are profusions of precious gems and all sorts of shapes in the forms of prisms, cubes and pyramids. But our Lord is the precious Living Stone (1 Peter 2:4,6). In Botany who could amply define the variety of the fabulous colours, nectars, aromas and odours of plants? But our Lord is the tender plant (Isaiah 53:2), and is the plant of renown (Ezekiel 34:29).

In Ornithology the eagle is unhindered by obstacles and can soar as no other. As with the eagle, so with the Lord (Deut 32:11). In Philology, the science of language, the alphabet is indispensable. Our Lord is the Alpha and Omega (Rev 1:8). In Biology, the origin of life is a huge question. Our Lord is the answer to it for He is "The fountain of life".

Get out there today and declare His glory.

November *sixteenth*

"Declare ... His wonders among all peoples"
(1 Chronicles 16:24)

The wonders of God's ways through nature, even in its most intricate actions are amazing. For example the time of incubation for a canary is fourteen days, for a chicken, twenty-one, and the eagle is, forty-two days. All the gestation periods in bird life are in periods of seven; the kitten is born on the fifty-sixth day, the pup on the sixty-third and right up to the whale on the three hundred and first. All, again, in periods of sevens.

Our Lord Jesus was the one who inaugurated time. And so it was in the exact fullness of time God sent His Son, born of a woman (Gal 4:4). It was "In due time Christ died" (Rom 5:6). As Christ inaugurated time so it will be Christ who will consummate it. And He has your times in His hand. Nothing comes from Him too late or too early. But remember; there is no way on earth to save time, all you can do is spend it.

November *seventeenth*

"Give the Lord the glory due His name"
(1 Chronicles 16:29)

Recently, I met a Jewish doctor, and, over a cup of tea and some delicious scones we fell to talking about the name of God. I asked her a question I have always wanted to ask a Jew; "What do you call God in general conversation?"

The doctor answered, immediately. In prayer she said "I say 'Baruch ata adonai' meaning 'Blessed art Thou O Lord'. When I have to refer to God in general conversation I say 'Baruch ata adoshem', which, roughly translated means 'Blessed art Thou of the name'". She told me that she would not even write the name of God in a letter but would simply put G-d. Such is the sacredness of the name of God with orthodox Jews.

What a name, God's name is! From Genesis 1:1-2:4 he is called "Elohim" thirty-five times. "Elohim" expresses the idea of greatness and glory and contains the idea of creative and governing powers. He is called "Jehovah", the one who is absolutely self-existent 6,823 times in the Old Testament. "Jehovah" means the one who always exists, who is eternal, unchangeable, the one who is a God of moral and spiritual attributes.

He is called "El-Shaddai", the one who nourishes, supplies, and satisfies; the all-sufficient one. He is "Jehovah Jireh"; the God who provides. He is "Jehovah-Rophe"; meaning, Jehovah heals. He is "Jehovah-Nissi"; the Lord is my banner. He is "Jehovah-Mckaddish"; the Lord who sanctifies. He is "Jehovah Shalom"; the Lord is peace. He is "Jehovah-Tsidkenu"; the Lord our righteousness. He is "Jehovah-Rohi"; the Lord is my shepherd. He is "Jehovah Shammah"; the Lord is there. Let's heed David's advice and give to the Lord the glory due his name.

November *eighteenth*

> *"For the Lord is great and greatly to be praised. He is also to be feared above all gods"*
> (1 Chronicles 16:25)

There is very little of the fear of God around. Swearing is all too common and it is lack of the fear of God that makes it so sadly prevalent in our world. What is the difference between swearing and cursing? Swearing involves the irreverent use of God's name as a witness or party to some statement and cursing implicates God's name with another's damnation. Often, in anger, people swear or curse. It is so pointless because it neither honours God nor brings honour to the person swearing or cursing.

A travelling salesman was once asked "Are you paid anything for swearing?" "No", he replied. "Well", came the answer, "you certainly work cheap. You lay aside your character as a gentleman, inflict pain on your friends, break a commandment, lose your soul and all for nothing!" Let's, then, control our anger and cultivate a sense of reverence. Let us remember how very serious swearing and cursing are. If there were only two sins in the world and those two sins were swearing and cursing Jesus Christ would still have died to pay for them. May the fear of God rule our tongues.

November *nineteenth*

> *"For all gods of the peoples are idols but the Lord made the heavens"*
> (1 Chronicles 16:26)

It must have been a great moment when the smitten children of Israel looked to the serpent on the pole and were healed (See Numbers 21). But do you know what happened to that metallic snake? If you don't you are in for a big surprise. In 2 Kings 18:4 we learn that for eight hundred years the children of Israel had kept it. They preserved it, protected it, and polished it and finally made an idol out of it. They called it Nehushtan meaning "A piece of bronze". That's all it was but they worshipped it, none the less. Crazy, isn't it? Yet, sadly true.

Such things happen, even today. Your child, your partner, your business, your house, your education, your holidays, your ambitions can so grip your heart that they can become your Nehushtan. Consumer religion all around us shows that the service of Mammon outstrips the service of the Master. "In ten hours we fly you to where Jesus walked" runs the El Al advertisement over a shot of the Lake of Galilee with the text "Come you after me and I will make you to become fishers of men". If you take that one seriously you have come a long way but the El Al "Pilgrimage Department" winks all the way to the bank. Is it any wonder that Kierkegaard the atheistic Dane wrote; "In every way it has come to this that what one now calls Christianity is precisely what Christ came to abolish"? Could you blame him? The preacher Jim Jones, who led so many of his congregation to commit suicide, once held up a Bible and said "Too many people are looking at this instead of looking at me!" Nehushtan, indeed.

"Happiness, what is it?", said Greta Garbo. "I have never known it. I have messed up my life and it's too late to change that". She once said to a friend; "Promise me that you'll never let money or glory rule your life". Good advice, for as David tells us "All the gods of the peoples are idols (worthless things) but the Lord made the heavens". Happy is the person who worships Him.

November *twentieth*

> *"Honour and majesty are before Him; strength and gladness are in His place"*
> (1 Chronicles 16:27)

God has not got any strong points for the simple reason that He does not have any weak ones. He is, in his character, perfectly balanced. When the Lord Jesus came to earth he was the exact image of his Father's person; all that his Father is, he displayed it.

David pinpoints four attributes of God in today's text. Did the Lord Jesus show these four attributes anywhere in his earthly life? He certainly did. Take the attributes of honour and majesty. Honour means personal integrity, a sense of what is right; majesty, a sense of stateliness and true grandeur. Taken by Satan to a high hill Christ was shown the kingdoms of this world and their glory. Notice Satan didn't say "Sing me a few choruses to my glory". No, he told Christ if he would bow down and worship him he would give him those kingdoms. It was a very subtle temptation but honour was before Christ and true majesty; "Away with you Satan. For it is written, 'You shall worship the Lord your God and him only shall you serve'", said Christ.

David also highlights strength and gladness as two further attributes of God. These lovely attributes are seen perfectly in the way the Lord Jesus dealt with the woman who had been bent over for eighteen years. "Woman", said Christ, "you are loosed from your infirmity". She was made straight immediately. The ruler of the synagogue protested that this was work on the Sabbath day but, with strength, Christ said to him "Hypocrite. Does not each of you on the Sabbath loose his ox or his donkey from the stall and lead it away to water it? So ought not this woman being a daughter of Abraham whom Satan has bound - think of it - for eighteen years be loosed on the Sabbath"?

The Sabbath was set up to commemorate freedom from slavery (See Deut 5:14-15; Lev 26:13) and the stance of the slave was to be bent over (See Luke 26:13). God had set his people free then and he still sets them free, now. If ever there was a day for setting folk free the Sabbath was that day. The result of Christ's action was sheer gladness on the part of the woman who had been straightened. Honour, majesty, strength and gladness. What a place, to borrow from today's text, is His place!

November *twenty-first*

> *"Give to the Lord,*
> *O kindreds of*
> *the peoples"*
> (1 Chronicles 16:28)

David certainly gave to the Lord. He gave Him his time, his energy, his pen, his very heart. Did he lose? He got back everything, one hundredfold.

"I gave God spoonfuls", said John Wesley, "and he gave me back shovelfuls". Are you giving God what is right, or what is left? We certainly make a living by what we get but we make a life by what we give. The best thing, though, which you can give to the Lord is your self. There is only one you. Your face, your features, voice, style, characteristics, abilities, walk, handshake, manner of expression, everything about you is found in only one individual since man first began - you!

Amos, the fruit picker from Tekoa was called to bring messages in the king's sanctuary up at the palace. The problem was the image keepers of Israel didn't like his rugged style. That didn't stop him giving himself to the Lord's will for his life. Just because Amos was outnumbered didn't mean he had to change, did it?

"I was no prophet, nor was I a son of a prophet but I was a herdsman and a tender of sycamore fruit. Then the Lord took me as I followed the flock. And the Lord said to me, 'Go, prophecy to my people Israel'". Amos gave himself to the Lord in his work no matter what the king's image builders, or spin doctors as they are now called, said or thought. Is it any wonder we are still reading his book, today? In this world it is not what we take up but what we give up that makes us rich. So give.

November *twenty-second*

> *"O worship the*
> *Lord in the beauty*
> *of holiness!"*
> (1 Chronicles 16:29)

Mark well what David is saying. He is saying that holiness is beautiful. We somehow imagine that holiness is drab, colourless, stern, critical, and cold; we forget that God is holy and being that is in every way, beautiful. Look around the tabernacle from the colourful gate of entry to the curtains of the inner sanctuary, to the gold and silver and the shining candlesticks. Every facet of these things speak of the holiness of God but it is anything but colourless; it is breathtakingly beautiful. Why, even the very top of the pillars that held up the white linen surround of the tabernacle were made of ornamented silver. The white linen certainly spoke of holiness but that which held it up was also beautiful in its intricacy.

Christians are to hold up the white linen of holy living as a testimony to the God they have trusted, but they need ornamentation too; the ornamentation of joy and gladness, of wholesome and happy marriages, and the obvious qualities of integrity, truthfulness and dependability. Their words should be their bond. Such lives attract. If our worship is backed up by holy living its potent force in the world cannot be underestimated.

November *twenty-third*

"The world also is firmly established, it shall not be moved"
(1 Chronicles 16:30)

Some would find our text a contradiction. They would refer to Peter's affirmation that "The elements will melt with fervent heat; both the earth and the works that are in it will be burnt up" (2 Peter 3:10). A little reflection will show that both David and Peter are right.

Any secondary school child will tell you that if you burn a table you cannot destroy its atoms. So it is with the earth. In a coming day it will be burnt up for sure and there will be, the Bible assures us, a new earth. But there will be something of the old earth in the new one. You cannot redeem something if there is not something of the original there. God is not going to say "I made a terrible mistake in creating the earth, Satan got the better of me, now away with it all". No, He is going to redeem the earth just as He is going to redeem our very bodies. That implies that there will be something of you, the original you, Christian, that will remain when you reach Heaven in a glorified state. It also implies that we will know one another in Heaven. Quietly study Romans 8:18-28 and if it doesn't cheer your day, what will?

November *twenty-fourth*

> *"Let them say*
> *among the nations,*
> *The Lord reigns"*
> (1 Chronicles 16:31)

Do you think the nations recognise the truth of our text? David is urging that they should, but sadly, few do. Recently in a study of the book of Daniel I was intrigued by the two great images of the governments of the world that are given there. One was an image of government as being like a beautiful statue with a head of gold and the other was the image of nations as being like animals. This is not a contradiction; governments can sometimes behave like animals and take just what they want when they are threatened, at other times they can behave well and do very intelligent and useful things.

The great image of Nebuchadnezzar's dream in Daniel 2 telling of coming world empires had an outstanding feature; it had feet of clay, it was unstable. This tells us a plain fact about all nations and all governments; they are basically unstable. Whether it be democracy, or communism, feudalism or dictatorships, all make great promises but cannot entirely deliver. The book of Daniel tells us that one day the Anti-Christ will rise and his government would destroy everything, even life itself, if God did not intervene (See Daniel 2:34-35; Daniel 11:36-12:3; 2 Thessalonians 2:3,12). So, don't put your trust in princes, or governments, or nations; put your trust in the Lord.

November *twenty-fifth*

> *"Let the sea roar*
> *and all its fullness"*
> (1 Chronicles 16:32)

I'm not often in Buckie. The truth is, I am not often in Findochty either - Banffshire on the Moray Firth is a jewel of a place where I came across a rather haunting thing, recently. Church of Scotland minister Bill Ross took me on a tour of the little fishing village of Findochty where the church building, set high on a rock overlooking the cove, is a guiding point for boats coming home, just as they have done for decades.

Bill greeted an old man walking by the sheltered side of the building. "Aye", he said. "Aye", said the other, (local talk for "Hello"!). "Watch him, Derick", said Bill, "he'll come back". Sure enough, he came back on his tracks. "Now he'll continue the same pattern", said Bill. Sure enough, back and forward, back and forward, he went.

"It has to do with a lifetime at sea", explained Bill. "He is walking the width of his boat". Soon another man joined him, and then a third, all of them looking out every now and again to sea. It was haunting to watch them. I have to confess that I have never understood why Revelation 21:1 says that in the new heaven and earth "there shall be no more sea". The men of Findochty have at last explained it for me. The absence of sea is a God-given symbol telling us that in Heaven there will be no more restlessness. Those old salts of Banffshire cannot rest because they have spent the best part of their lives heaving up and down on the sea. Similarly, millions cannot rest because of the continuing pressure and problems that living in a sinful world brings. In Heaven there will be perfect rest. Men of Findochty, I thank you.

November *twenty-sixth*

> *"He is coming to judge the earth"*
> (1 Chronicles 16:33)

For months an image has been playing over and over again on television, world-wide. It has been an eighty-one second video tape of a blackman called Rodney King writhing on a pavement in Los Angeles being kicked by uniformed policemen, jolted with a sten gun and hit with night sticks fifty-six times. Yet, seeing for the jurors was not believing. A superior court jury in Sinni Valley, north west of Los Angeles had acquitted on all but one count the four white Los Angeles policemen on trial for mistreating black motorist Rodney King. That judgement sparked the worst race riots in the United States this century. More than 3,700 fires were started and fifty people died.

David tells us in this Psalm that when God comes to judge the earth, things will be different. It will be some Judgement Day. No riots will be started, no voice will be raised in protest, no murmur will be heard when the Judge of all the earth gives His verdict. No judge on earth ever gave a judgement, yet, that wasn't criticised. When God judges the earth every mouth will be stopped. When that great day comes will you be found in Christ?

"When as a child I laughed and wept,
Time crept,
When as a youth I grew more bold,
Time strolled,

When I became a full grown man,
Time ran,
Soon I shall find as I journey on,
Time gone,
Wilt Thou O Christ have saved me then?
Amen."

November *twenty-seventh*

*"O give thanks to
the Lord for He is
good"*
(1 Chronicles 16:34)

When you are disappointed, when circumstances do not work out for you, the Bible reminds you that the Lord still preserves your going out and your coming in. The Lord is not controlled by circumstances but reminds you that circumstances are controlled by Him. When you are worried, He reminds you not to let your heart be troubled, that He will not leave you, comfortless. He is not ignorant of your needs. You are told to cast all your care upon Him for He cares about you. That word means to turn over to somebody else, to take your hand off it and let somebody else bear it for you.

When you doubt, you are reminded of Thomas, Christ's disciple, who doubted. What changed Thomas from being a doubting Christian to one who looked into Christ's face and said "My Lord and my God"?; the personal intimate presence of Jesus Christ. You can't keep doubts from coming into your mind but you can bring them into the living presence of Christ and the light of His countenance will cause the darkness of doubt to disappear. When your mind is subjected to the mind of Christ, darkness will be dissipated.

When you are discouraged, when you have lost heart, when you have lost the will to fight, you are asked to look to Jesus, the author and finisher of your faith and He will inspire you to keep going. You are reminded that you are in God's hands, that He will fulfil His purpose and accomplish His perfect will in and through you.

There is not a circumstance that the Lord will not meet you in and pull you through. David, of all men, proved it. No wonder he calls us to give thanks to the Lord, for He is good.

November *twenty-eighth*

*"His mercy endures
forever"*
(1 Chronicles 16:34)

Mercy means two things. It first of all means forbearance from inflicting punishment upon an adversary or a lawbreaker and secondly it means compassion to help the weak, the sick or the poor.

Of all the truths in the Bible the one that moves me most is the truth of the self-substitution of God. There is a fundamental difference between penitent substitution in which the substitute offers what we could not offer and penal substitution in which the substitute bears what we could not bear. Let Dr. Packer define the latter from his book "What did the Cross Achieve?"; "That Jesus Christ our Lord, moved by love that was determined to do everything necessary to save us, endured and exhausted the destructive divine judgement for which we were otherwise inescapably destined and so won us forgiveness, adoption and glory. To affirm penal substitution is to say that believers are in debt to Christ specifically for this and this is the mainspring of all their joy, peace and praise both now and for eternity". What mercy we have been shown and the great thing is, as David reminds us, that mercy endures for ever.

November *twenty-ninth*

*"Save us, O God of
our salvation"*
(1 Chronicles 16:35)

What are the great images of salvation in the Bible? There are four major images. There is "propitiation" which means to appease or pacify someone's anger. The death of the Lord Jesus has averted God's wrath against us, so that as far as the person who has received Christ as Saviour is concerned, God can look upon them without displeasure and they can look on God without fear. There is "redemption" which means that through his death Christ has bought us at a huge price, the price of His blood, and set us free from slavery to sin. We are now the slaves of Christ and find in His service perfect freedom.

There is "justification" whereby the believer is no longer condemned, but now has, given to them, a righteous standing before God. What a relief! But more, there is "reconciliation". It is the most popular of the four great images of salvation in the Bible because it is so personal. An original relationship with God had been broken, alienation and enmity had come, but Christ came, as the agent of reconciliation and brought the two parties together.

Find some quiet spot today, Christian, and thank God for His salvation for, though in creation God has shown us His hand, in salvation, He has shown us His heart.

November *thirtieth*

> *"Blessed be the Lord God of Israel, from everlasting to everlasting"*
> (1 Chronicles 16:36)

In March 1972 the persecuted writer Alexander Solzhenitsyn invited the Moscow correspondents of 'The New York Times' and 'The Washington Post' to interview him. This was a rare occurrence, indeed no journalist had observed him closely for five years. He was enduring the full wrath of the Soviet leadership of the time and he talked about the fact that he and his family were "a kind of contaminated zone" in the eyes of that leadership.

It was a most graphic and pained interview but one thing deeply impressed me when I read of it. Asked for his opinion of two young Russian writers who had aroused interest in the late 1950s, Solzhenitsyn pointed out that writers who deal with highly topical questions as opposed to "Themes of eternal significance" naturally fade from the limelight together with the issues they have treated.

I read, the other day, of the Solzhenitsyns looking for a new home in Moscow. Their long exile from their native land is over and the Soviet Union is no more. Solzhenitsyn's statement in 1972 was true, wasn't it? He dipped his pen in a theme of eternal significance and it outlasted the very regimes that had tried to rub out what he had written.

David, in the beautiful psalm we have studied together this month, would bear out the truth of Solzhenitsyn's statement. He too wrote of themes of eternal significance. In fact he wrote of that which is most eternally significant of all; the God who is from everlasting to everlasting. Worship Him! Give your heart to Him! Be ambitious for His truth! Live for the immediate and soon it will be gone. Serve the everlasting God and the results will be as everlasting as the one you serve. It is the best gilt edged security available.

DECEMBER

It was to the Mount of Olives that the Lord Jesus led His disciples before he ascended to the highest place of all. The name "Mountain of Three Lights" was given in the past to the Mount of Olives because of the glow of the flaming Temple altar reflected on the hillside by night, the first beams of sunrise gilding the summit and the oil from the olives which fed the temple lights.

The Saviour came so gently and quietly to Bethlehem through Mary's womb. He had come to do a mighty work and now it was finished. Before He ascended, though, He spent some precious time with His own, particularly with Thomas and Peter. He taught very useful lessons for a Christian's life and witness in those few days before He went to be with his Father. As December days pass and we remember the Saviour's advent let's also learn from those lessons He taught just before He ascended, far above all.

December *first*

> *"But Thomas ... was not with them when Jesus came ... he said to them, 'Unless I see in His hands the print of the nails, and put my finger into the print of the nails, and put my hand into His side, I will not believe'"*
> (John 20:24-25)

Let no-one ever say that the Scriptures are removed from reality. There is nothing more real than God's Word. If some romantic writer were handling this story I doubt if he or she would ever insist that the whole thing was called into question by one of Christ's nearest and dearest followers. Let's never forget that Thomas had been perfectly prepared to die for Christ. He had said so (See John 11: 16). But he like the rest had run away and now, no doubt, filled with grief and remorse, on hearing the disciples speak of the Saviour's resurrection, he reacts with great caution and doubt.

I don't think Thomas was a natural sceptic. He didn't doubt everything as a matter of principle. Rather Thomas was a man who had a faith in two minds. His questions were from the standpoint of faith. Faith and doubt aren't mutually exclusive but faith and unbelief are. Thomas did not say he did not love the Saviour or deny belief in His teaching. What he did do, though, was doubt that Christ could have survived the awful treatment and wounding He had received at the cross. He must see and touch those wounds or he would not believe. After all he had not been present at Christ's appearing and he was no more unbelieving than the disciples had been before it. It proves one thing, though; the resurrection of Christ was subjected to the severest tests at the time of the resurrection.

You doubt the resurrection? Then remember this statement of Francis Bacon: "If a man will begin with certainties, he will end in doubts; if he is content to begin with doubts, he will end in certainties"

December *second*

"After eight days His disciples were again inside, and Thomas with them. Jesus came, the doors being shut, and stood in the midst, and said, 'Peace to you!'"
(John 20:26)

Long have I seen and known it: Christ does not, as Isaiah teaches, break bruised reeds and throw them away, nor does He quench smoking flax despite its fitful burning. If He turned away from every doubter He would have to turn away from the entire Christian church. Life is, as any medical practitioner will tell you, a permanent battle against all sorts of diseases and good health is an ability to keep disease at bay. The life of faith is a permanent battle against doubts. Most Christians doubt at some stage in their life of faith. To doubt is not a sin, it does not invalidate your conversion experience. Just study how Christ handled the doubts of John the Baptist, if you don't believe me.

Christ did not come to damn Thomas. He didn't even come to scold him. For eight whole days Thomas had heard the disciples speak of the risen Lord and how he must have tossed and turned in his soul that week. And now Christ appears again and who would doubt that He appeared just for Thomas' sake? He had come to restore him. Would He do such a thing? He certainly would. If there had been no-one on this earth but you, He would have come all the way and died just for you. Christian, walk in the common knowledge that you are beloved of the Lord, doubts and all.

December *third*

> *"The disciples therefore said to him, 'We have seen the Lord'. But he said to them, 'Unless I see in His hands the print of the nails, and put my finger into the print of the nails, and put my hand into His side, I will not believe'"*
> (John 20:25)

The pathos and emotion of this incident is a lot deeper than words. Yet, apart from the feelings it stirs in all of us, a principle of the spiritual life lies at the very heart of it. The principle is that Christ hears all our conversations, even though we don't see Him. The Lord knew exactly what Thomas said when expressing his doubts about the resurrection even though he was not physically present in the room at the time. Indeed, not only does the Lord know our private conversations, He knows our every thought.

I doubt if Thomas availed himself of Christ's invitation by coldly scrutinising the wounds of the Saviour. Such an act would be incompatible with the immediate spontaneous words he spoke, "My Lord and my God". Thomas may have appeared a hopeless case to those who might have heard him express his doubts during that momentous week but of all the disciples he made the greatest confession of any. He reached a higher level than all the rest. Don't judge a doubter too hard for "when the Queen of Sheba heard of the fame of Solomon concerning the name of the Lord, she came to test him with hard questions". Before she was finished she was saying, "Blessed be the Lord your God, who delighted in you, setting you on the Throne of Israel". Sometimes the toughest of doubters become the greatest of believers.

December *fourth*

> *"Jesus said to them, 'Thomas, because you have seen Me, you have believed. Blessed are those who have not seen and yet have believed'"*
> (John 20:29)

Here is the Saviour's last beatitude. He is not talking to His disciples, now. They had experienced the privilege of seeing Him and believing on Him. Just like Thomas they had not believed until they saw; if they had believed a week earlier than Thomas, it was simply because they saw the resurrected Lord a week earlier than he did. The Lord is now looking down the coming centuries seeing all those people from every corner of the earth who would believe on Him without seeing Him. They are pronounced "Blessed", i.e., not simply "happy" but "accepted by God".

Peter put it beautifully, later. "Whom not having seen you love. Though now you do not see Him, yet believing, you rejoice with joy inexpressible and full of glory, receiving the end of your faith - the salvation of your souls". And how do we believe, even though we don't see? Particularly through the reading and teaching of the Scriptures, for, "Faith comes by hearing and hearing by the Word of God". Keep on reading and teaching the Word of God, Christian, and just as you love the one you have never seen, others will come to love Him too.

December *fifth*

> *"And truly Jesus did many other signs in the presence of His disciples, which are not written in this book; but these are written that you may believe that Jesus is the Christ, the Son of God, and that believing you may have life in His Name"*
> (John 20:30-31)

I once knew a man in my youth who said that he was only interested in the Bible from a historical point of view. He read it for its history, he said. Poor man! Notice how John's purpose is not academic or merely historical, it is evangelistic. He carefully selects his material from all the material available in order that people might personally believe the truth at the heart of it all. He deliberately set out to show that the Messiah is the Jesus he has just written a beautifully drawn portrait of in his Gospel. The end result of such belief was "life in His Name", not just a lot of facts in his readers' heads.

To say that John was successful in his noble purpose is an understatement. In the intervening centuries millions have taken up his invitation to believe the message. John's goal in evangelism is the goal of all evangelism. In this area, as Christians, we dare not be tepid. God forgive us if we have no emotion, no enthusiasm, no urgency and no compassion regarding the lost. How can we ever possibly say we are evangelical without being evangelistic? Leon Morris once said, "When Christians evangelise, they are not engaging in some harmless and pleasant past-time. They are engaging in a fearful struggle, the issues of which are eternal". We would also be well reminded of the words of Vance Havner when he stated that, "The Gospel is for lifeboats, not showboats, and a man must make up his mind which he is going to operate".

December *sixth*

> *"After these things
> Jesus showed
> Himself again to the
> disciples at the Sea
> of Tiberias, and in
> this way He showed
> Himself"*
> (John 21:1)

Is not the resurrection the climax of John's story? Yes, it certainly is. Yet, here we are given a demonstration of the reality of the resurrection. There were at least twelve post-resurrection appearances of the Lord Jesus and this is number seven. It is an interesting study. He appeared to Mary Magdalene (Matthew 16: 9), to the women (Matthew 28: 9), to Cleopas and his companion (Luke 24: 13-35), to Simon (Luke 24: 34), to the disciples with and without Thomas (John 20: 24-29), to the seven at the sea of Tiberias (John 21: 1-14), to the disciples on a mountain (Matthew 28: 16-20), to the five hundred (1 Corinthians 15: 6), to James the Lord's brother (1 Corinthians 15: 7), to the eleven on Olivet (Acts 1: 4-11) and to Paul (Acts 9: 3-7). They all show that the resurrected Christ was not a spirit, not an hallucination, not a vision but a real, live, flesh and blood person. The pre-resurrected Jesus has come back as the very same Jesus. He has forced open a door that had been locked since the death of Adam. He has beaten him who had the power of death, that is the devil, and now everything is different.

December *seventh*

> *"Simon Peter,
> Thomas called
> Didymus,
> Nathanael of Cana
> in Galilee, the sons
> of Zebedee, and two
> others of His
> disciples were
> together"*
> (John 21: 2)

I like to meditate on the fact that Nathanael was there at the end of Christ's public ministry because he had been there at the beginning. The man whom Christ said was guileless, who had first wondered if any good thing could ever have come out of Nazareth, who had then declared to the Saviour, "You are the Son of God, you are the King of Israel!" had remained faithful, right to the end.

How many there are who begin well. They flourish in the things of God, they enthuse about the joy of sins forgiven and peace with God, they witness for their Master, they give to His work, they live for Him. Then they go missing from their usual place of worship, they no longer raise a song to Christ at the unusual hour, never to speak of the usual. They have grown cold. They are "splendidly null". They have left their "first love" for Christ. There is some disease at the root of their faith and the lovely blossom is gone. I tell you it is impossible to witness for Christ in the darkness of the world except in the power of first love. Nathanael never forgot his beginnings, that's why he was there at the end. Don't you think consistency is one of the best jewels you could possess?

December *eighth*

> *"Simon Peter said to them 'I am going fishing'. They said to him, 'We are going with you also'"*
> (John 21:3)

People have always disagreed as to whether or not to blame Peter and his friends for going fishing on this occasion. Surely he had to eat, so the action in itself was not wrong. It would not be unreasonable to assume that they had gone to Galilee in obedience to their Lord's command and there is no indication that they had gone there to assume their old career as fishermen.

There is, though, an underlying restlessness in this story. Peter was a man of action, a leader, and he must do something. When you are restless you can find relief in action. They knew too much to go back, and not enough to go on, it was the waiting that was a killer. Jesus had told them to wait. I can't see anything wrong in filling in waiting time with something useful. But we must beware of restlessness. Just last evening I was involved in a very public way in evangelistic preaching and when I got to my bed I tossed and turned in the wee small hours over what I had just done and said. I was very restless when suddenly a verse from the Bible entered my mind like lightening. It simply said, "My Word shall not return to Me void". I was suddenly filled with this incredible calm at the thought that God's Word always fulfils that purpose for which God sent it. God was saying, "Trust Me on this". I rolled over and slept like a baby. You can wait for the fulfilment of a promise like that, can't you? But you don't need to be restless in the interim.

December *ninth*

> *"They went out
> and immediately
> got into the boat,
> and that night they
> caught nothing"*
> (John 21:3)

What good can failure do? A lot. All things that happen to us as believers are not necessarily good but they all work together for good. There is not a loss, not a disappointment, not a failure, not a heartache, not a difficulty, not a turn on the road of your life but a loving Saviour can, through it all, teach you a lesson. Was it by chance that Peter and his friends caught nothing? No, it had been carefully arranged by the Lord. Lessons were about to be taught which would not only help these men but which would enrich the whole church of Christ forever.

So, you caught nothing? So, you have outwardly failed in some enterprise for the Master? Read then, these words by F. B. Meyer: "But what good can failure do? It may shut up a path which you were pursuing too eagerly. It may put you out of heart with things seen and temporal, and give you an appetite for things unseen and eternal. It may teach you your own helplessness, and turn you to trust more implicitly in the provision of Christ. It is clear that Christians have often toiled all night in vain, that Christ may have a background black and sombre enough to set forth all the glories of His interposition".

December *tenth*

> *"But when the
> morning had now
> come, Jesus stood
> on the shore; yet
> the disciples did
> not know that it
> was Jesus"*
> (John 21:4)

It was most probably the early morning mist that obscured the Saviour. I don't think it was unbelief that had closed their eyes, do you? Yet, how often the Lord is near us and we don't know Him? There He is in your place of work, today. There He is by the bedside of that sick patient as you do your best to help them. There He is, standing, despite your marital row, or family disagreement, or heartbreaking exam failures. There He is when you were passed over

288

FAR ABOVE ALL

for promotion. There He is, standing on the shore, when your nets are empty.

Learn to discern the presence of the Lord. You will reach no shore in life where He isn't present. As David put it long ago: "Where can I flee from Your presence? If I ascend into Heaven, You are there: .... if I take the wings of the morning, and dwell in the uttermost parts of the sea, even there Your hand shall lead me, and Your right hand shall hold me. If I say, 'Surely the darkness shall fall on me', even the night shall be light about me: indeed, the darkness shall not hide from You, but the night shines as the day, the darkness and the night are both alike to You". See your Lord everywhere, Christian. If you truly love Him, as Peter soon showed, you will detect His presence.

December *eleventh*

"Then Jesus said to them, 'Children, have you any food?'. They answered Him, 'No'. And He said to them, 'Cast the net on the right side of the boat, and you will find some'. So they cast, and now they were not able to draw it in because of the multitude of fish"
(John 21: 5-6)

D.A.Carson makes a very interesting point regarding this command, which was obviously given by a Man whom the disciples did not recognise! Why should they listen to the voice of someone calling in the early dawn mist from the shore of the lake? Carson points out that since the disciples did not recognise the Lord, "It is hard to see how Jesus' exhortation to throw the net on the starboard side greatly differs from advice that temporary sports fishermen have to endure: 'Try casting over there, you often catch them over there'". He says if there are those who haven't experienced this delight he recommends they take his children with them on their next fishing trip! (D.A. Carson, 'The Gospel According to John' IVP, Eerdmans, 1991, p. 671).

The point was, of course, that there was a shoal of fish on that side of the boat and Jesus knew all about them. Just like He knew there was a coin in the fish's mouth so that Peter could pay his tribute money, just like

He had earlier in His ministry asked Peter, in whose boat He had preached, to "launch out into the deep and let down your nets for a catch". It is obvious that the Lord Jesus knows the flip of every tail of every fish in every ocean on earth. If He knows that much detail about fish, how much more does He know about you? Talk about fish: His thoughts about you are more, says Scripture, than the sand on the seashore! As for those lonely, bewildered disciples, He is able to do for you, too, exceedingly, abundantly, above all that you could ever ask or think.

December *twelfth*

> *"Therefore that disciple whom Jesus loved said to Peter, 'It is the Lord!'"*
> (John 21: 7)

The relationship between Peter and John is full of lessons. They were obviously great friends. They are recorded in Scripture as often being together (John 1: 35-41; 13: 23-24; 18: 15-16; 20: 1-10; 21: 2, 7, 20-22; Acts 3: 1-4; 8: 14-17; Galatians 2: 9). They were as great friends often are, very different. Peter was the man of action, John the man of insight. Quick action and quick insight in the hand of God, in the Kingdom of God, are a great complement to one another.

Why, so often, do so many people want to stereotype Christians? Why do people think that when a person finds Christ he or she loses their personality, their "colour and flair"? Look at these two: Peter the impulsive, articulate, fervent, spontaneous leader: John the literate, pondering, sensitive, retiring visionary. Between them they and their friends were about to turn the Roman world upside down for Christ. You are in your personality the person God made you, don't try to be anyone else. You are, in all the world, the person best qualified to be you. Let God use you to His glory just like Peter and John.

December *thirteenth*

"Now when Simon Peter heard that it was the Lord, he put on his outer garment (for he had removed it) and plunged into the sea"
(John 21: 7)

Let no-one ever say that deep in his heart Peter did not love the Lord. Cowardly, wayward and weak he had been. Sinful, certainly. A disastrous denial of his Lord had no doubt led to the dark night of his soul. Who of us is there who have not known it? Pressurised by this, that or the other, instigated by Satan, we have let the Lord down. We have, like Peter, gone out and wept. As Dr. Alan Redpath said one evening as he and I were preaching together in Greystones in Co. Wicklow, "There is no sin that I am not capable of committing two minutes after this service is over". I have long thought on that statement by that great servant of God.

The meaning of our text seems to be that Peter put on his outer garment when he knew it was the Lord. He had obviously stripped to his loincloth for fishing purposes. He did this out of respect tucking up the lower part of his outer garment into his belt, so as not to impede his legs, and swam for the shore. "It is the Lord!" was all he needed to hear. Gone was fear, gone was hopelessness and restlessness, the Lord was there and that was enough. He couldn't wait to see Him. He didn't even wait to help with the immediate haul of fish, he must see the Lord. He must welcome Him.

We know that Peter had said on one occasion previously, when he had failed, "Depart from me for I am a sinful man, oh Lord". He had asked the Lord to give him up because of his personal failure. But the Lord will never leave us nor forsake us. So then, discouraged, broken, down-hearted Christian, be up with you and away to your new risen Lord. He loves you still with the very same love as He showed you at Calvary. He is Jesus Christ, the same yesterday and today and forever.

December *fourteenth*

> *"Then, as soon as they had come to land, they saw a fire of coals there, and fish laid on it, and bread. Jesus said to them, 'Bring some of the fish which you have just caught'"*
> (John 21:9-10)

You may have had a bad night but the Lord Jesus can give you a good morning. How very typical of the Master to show His servant nature as much in post-resurrection days as pre-resurrection days. And when we pass through the chill waters of death, or we are called by the Lord's shout at the Second Coming, we shall dine with Him as these men did.

We shall, we are told, gather from every clime and nation. Not, then, by a fire with its curling smoke on a stretch of deserted beach in Galilee, but on a celestial shore on Heaven's morning. We shall hear stories which will thrill our hearts as to how multitudes were found by the Saviour, and who will serve at the table? The Lord will. We serve a Servant-King who came not to be ministered to, but to minister. Have we the same nature? Ask not what your local church or community can do for you but rather what you can do for your local church or community, for the Lord's sake.

December *fifteenth*

> *"Simon Peter went up and dragged the net to land, full of large fish, one hundred and fifty-three"*
> (John 21:11)

He has not been nicknamed "The big fisherman" for nothing, has he? Peter, single-handedly, hauled the net with one hundred and fifty-three fish up the beach. Interesting interpretations, especially from some of the early church fathers, have been given as to the significance of the number of fish: obviously somebody thought to count them and remembered how many there were.

It is very hard not to catch a subliminal message through this haul of fish. Surely it was a parable to the disciples of the kind of work in which they would be involved in the future. Not only would the Lord provide for their needs but they were going to become fishermen for the Lord and catch people. They will have to learn to cast their nets by His direction, they will have to learn great patience, as they go through the contrasts of storm and calm, wind and sunshine, summer and winter, for His sake. One thing is certain, though, the Gospel net will never break no matter how many fish you land. The net may have broken in the haul recorded in Luke 5: 1-11 but not here. So, Christian, keep casting! Remember though these four little rules as you fish:

"Keep your face towards the sun,
Study the fishes' curious ways,
Keep yourself well out of sight,
Study patience all your days".

December *sixteenth*

"Jesus said to them, 'Come and eat breakfast,' yet none of His disciples dared ask Him, 'Who are you?' - knowing that it was the Lord"
(John 21:12)

When the Lord calls you to do something for Him, He means it. He decided you should do it, He provided the circumstances in which to call you, He organises the sphere in which you should serve Him. Sometimes the events of life are so overwhelming that we forget our calling. The pressures of the immediate crowd out the big picture, we lose our sense of direction.

Look at these men sitting by a fire of crackling charcoal which is chasing away the morning chill. Every word of their Saviour is hung upon eagerly, every movement watched. Notice that John does not merely say that they did not ask Him who He was, He tells us that they dared not ask Him.

There is no doubt that Christ's presence by that fire that morning reminded them of something vitally important - their calling. He had called them to serve Him three years before and that calling still stood. So does yours. Don't let anything obscure that which the Lord has called you to do.

December *seventeenth*

"Jesus then came and took the bread and gave it to them, and likewise the fish. This is now the third time Jesus showed Himself to the disciples after He was raised from the dead"
(John 21:13-14)

Two things are important to note in this part of this beautiful epilogue of John's Gospel. The first is that the Lord personally does the feeding here. Back in Jerusalem they gave Him a piece of "broiled fish" and He strengthened their faith by eating it. Here the Lord Jesus feeds them symbolically, showing as He did by the lake with the multitudes, that this is what He loves to do.

How many times, weary with life's burdens and heartaches has He said to you, as He did to those men that morning, "Come and eat"? He has fed you on food this world knows nothing of for it suffers from a wasting disease called, by the French philosopher, Albert Camus, "absurdism". Life, such people believe, is a bad joke. Millions more suffer from a complaint called "Marie Antoinette's fever". She who could have virtually anything she wanted complained that "Nothing tastes". So many are like the Duchess of York who recently told Alexandra Shulman of "Vogue" Magazine: "You know what, when you're down and you've got nowhere to go, you're going to try everything." She talked of her search for "inner peace" and the "mammoth journey" she had embarked upon. To all such, the Saviour of the world says, "Come and eat." When He feeds you there is a satisfaction which results which cannot be beaten. Taste and see, said the Psalmist, that the Lord is good. You need journey no more. He has what you need.

December *eighteenth*

> *"So when they had eaten breakfast, Jesus said to Simon Peter, 'Simon, son of Jonas, do you love Me more than these?' He said to Him, 'Yes, Lord; you know that I love You'. He said to him, 'Feed My Lambs'"*
> (John 21:15)

And how did it fare with Peter? How did he feel in his heart and mind as he gazed into the face of the one who died for him and whom he had so cruelly and selfishly denied? What right had he to serve the one he had caused the enemy to blaspheme? Was Peter finished?

The Lord singled him out from the rest and, notice, He addressed him by his old name. He was taking him right back to his natural roots, right back to where he had been, where He had found him and He re-issues the call to serve Him. He is the God of second chance.

Notice, though, the basis on which all Christian service rests. He didn't say, "Do you believe in Me?", or "Will you obey Me?" or even "What on earth were you doing denying Me?" There was no scolding, no checking out his present doctrinal position, He simply said, "Do you love Me?"

The story is told of a young woman in Edinburgh who applied for fellowship in a church but the minister was not happy with her inability to answer certain basic questions. On his third refusal she answered, "Weel, sir, I mayna and I dinna ken sae muckle as mony: but when ye preach a sermon aboot my Lord and Saviour, I fin my heart going out to Him, like linseed out of a bag". If you have ever seen the process you'll understand why the minister admitted her to the fellowship of that local church immediately.

December *nineteenth*

> *"He said to him a second time, 'Simon, Son of Jonas, do you love Me?' He said to Him, 'Yes, Lord; you know that I love You'. He said to him, 'Tend my sheep'"*
> (John 21:16)

Being a shepherd is not the easy pastoral idyll it always appears. In Romania I was up a mountain at 10,000 feet with some friends when we met a shepherd. He told us with great animation that a bear had come upon his flock in the night and I could very clearly see that being a shepherd was not all quiet meadows and sheep grazing safely. Shepherding is not always done beside still waters. It may mean having the wolf burying his fangs in you to save the lambs.

The Lord had spoken earlier of the sheep He would bring into His fold and now Peter is specifically given the job of shepherding them. No-one did a better job than Peter was to do in this very special area of ministry. He was to write two letters in the New Testament addressed to Christians who were facing hostility and suspicion in the Roman Empire and who were being reviled and abused for their lifestyles. His letters are filled with encouragement and inspiration for the suffering lambs and sheep of Christ's fold. His letters minister to millions of Christians today. Standing on the shore of Galilee that misty morning Peter had no idea of the ministry that lay ahead of him. Neither do you. Never say that you know the will of God for the rest of your life. You don't. Your greatest work for the Lord may lie just ahead of you.

December *twentieth*

> *"He said to him the third time,'Simon, son of Jonas, do you love Me?' Peter was grieved because He said to him the third time, 'Do you love Me?'"*
> (John 21:17)

A lot of textual discussion has taken place around the different levels of meaning of the word "love" in the Lord's questions to Peter. I am not scholastically qualified to adjudicate on it all but surely the point of the three questions is that as Peter had denied his Lord three times, he is now required to profoundly confess Him three times. Peter is grieved that the Lord asked him the third time about his love for Him but it must be done. Peter, on his third confession, is now fully restored for service.

Have you, like Peter, let your Lord down? The Lord would draw you back to the point where you went wrong and there He would restore you. At Bethel Abraham went astray and went off into Egypt to lie his way out of a crisis. He had to be brought back to Bethel and restored to his calling. He built an altar there and became the epitomy of faith in all generations.

"No chastening", says the Bible, "seems to be joyful for the present, but grievous; nevertheless afterward it yields the peaceable fruit of righteousness to those who have been trained by it". The Lord's chastening grieved Peter but what incredible fruit it produced. So, be patient, Christian, if you are experiencing the chastening of the Lord, it will yield a great harvest in your life.

December *twenty-first*

> *"Jesus said to Him,*
> *'Feed my sheep'"*
> (John 21:17)

For the third time Peter is told of the work the Lord has for him. Aware of his great weakness and failure it must have been one of the greatest revelations of his life to discover that the Lord still loved him and wanted him to continue in Christian service.

Time changes us all. Affections between people cool, opinions alter, but the Lord Jesus does not change. He loved Peter just as He loves you, as much as He ever did. Time has no effect on Him whatsoever. Our moods change, we are "like oranges one day and lemons the next". But not with the Saviour - He is never put out, He is never variable. He is, says Scripture, "without shadow cast by turning".

Have you not found that circumstances change people? Someone gets promoted and suddenly forgets their roots and doesn't want to know their old friends. New surroundings, new friends, new opportunities alter people. But the Lord Jesus, though, now exalted to the highest place in the Universe is just the same Lord Jesus as He was here on earth.

Even sin and provocation from Peter did not change the Saviour's attitude to him. Peter must have been staggered at the Lord's constancy. He certainly found out in no uncertain terms that his Lord was the same yesterday, today and forever.

Peter's Lord is yours, "He who has begun a good work in you will complete it until the day of Jesus Christ", wrote Paul. Nothing will stop the Lord's determination to make you holy. Nothing.

December *twenty-second*

> *"Most assuredly, I say to you, when you were younger, you girded yourself and walked where you wished; but when you are old you will stretch out your hands, and another will gird you and carry you where you do not wish"*
> (John 21:18)

By the time John wrote this Gospel Peter had been martyred and he now well understood the meaning of the Saviour's words to Peter. The Lord contrasts Peter's youth with what lay ahead. As with any young person Peter was free to move as he wished; literally, the words mean "you used to put on your belt, you used to get dressed to travel". Peter could have walked wherever he wished to walk. The hour was coming, though, when Peter would have to raise his arms so that a rope could be tied around him as he was prepared for crucifixion. Then Peter would later have to stretch out his hands on the cross-beam of a cross.

Serving God, would, for Peter, not be to go where he wished. He would have to be prepared to go to a place where he did not wish to go. So often that is how it is in God's work. Ask people who have obeyed the Lord in service if their sphere of activity is where they would have naturally chosen to serve and you will find almost, invariably, that it isn't. They are given grace to do it, though. The question, "Would you be prepared to die as a martyr?" is sometime used. The answer is that if you have to die for Christ you will get the grace from God to do so. Meanwhile you will get the grace from God to live for Him and that is often just as difficult.

December *twenty-third*

> *"This he spoke, signifing by what death he would glorify God"*
> (John 21:19)

Dying a good death for the Lord is just as possible as living a good life for Him. I know we have arrived at the Christmas season and you are probably surrounded with every sign of life but, then, we do not know the moment our earthly life will be taken from us. Even Bethlehem's manger had the shadow of death upon it and as the Lord Jesus brought glory to the Father in His death (see John 13: 31-32; 17: 1) so Peter was to do the same.

There is a message of tremendous hope here. Do we despise Peter forever for his dreadful denial of the Lord Jesus? Certainly not. In fact we love his tender, sensitive and sympathetic writing in the New Testament letters. He became a pillar in the church. Peter's dreadful and shameful denial was overcome by thirty years of dedicated service that followed the faithfulness to his Lord, even to the point of martyrdom. If you have failed your Lord, repent, be restored and live the rest of your days to His glory and, if the Lord be not come, die a death to His glory. I tell you it is harder to live for the Lord Jesus when you are older than it is when you are younger, but remember the young are looking to see if it works. By God's grace, show them.

December *twenty-fourth*

"And when he had spoken this, he said to them, 'Follow Me'"
(John 21:19)

This verse could immediately mean that the Lord invited Peter for a walk and a private conversation along the seashore but surely there is more to it than that. Just as Peter had been recommended to service, so now the Lord re-issues that original simple, clear, unequivocal call. Peter had first heard it when he and Andrew had been casting a net into the Sea of Galilee three and a half years before (See Matthew 4; 18). The words, I'm told, more literally mean "travel with Me".

Those words come to you and me on this Christmas Eve. Love always involves sacrifice, always. The Saviour's love for us involved His coming from unimaginable glory to a lowly stable, making Himself of no reputation. He lived for thirty-three and a half years with the reality of the cross over His head. Peter in turn lived for Christ for thirty years knowing it would cost him his life. We too know that it will be costly for us in the coming days to live for the Lord Jesus. Yet, as we stand by Bethlehem's manger and by Calvary's cross and hear that incredible call of our Saviour saying, "Follow Me", we gladly say, by God's grace, "Anywhere with Jesus we will follow on".

December *twenty-fifth*

> *"Peter, turning around, saw the disciple whom Jesus loved following, who also had leaned on His breast at the supper, and said, 'Lord, who is the one who betrays you?'"*
> (John 21:20)

John, from the very beginning of his Gospel, constantly veiled himself but what better description to be veiled by than this one? It does not imply in the slightest that Jesus did not love the other disciples. Our reading of John's Gospel shows that without any doubt. It was, though, the phrase that John wanted to be known by.

On this Christmas Day the T.V. listings will be full of programmes featuring famous people, highlighting actors famous for their part in the films shown, interviews given with interesting people who have accomplished great things, etc. Who, in any of the films will be highlighted as having one great feature above all others, the feature that they are loved by the Lord? On this day millions are reminded of Christ's birth but how many have personally responded to the incredible love that led Him to Bethlehem and Calvary? How may count it the greatest distinction of all to be loved by the Lord? On every continent there are such and if you and I are amongst them then there is one call we should heed above all others today. In the light of such love that call says, "Come, let us adore Him".

December *twenty-sixth*

> *"'But Lord, what about this man?' Jesus said to him, 'If I will that he remain till I come, what is that to you? You follow Me'"*
> (John 21:22)

Peter had just been told what following Christ would cost him. It would cost him his life. Peter's question about what would happen to John was understandable. These two were very close and if Peter was going to die he was concerned about John. The Lord saw deeper into Peter's heart than anyone else. He saw that Peter had not fully understood what He had meant by the words "Follow Me". He meant that Peter had a task to accomplish and it would be well for him to concentrate on it rather than on what another should be doing and what might happen to him.

The answer was very straight. He had obviously told Peter to mind his own business. It was a call not to interfere in the life of another. And isn't it a message to all of us? We can be so busy asking questions about others that we fail to fulfil the mission to which we are called ourselves. We are to be faithful to our own commission and that will take all our time and energy. It is not necesssary for me to know the Lord's plans for others. His plan for me is enough to be getting on with. I am called to play out the part He has written for me, not to be spoiling my own soul's condition by fussing about another's part.

December *twenty-seventh*

"Jesus said to him, 'If I will that he remain till I come, what is that to you?'"
(John 21:22)

This amazing statement shows very clearly that our lives are not the victims of chance nor the creatures of circumstance. Our steps are ordered by the Lord. He has adapted our lives in such a way that our past is suited to our limitations, temperaments and capabilities. The words, "If I will" shows the sovereignty the Lord has over our lives and deaths. We can now look back upon the amazing paths the Lord laid out for these two men. They had no idea, that misty morning by the sea, just how significant they were to be. Peter was to see huge success as a preacher of the Gospel but even more as a writer to sufferers. His pastoral ministry through his letters will be a help to people "going through the mill" to the end of time. Yet, how could he have ever been such a pastor if he had not proved God to be his comforter as he lived out his ministry with the anticipation of his martyrdom hanging over his head?

John, though, was to write the book of Revelation. He became a lonely exile on the island of Patmos and lived through the time of the fall of Jerusalem, the destruction of the Temple and the scattering of the Jews worldwide. It was because of his lonely exile that he was able to write of those sublime visions given to him by God and his great emphasis on the unchanging Saviour. It was his personal circumstances that gave his writing such potency, even to this day. The words, "If I will" should not make us afraid, rather they should comfort us in that they remind us that the Lord knows what He is doing with our lives. All our circumstances are used to bring about His purposes.

December *twenty-eighth*

> *"Then this saying went out among the brethren that this disciple would not die. Yet Jesus did not say to him that he would not die, but, 'If I will that he remain till I come, what is that to you?'"*
> (John 21:23)

People do not always listen to what is being said, do they? The disciples did not pay close enough attention to the Lord's words and for many a day it was believed by them and through them by the wider Christian circle that John would not die until the Second Coming. Therefore the longer John lived the closer they felt the coming of the Lord to be. You can imagine the sense of anticipation must have reached fever pitch as John grew older! On his death Christians were bound to be disappointed and non-Christians caused to mock. That's why this verse is carefully included in John's Gospel to warn us to pay close attention to the detail of Scripture.

How many another person have you heard saying that they believe they will not die until the return of Christ? How many have through the generations predicted a date and a time for His coming? When those Christians died and when those many predictions did not happen it all led to mockery from the unconverted. Jesus told us that only the Father knows the day and the hour of His return. Nobody else does. So let's stick by His words. If He wills that we remain until His coming, or if He wishes us to pass through death, His will is paramount. Believing this will bring confidence to us and stop un-necessary mocking from the unconverted.

December *twenty-ninth*

> *"This is the disciple who testifies of these things, and wrote these things ..."*
> (John 21:24)

Today's text establishes beyond all doubt that "the beloved disciple" whom we have met through this Gospel is none other than John. It also indicates that he was still orally testifying for Christ even after he had written his Gospel. Right through his long life he still spoke far and wide of the years of communion he had had with the Saviour and also of that turning point in his life when, because of the way the clothes lay, he had first believed that Christ had risen from the dead.

Don't you love the way John's tongue and pen are linked in our text? His Gospel writing is unsurpassed, indeed as a friend of mine said to me just yesterday, "If we had nothing but John's Gospel it would be enough". John's writing has left its mark. Indeed checking on the Internet for references to John's Gospel recently I found there were tens of thousands of references. I have tried to imagine what it must have been to hear John speak. As he wrote in one of his letters, "What we have seen and heard we declare to you also", but as he declared it what must have been the look in his eye? What must have been the tone in his voice? He who had seen Him, bore Him an incredibly faithful witness.

And you and I? Christ declared that we who have not seen yet who have believed are more blessed. How, then, runs our pen and our tongue? John's witness to his Saviour lasted consistently to the end of his life. How will ours be? Is ours Wesley's cry?

> "Happy, if with my latest breath,
> I may but gasp His Name:
> Preach Him to all and cry in death,
> 'Behold, behold the Lamb!'"

December *thirtieth*

"... and we know that his testimony is true"
(John 21:24)

Who are the "we" in our text? Some say the church to which John belonged, some say the church at Ephesus, some say a group of John's disciples who preserved his record and gave it to the world. Others suggest it is an editorial "we", a form by which the writer is underlining the truthfulness of his own witness. In the end, though, whoever the "we" refers to, they could not have known John's witness was true because they were not present at the events he writes about. They weren't there! It surely must refer to what F.F. Bruce calls, "the inward witness of the Holy Spirit ... that witness had begun to validate itself in their personal experience and thus they knew it to be true".

We too, in our day and generation, also know the very same experience. There is a ring of authenticity in this Gospel that touches our lives as we face a new millennium as it has touched millions in the last two. The Spirit of God witnesses with our spirit that this Gospel is true. What we once guessed about we now know, through John, as a fixed guiding pole star in our journey to eternity. As the great preacher W.E. Sangster was dying of a wasting disease, he wrote to the evangelist Dr. Billy Graham and said, "Tell them it's true, Billy, tell them it's true".

December *thirty-first*

"And there are also many other things that Jesus did, which if they were written one by one, I suppose that even the world itself could not contain the books that would be written. Amen"
(John 21:25)

At the very beginning of this Gospel, John wrote of the Saviour who "was in the world, and the world was made through Him, and the world did not know Him". Through his wonderful Gospel John testified of the Saviour, of His words, His deeds, His acts. He then tells us that his Gospel was one great invitation to believe that Christ is the Son of God. Now, at the very end of the greatest story ever told, John re-asserts himself and for the one and only time in his Gospel refers to himself as "I". (See 1 John for John's use of "we" and "I"). He says that the world that did not know Christ when He came, would be a very small library to contain all the books that could be written if all of the Saviour's deeds were put into writing.

Let us be reminded again that God never ends with an end but always ends with a beginning. As C. S. Lewis pointed, the story goes on forever and, in fact, each chapter is better than the last one! John's invitation comes down the centuries to us again. Are we going to be part of this unending story too or are we going to live merely for ourselves? John's one aim in life had been to glorify Christ. In that he gloriously succeeded. May we do the same.

BIBLIOGRAPHY

F. F. Bruce, *The New International Commentary on the New Testament,*
 (Wm. B. Eerdmans Publishing Co., Grand Rapids, Michigan) 1984

D. Stuart Briscoe, *"Let's get moving"*
(Regal Books, Ventura, CA) 1978

John Calvin, *Galatians - Ephesians, Calvin's Commentaries,*
(Wm. Eerdmans Publishing Company Co., Grand Rapids, Michigan)

D. M. Lloyd-Jones, *An Exposition of Ephesians*
(Banner of Truth, Edinburgh, Scotland) 1976-79

A. T. Lincoln, *Ephesians. Word Biblical Commentary*
(Word Books, Dallas, Texas) 1990

W. L. Liefield, *Ephesians,*
Inter Varsity Press (Downers Grove, IL) 1997

Klyne Snodgrass, *NIV Application Commentary,*
Zondervan Publishing House (Grand Rapids, Michigan) 1996

J. R. W. Stott, *The Message of Ephesians,*
 Inter Varsity Press (Leicester, England) 1989